STATE AND LOCAL TAXATION AND FINANCE

IN A NUTSHELL

Third Edition

By

M. DAVID GELFAND
Ashton Phelps Chair in Constitutional Law
Tulane University, School of Law

JOEL A. MINTZ
Professor of Law
Nova Southeastern University
Shepard Broad Law Center

PETER W. SALSICH, JR.
Professor of Law
Saint Louis University, School of Law

Mat #40631349

COPYRIGHT © 1986 M. DAVID GELFAND & PETER W. SALSICH, JR.
© West, a Thomson business, 2000
© 2007 Thomson/West
      610 Opperman Drive
      St. Paul, MN 55123
      1–800–328–9352

Printed in the United States of America

ISBN: 978–0–314–18387–3

TEXT IS PRINTED ON 10% POST
CONSUMER RECYCLED PAPER

To our wives, Mary, Meri-Jane, and Barbara,
and
to the memory of our dear friend and
co-author, David Gelfand, whose sudden,
untimely passing preceded the
publication of this edition

*

PREFACE

Public finance has taken on new significance in the past several decades. Serious fiscal crises in several major American cities, shifts in attitudes regarding state and federal social programs, and an explosion in the use of tax-exempt bonds have brought a topic once thought to be the exclusive province of public finance specialists to the attention of the American public at large. Law schools, in particular, have added courses on state and local taxation and finance to their curricula, and law students increasingly view municipal bond firms and state and local government agencies as respectable potential employers. Business schools and public policy schools have continued to give attention to the important topic of public finance.

Against this backdrop, the authors have prepared this "nutshell" on State and Local Taxation and Finance. Like others in the West Nutshell Series, this book was originally intended primarily for the law student confronting the topic for the first time. Many readers' comments on the First Edition, however, assured us that public policy and business school students, practicing lawyers, and public officials have found much of the book useful.

The book should be read as it was written—as an initial discussion and analysis of the main points of law and policy in a highly technical and diverse field. It is not designed as a substitute for careful study of the applicable statutes and local ordinances, the case law interpreting those provisions, and the public policy background. Moreover, the authors hope that many students will use this Nutshell as an adjunct to—but not a substitute for—the texts and treatises they are assigned in their law, business, or public administration courses.

Law students and lawyers entering the field of public finance will soon find themselves immersed in volumes of very detailed material (bond transcripts can run into the hundreds of pages) that require technical mastery of the subject. However, a full understanding of the relevant documents also requires an appreciation of the interrelated social and political issues. Thus, many public policy questions—ranging from the appropriate role of government in society to the appropriate location of new capital facilities—frequently are central to the approval and implementation of a particular taxation, expenditure, or borrowing proposal. Moreover, responses to periodic fiscal crises (many of which are analyzed in this book) require both imagination and respect for settled expectations. Therefore, lawyers and others involved in public finance must be fully conversant with both technical legal rules and the broader public policy issues.

This book focuses upon three main concerns: (1) the requirements contained in state laws controlling whether a particular tax or debt obligation is authorized; (2) federal and state constitutional limitations upon the exercise of taxing and borrowing powers; and (3) the rules for actually engaging in taxation, expenditures, or debt financing. Whenever possible, within the space constraints, the authors have attempted to place these rules and policies within their social and historical context.

M. DAVID GELFAND
JOEL A. MINTZ
PETER W. SALSICH, JR.

New Orleans,
Fort Lauderdale,
and St. Louis,
Spring 2007

*

ACKNOWLEDGEMENTS

Duquesne Law Review for permission to paraphrase material from Herman C. McCloud, *Sales Tax and Use Tax: Historical Developments and Differing Features*, 22 DUQUESNE LAW REVIEW 823, 825-827, 835-838 (1984).

Matthew Bender and Company, Inc., one of the LEXIS Publishing companies, for permission to cite and paraphrase material from MANDELKER, NETSCH, SALSICH, WEGNER, STEVENSON AND GRIFFITH, STATE AND LOCAL GOVERNMENT IN A FEDERAL SYSTEM, (6th ed. 2006).

THE URBAN LAWYER for permission to use material from *New Federal Tax Legislation Affecting Tax Exempt Obligations*, by Neil P. Arkuss; reprinted with permission of THE URBAN LAWYER, the national quarterly journal on state and local government of the American Bar Association, as it appeared in Volume 16, Number 4 (Fall 1984), Robert H. Freilich, editor.

New York University School of Law for permission to paraphrase material from Shores, *State Taxation of Interstate Commerce—Quiet Revolution or Much Ado About Nothing?* 38 TAX LAW REVIEW 127, 131-136, 167-168 (1982) (1982). Copyright © 1982 by New York University School of Law. All rights reserved.

ACKNOWLEDGEMENTS

Foundation Press for permission to reprint material from OLDMAN and SCHOETTLE, STATE AND LOCAL TAXES AND FINANCE 856-857 (1974). Copyright © 1974 by Foundation Press, Inc. All rights reserved.

West Group for permission to paraphrase material from STATE AND LOCAL GOVERNMENT DEBT FINANCING (1991 & annual supps.), Edited by M. David Gelfand.

————————

The authors would like to thank Kent Bartholomew, Laura Ford, Kate Kmiec, Keith Sonderling, and Connor Sperry for their invaluable research assistance. The careful word processing work of Andrea Brigalia, Leslie Deckelbaum, and Jesse Monteagudo is very much appreciated.

OUTLINE

OUTLINE

OUTLINE

XVIII

TABLE OF CASES

References are to Pages

A

D

DaimlerChrysler Corp. v. Cuno, ___ U.S. ___, 126 S.Ct. 1854, 164 L.Ed.2d 589 (2006), *53, 143*

DeFazio v. Washington Public Power Supply System, 296 Or. 550, 679 P.2d 1316 (Or.1984), *258*

Department of Revenue of Oregon v. ACF Industries, Inc., 510 U.S. 332, 114 S.Ct. 843, 127 L.Ed.2d 165 (1994), *40*

Dolan v. City of Tigard, 512 U.S. 374, 114 S.Ct. 2309, 129 L.Ed.2d 304 (1994), *121, 122*

Downingtown Area School District v. Chester County Bd. of Assessment Appeals, 913 A.2d 194 (Pa.2006), *16*

E

Energy Reserves Group, Inc. v. Kansas Power and Light Co., 459 U.S. 400, 103 S.Ct. 697, 74 L.Ed.2d 569 (1983), *235*

Exxon Corp. v. Wisconsin Dept. of Revenue, 447 U.S. 207, 100 S.Ct. 2109, 65 L.Ed.2d 66 (1980), *34, 35, 36*

F

Fair Assessment in Real Estate Ass'n, Inc. v. McNary, 454 U.S. 100, 102 S.Ct. 177, 70 L.Ed.2d 271 (1981), *141*

Federal Maritime Com'n v. South Carolina State Ports Authority, 535 U.S. 743, 122 S.Ct. 1864, 152 L.Ed.2d 962 (2002), *23*

Fitzgerald v. Racing Ass'n of Central Iowa, 539 U.S. 103, 123 S.Ct. 2156, 156 L.Ed.2d 97 (2003), *15*

Fitzpatrick v. Bitzer, 427 U.S. 445, 96 S.Ct. 2666, 49 L.Ed.2d 614 (1976), *24*

Flushing National Bank v. Municipal Assistance Corp. for City of New York, 390 N.Y.S.2d 22, 358 N.E.2d 848 (N.Y.1976), *181, 222, 224*

F.W. Woolworth Co. v. Taxation and Revenue Department of New Mexico, 458 U.S. 354, 102 S.Ct. 3128, 73 L.Ed.2d 819 (1982), *34, 35*

G

Garcia v. San Antonio Metropolitan Transit Authority, 469 U.S. 528, 105 S.Ct. 1005, 83 L.Ed.2d 1016 (1985), *23, 24, 25*

L

M

N

O

P

Q

R

S

T

U

W

TABLE OF CASES

*

STATE AND LOCAL TAXATION AND FINANCE

IN A NUTSHELL

Third Edition

*

CHAPTER I

HISTORICAL INTRODUCTION

PART A.   HISTORICAL DEVELOPMENTS

The early features of American state and local government taxation evolved out of the fiscal systems of the American colonies. These systems varied somewhat, depending upon the economic conditions present in those various colonies. For example, in the New England colonies taxes were levied based upon ownership of land. (However, the modern property tax was not fully developed until the Nineteenth Century.) The Southern colonies, by contrast, primarily taxed imports and exports.

From the beginning, the state and local governments that relied upon a form of property tax had to supplement it with other kinds of taxes. The extent of diversification of revenue sources depended upon the economic conditions in particular geographic regions and the changes in those conditions over time. The most popular forms of diversification are taxes on production, use, or consumption of goods and services (sales, excise, use and gross receipts taxes). Diversification of revenue sources has permitted state and local governments to stabilize and increase their tax yields.

The first widespread use of debt financing by state and local governments came in the early Nineteenth Century. As the shape of the American economy changed, the need for development of infrastructure, communication networks, and transportation greatly increased. Public debt financing of such infrastructure increased dramatically where private enterprise was unable to raise sufficient capital.

Initially, very few controls were imposed on state debt financing, so several states financed transportation and commercial projects with their bonds in the early Nineteenth Century. In the wake of the economic panic of 1837, tax and project revenues declined, and several states defaulted or suspended payments on their obligations during the 1840s. Some states even repudiated portions of their debt. In response, debt ceilings (see IV I(1)-(3), below) and lending of credit limitations (see IV C(1)(b) and IV F(2), below) were later added to the constitutions of these states and of states that subsequently entered the Union.

Because these early restrictions did not apply to local governments, they were free to finance the railroad boom of the mid-Nineteenth Century by floating general obligation debt. Soon, however, many municipalities became overextended, just as several states had been earlier in the century. Many municipal bond defaults occurred during the depression of 1873–1879 and the panic and depression of 1893. As a result, local government lending of credit prohibitions, debt ceilings, and referenda requirements were added to state constitutions and statutes to restrict municipal debt financing, just as policymakers had added the earlier limits to restrict state debt-financing activities. Over time, exceptions to these restrictions have been developed, and it has become clear that neither debt ceilings nor referenda requirements are sufficient to ensure state and local fiscal integrity or to prevent periodic financial crises.

PART B.   THE INCREASING SIGNIFICANCE OF STATE AND LOCAL GOVERNMENT TAXATION AND FINANCE SINCE WORLD WAR II

State and local government taxes, expenditure patterns and debt financing have become increasingly important since World War II, because the state and local sector of the U. S. economy has expanded greatly during this period. The fairly high level of state and local government borrowing has important effects upon the banking industry, credit markets, and other aspects of the national economy. Developments in state and local taxation and spending can also have significant impacts upon the expansion or decline of private businesses. Therefore, the substantial publicity surrounding the 1982 Washington Public Power Supply System default and the local government fiscal crises of the last three decades—in Orange County, California, Camden, New Jersey, Cleveland, Ohio and New York City—is not surprising. (See III E, IV F(1), and IV H (3)–(4), below.)

In addition to these economic effects, state and local government financial affairs have an important effect upon the quality of life experienced by Americans, because these governments provide many significant public services. Contractions in tax revenues and intergovernmental aid since the mid–1970s have resulted in pressures upon these governments in their attempts to maintain, from current revenues, the services demanded by their citizens. In addition, in recent decades, state and local governments have been called upon to borrow to finance economic development programs, low-and-moderate-income housing, pollution control facilities, and student loans, as well as traditional capital infrastructure products.

State and local taxation and finance also have important ramifications for many areas of the law. In addition to their obvious effect upon the development of local government law, cases involving state and local taxation and finance also figure prominently in the fields of constitutional and administrative law.

This Nutshell begins with general revenue sources, then reviews budgetary matters and concludes with debt financing. Chapter II This Nutshell first discusses state and local government revenue sources, including various forms of taxes, license fees, special assessments, "gaming" revenues, fines, and intergovernmental aid (see Chapter II). The next Chapter III considers state and local government expenditure patterns (for current, ongoing expenses), including budgetary requirements and responses to fiscal crises. The fourth and final chapter describes and analyzes state and local government debt financing and capital spending.

CHAPTER II

STATE AND LOCAL GOVERNMENT REVENUE SOURCES

PART A.   OVERVIEW

Revenue sources employed by state and local governments can be classified as taxes, license fees, special assessments and service charges, "gaming" revenues, fines, or intergovernmental aid. Taxes include real property, personal property, income, sales, severance, and estate and gift taxes. The mix of revenue sources varies from one type of government to another. For example, most school districts rely upon real property (ad valorem) taxes and some service charges (user fees), but cities, particularly larger ones in metropolitan areas, employ nearly the whole range of revenue sources to fund their municipal services.

The use of service charges (user fees) rather than taxes to pay for a particular service may be more or less equitable (fair), depending upon the type of service involved and the method of structuring the service charges. (See II H, below.) A fairly new revenue source involves funds derived from legalized gambling, such as profits from state lotteries or taxes upon casinos. (See II I, below.)

Section 1. Economic Classifications

Taxes can be classified as progressive or regressive; income elastic or inelastic; and cyclical, countercyclical, or non-cyclical.

A tax is "progressive" if its rate increases as the taxpayer's income (or wealth) being taxed increases. The classic example is the federal income tax, which has higher marginal rates for persons in higher income brackets. A tax is "regressive" if its burden is greater for persons with lower incomes (or wealth) than for persons with higher incomes (or wealth).

A tax is said to be "income elastic" if it is directly related to changes in the taxpayer's income. Income taxes are inherently income elastic because they are based on taxpayer income, which can fluctuate up or down, but residential property taxes tend to be fairly inelastic, because homeowners do not buy or sell their homes as frequently as their income may change. Also, real property taxes are based upon assessment levels, which do not always keep pace with increases in property values let alone increases (or decreases) in property owners' incomes. (See II B(1), below.)

A tax (or intergovernmental aid payment) is classified as "cyclical" when it rises and falls with the business cycle, as "countercyclical" when it varies in inverse proportion to the business cycle, and as "non-cyclical" when its variations are unrelated to the business cycle. Sales taxes are generally cyclical, because purchases—and therefore sales taxes—increase when the economy is in a period of upswing, and they decline during periods of economic downturn. By contrast, the real property tax is basically non-cyclical, because it remains a fairly stable revenue source during both upswings and downturns in the business cycle. Some business owners have complained that personal property taxes on inventory are countercyclical, because they tend to be higher during recessionary periods when businesses are forced to carry larger inventories.

Section 2. State and Federal Constitutional Constraints

The federal Constitution and state constitutions place various restrictions upon the taxing power of state and local governments. The principal state constitutional constraints are contained in provisions restricting the types of taxes and limiting their rates, public purpose requirements, and uniformity and equal protection provisions. (Many restrictions upon local taxation also appear in state statutes.) The United States Constitution places several constraints upon the operation of state and local taxes. The principal provisions involved are the equal protection, due process, and commerce clauses. Also, some cases arise under the supremacy clause or the privileges and immunities clause.

Courts, though, presumably under the separation of powers principle, have been reluctant to strike down tax laws. The resulting "presumption of constitutionality" has led commentators to conclude that "constitutional law has played a relatively minor role in the development of tax laws in the United States." Stephen W. Mazza & Tracy A. Kaye, *Restricting the Legislative Power to Tax in the United States,* 54 AM. J. COMP L. 641, 641 (2006).

Subsection a.   General Authorization and Rate Limitations.

The power to tax is an inherent attribute of state authority. But this power is not limitless. Federal and state constitutional provisions place important restrictions on the power to tax. For example, several state constitutions place limits upon the rates of state real property or sales taxes. Local governments, as creatures of the state, do not have inherent power to tax but must be specifically authorized to impose taxes by state statutory or constitutional provisions. These authorizing provisions, in turn, regulate the rates and operation of local government taxes. Courts in some states, however, have ruled that the power to impose certain taxes can be implied from broad "home rule" grants (general state constitutional provisions which grant partial autonomy to local governments). Municipal charters often place additional restrictions upon local taxing power, *e.g.,* a requirement that increases in the municipal sales tax rate must be approved by the local electorate.

Subsection b.   Public Purpose Requirements.

Most state constitutions contain a provision requiring that taxes be levied and collected for public purposes only. The term "public purpose" is inherently vague, and courts have given it a wide variety of interpretations when considering challenges to specific taxation proposals.

The starting point for analysis is the general principle that taxation should be imposed only for the support of a governmental activity or to promote the welfare of the community. Activities that do not serve these purposes but instead foster purely private interests should not be funded by tax dollars. The line drawn between public and private is rarely clear or distinct. Changing community, social and economic concerns, as well as the judiciary's perception of its role in the definitional process, influence the outcome of particular controversies over the public purpose requirement. Both federal and state courts generally give deference to legislative pronouncements on the subject. See, for example, *Appeal of Town of Bethlehem,* 911 A.2d 1, 9–10 (N.H. 2006) (state pollution control property tax exemptions served public purpose and did not unconstitutionally confer private benefits). However, when specific taxing or spending schemes are reviewed, state courts are far more willing than federal courts to examine—and, sometimes, second guess—the legislature. For example, in *Sun 'N Lake Imp. Dist. v. McIntyre,* 800 So.2d 715, 722 (Fla. 2d DCA 2001) the court held that "active marketing of [publicly-owned] lots to private interests for use as private homesites overcomes the presumption that vacant land is held exclusively for a public purpose."

Because the decision to tax is made by a legislative body and is generally viewed as a policy decision affecting the governmental values and policies of the community, a strong presumption of validity attaches to the decision. A specific statement of the public purpose sought to be achieved is not necessary, but a legislative determination will be upheld unless "manifestly and palpably incorrect." As a result, the party challenging the tax has a heavy burden to overcome. The courts, however, in their role as enforcers of constitutional limitations on legislative power, must make the ultimate decision regarding what constitutes a public purpose.

Though a "slide-rule definition ... cannot be formulated," commentators have observed that a number of factors have been used by courts to analyze the public purpose requirement, including prior characterization by the courts, legislative or voter approval, the likelihood of general economic benefit, the potential for significant competition with private enterprise, the number of persons who will benefit, and whether government action is deemed necessary because of the private sector's inability to respond to the particular problem.

Subsection c. *Uniformity Provisions.*

Most state constitutions require that taxes be "uniform." The "uniformity" provisions are closely related to the equal protection concept and generally require that similarly situated persons or objects subject to taxation be treated in a similar manner. The uniformity requirement tends to be implicated in situations that raise one or both of the following two questions: (1) whether some, but not all, persons (or activities) in the taxing jurisdiction can be taxed in a particular manner, and (2) whether differential rates of taxation can be imposed. The first issue might arise, for example, in cases or debates regarding property tax exemptions for particular business activities, sales tax exemptions for specific items such as food and medicine or special benefit assessments (which apply only to certain landowners). The second issue is illustrated by graduated income tax rates, differential gross receipts and license tax rates, and partial property tax abatements.

The cases on this subject generally involve the organization or classification of taxable subjects into groups that receive varying treatment. In general, the courts answer uniformity questions by analyzing the classification scheme that the challenged tax utilizes. Unless a suspect class (such as race) or a fundamental interest (such as the right to vote) is involved, the courts usually apply the so-called "rational basis test" of equal protection jurisprudence to determine the validity of the classification (See II A(2)(d), below.), although some courts conclude that the uniformity clause "imposes more stringent limitations than the equal protection clause on the legislature's authority to classify the subjects and objects of taxation." *Sun Life Assurance Company of Canada v. Manna,* 858 N.E.2d 503, 512 (Ill. App. 2006).

If a legitimate governmental interest can be identified, and the particular classification can be said to bear a rational relationship to that interest, the test is satisfied even though the classification may not be the "most precise possible means of accomplishing [the] legislative purpose." Classifications based on "natural, intrinsic, or fundamental distinctions" have been upheld, while those designed to favor one group over another (such as local businesses competing with outsiders) have been rejected. In sum, the uniformity test is usually satisfied if the tax rates are the same for all persons or objects that fall within a particular (rational) classification.

Subsection d.　Equal Protection Clause.

The United States Constitution and many state constitutions contain an equal protection clause, which (like the uniformity requirement) generally requires that similar persons or objects must be taxed in a similar manner. If a particular tax infringes upon a fundamental interest, for example by taxing religious or free speech activities, the courts will employ the "strict scrutiny test," which requires the taxing governmental entity to prove that the tax is necessary to further a compelling state interest. In addition, if a tax system were to employ a suspect classification, for example by imposing substantial differences in the level of property tax assessment in minority neighborhoods from those in majority neighborhoods or by granting tax credits or other tax concessions to property owners in majority neighborhoods but not in minority ones, a constitutional challenge to that tax system likely would be analyzed under the strict scrutiny test. Taxes subjected to the strict scrutiny test usually are invalidated.

If a tax discriminates on the basis of gender (*e.g.*, by charging women more than men), it will be assayed under the "intermediate scrutiny test," which requires that the tax serve important governmental interests and be substantially related to the achievement of those interests. Most taxes reviewed under this test also will be invalidated, such as an income tax deduction for dependent care expenses available to women, widowers, divorces and husbands whose wives were incapacitated or institutionalized, but not to men who had never married. *Moritz v. Commissioner,* 469 F.2d 466, 470 (10th Cir. 1972), *rev. denied,* 412 U.S. 906 (1973) (classification is an "invidious discrimination"). The case is discussed in the *Mazza/Kaye* article noted above. However, the United States Supreme Court upheld a state statute that granted a real estate homestead exemption to widows but not to widowers. The Court ruled that the law was a legitimate form of benign differentiation designed to compensate women who had suffered economic discrimination in the past. *Kahn v. Shevin,* 416 U.S. 351 (1974). (See II B(5), below.)

Taxes that do not infringe upon fundamental interests and do not discriminate against suspect classes or against one gender will be tested under the "rational basis test," which requires simply that the taxing statute bear a rational relationship to a legitimate governmental interest. When applying this deferential standard, federal courts generally will uphold state and local taxation provisions, even those which differentiate among various classes of property. For example, in *Fitzgerald v. Racing Ass'n of Central Iowa,* 539 U.S. 103 (2003), the United States Supreme Court upheld an Iowa statutes imposing different rates of taxation on revenues derived from slot machines (20 percent from slot machines on on riverboats and 36 percent from slot machines at race tracks). Applying the rational basis standard, the Court held that "there is 'a plausible policy reason for the classification,' that the legislature 'rationally may have . . . considered . . . true' the related justifying 'legislative facts,' and that the 'relationship of the classification to its goal is not so attenuated as to render the distinction arbitrary or irrational.' ". *Id.* at 110, quoting *Nordlinger v. Hahn,* 505 U.S. 1, 11 (1992).

The Court, however, has sometimes relied upon the equal protection clause to invalidate unequal property tax assessment practices as well as state taxes that discriminate against nonresident individuals or corporations. For example, in *Allegheny Pittsburgh Coal Co. v. County Commission of Webster County,* 488 U.S. 336 (1989), the Court invalidated a county assessment practice in which recently purchased property was assessed at the purchase price while only minor annual changes were made to assessments of property not recently sold. *Allegheny* was applied by the Supreme Court of Pennsylvania to strike down a statutory property tax equalization procedure that limited tax assessment challenges to property owners whose assessments were more than fifteen percent different from the statutory standard. *Downingtown Area School District v. Chester County Bd. of Assessment Appeals,* 913 A.2d 194, 205 (Pa. 2006) (applying state uniformity clause).

In *Metropolitan Life Insurance Co. v. Ward,* 470 U.S. 869 (1985), the Court invalidated a statute that imposed a lower tax upon Alabama insurance companies than upon out-of-state companies doing business in Alabama, because it reflected "the very sort of parochial discrimination that the Equal Protection Clause was intended to prevent." (*Id. at 878.) See also Williams v. Vermont,* 472 U.S. 14, 23 (1985) ("residence at the time of purchase is a wholly arbitrary basis" for differential tax treatment).

Some states scrutinize tax provisions more closely under their state equal protection clause than under the federal equal protection clause. Often, state courts use the terms "uniformity" and "equality" almost interchangeably. (*See* II A(2)(c), above.)

Subsection e.   Due Process Clause.

Challenges to state or local taxes based upon the due process clause of the Fourteenth Amendment of the United States Constitution (and its counterpart in many state constitutions) rarely succeed. A common challenge is that a particular tax is so unreasonably high and unduly burdensome as to deny due process. The United States Supreme Court has consistently refused to accept this argument, unless the challenging taxpayer can show that the taxing power is actually being used to disguise some other exercise of power forbidden by the Constitution.

For example, in *City of Pittsburgh v. Alco Parking Corp.*, 417 U.S. 369 (1974), the Court upheld a twenty percent tax on the gross receipts of commercial parking facilities, rejecting arguments that the tax was so excessive as to threaten the taxpayers' businesses and that the City was engaging in unfair competition with the private sector (by operating its own parking facilities which were not subject to the tax). The Court stressed that the size of the tax and its impact upon businesses were matters for the legislature rather than the judiciary. The fact that a tax might threaten the existence of a business or occupation was not in itself sufficient to raise an inference that the legislature was attempting to exercise a forbidden power-confiscation—under the guise of a permissible power-taxation. With respect to the unfair competition charge, the Court concluded that so long as the City was engaged in a lawful activity (which would be subject to state court scrutiny under the state's public purpose doctrine and the authorizing statute) nothing in the federal due process clause prevented government from competing with private businesses or from taxing those businesses in a manner that helped the government enterprise to succeed.

The Supreme Court has employed a similar deferential analysis even in due process cases involving the taxation of interstate commerce. In *Moorman*

Manufacturing Co. v. Bair, 437 U.S. 267 (1978), the Court identified two basic due process requirements for a tax on interstate business: (1) there must be some minimal connection between the activities being taxed and the taxing state, and (2) the measure of the tax must be rationally related to "values connected with the taxing state." In *Norfolk & Western Railroad Co. v. Missouri State Tax Commission*, 390 U.S. 317 (1968), the Court explained that the relevant due process inquiry was whether the tax "in practical operation has relation to opportunities, benefits, or protection conferred or afforded by the taxing state.... Those requirements are satisfied if the tax is fairly apportioned to the commerce carried on within the State."

In reviewing these and other due process cases, the Court in *Commonwealth Edison Co. v. Montana*, 453 U.S. 609 (1981), noted that states have wide latitude in the imposition of general taxes, and it observed that there is no due process requirement that the amount of tax collected from a taxpayer be reasonably related to the value of the services provided to that taxpayer. Quoting from an earlier case upholding an unemployment compensation tax, the *Commonwealth Edison* Court noted that "a tax ... is a means of distributing the burden of the cost of government. The only benefit to which the taxpayer is constitutionally entitled is derived from his enjoyment of the privileges of living in an organized society, established and safeguarded by the devotion of taxes to public purposes."

In *Container Corporation of America v. Franchise Tax Bd.*, 463 U.S. 159 (1983), however, the Court ruled that the due process clause does not permit a state to tax income derived from an interstate business unless there is a "minimal connection" or "nexus" between the taxing state and the interstate activity and "a rational relationship between the income attributed to the State and the intrastate values of the enterprise." Nine years later, the *Court* in *Quill Corp. v. North Dakota,* 504 U.S. 298 (1992), concluded that the Due Process Clause "minimum contacts" test did not require a physical presence in order for an interstate mail-order business to be taxed, but that lack of such physical presence prevented the business from meeting the Commerce Clause's "substantial nexus" test that is a prerequisite for state taxation of such businesses. (See II A(2)(f)(ii), below.)

In addition to the due process issues just discussed and the Commerce Clause limits discussed below, taxing out-of-state companies at higher rates than comparable in-state companies performing the same activity can raise equal protection issues. (See II A(2)(d), above.)

Subsection f.   Commerce Clause.

The commerce clause, Article I, § 8, cl. 3 of the United States Constitution, provides: "The Congress shall have Power ... To regulate Commerce with foreign Nations, and among the several States, and with the Indian Tribes." It is the most significant constitutional limitation on the states' power to tax. From the early days of the American Republic, the United States Supreme Court has recognized the commerce clause as both a grant of power to Congress (the affirmative commerce clause) and a limitation on the power of the states and their local governments (the dormant or negative commerce clause).

Subsubsection i.   Commerce Clause as a Grant of Power to Congress—Federalism Constraints and Preemption. When Congress has already regulated in an area which a state or local government attempts to tax, the courts must first determine whether the legislation involved is within Congress' power to regulate under the commerce clause (or to tax under the taxing and spending clause). Second, they must determine whether the congressional law encounters federalism barriers. Third, the courts must decide whether the state or local taxing measure is consistent with the congressional regulation. If the federal regulation is valid and the state or local tax is inconsistent, the tax will be deemed preempted by the federal regulation, because of the supremacy clause. (See II A(2)(g), below.)

With respect to the first issue—whether Congress has authority to regulate or tax the particular subject—the courts are likely to rule in the affirmative in the vast majority of cases. Ever since 1937, the United States Supreme Court has ruled that Congress has extremely broad regulatory power—even if the regulation also involves intrastate activities, such as a farmer's personal wheat crop or a loan shark's intrastate transactions. During the same modern period, the Supreme Court has also acknowledged Congress' extremely broad power to tax interstate activities.

In 1995, however, the Supreme Court made it clear that there is an outer limit to Congress' regulatory power under the Commerce Clause. In *United States v. Lopez*, 514 U.S. 549 (1995), the Court invalidated the Gun–Free School Zones Act of 1990, because it exceeded Congress' commerce clause power. The Court concluded that the criminal prohibition of guns in school zones did not relate to " 'commerce' or any sort of economic enterprise, however broadly one might define those terms." (*Id.* at 561.) And in *United States v. Morrison*, 529 U.S. 598 (2000), the Court struck down a statute providing a federal civil remedy for victims of gender-motivated violence, holding that Congress "[has no power to[regulate noneconomic, violent criminal conduct based solely on that conduct's aggregate effect on interstate commerce." (*Id.* at 617.) *See also City of Boerne v. Flores*, 521 U.S. 507, 532 (1997) (Congress' power under § 5 of the Fourteenth Amendment was not broad enough to encompass the Religious Freedom Restoration Act of 1993, which "attempt[ed] a substantive change in constitutional protections," by altering the Court's prior interpretation of the Free Exercise Clause).)

The Court reemphasized Congressional commerce clause power in 2005 when it upheld application of the Controlled Substance Act (CSA) to California producers and consumers of marijuana for personal medicinal use. *Gonzales v. Raich,* 545 U.S. 1 (2005). Noting that *Lopez* and *Morrison* applied to regulations "outside Congress' commerce power in its entirety," the Court asserted that "the activities [production, distribution, and consumption of marijuana] regulated by the CSA are quintessentially economic." *Id.* at 23, 25.

Even if a regulation is within Congress' commerce clause (or other enumerated) power, it still might encounter a constitutional barrier based upon federalism constraints. During the last 25 years, there have been several twists and turns in the Supreme Court's decisions regarding when "state sovereignty" might serve as a judicially enforceable barrier to congressional regulation. The high point of this modern development was *National League of Cities v. Usery,* 426 U.S. 833, 852 (1976), in which a majority of the Court ruled that Congress may not "directly displace the States' freedom to structure integral operations in areas of traditional governmental functions." The *National League of Cities* Court added that "integral governmental services provided by" local governments were also "beyond the reach of congressional power under the Commerce Clause, just as if such services were provided by the State itself." (*Id.* at 855–56 n. 20.) Almost immediately, however, the Court began a process of delimiting and narrowing the scope of *National League of Cities* as a precedent, ruling that it did not prevent Congress from regulating land use, labor relations of a state-owned commuter railroad, and civil rights of various government employees. Indeed, in 1985, the Supreme Court overruled *National League of Cities*, in *Garcia v. San Antonio Metropolitan Transit Authority*, 469 U.S. 528 (1985).

Garcia, however, was not the end of this story. In *New York v. United States*, 505 U.S. 144 (1992), the Court invalidated a federal statutory provision that required states to accept ownership of certain waste products or to regulate disposal pursuant to specific congressional instructions. The United States Supreme Court held that the challenged federal provision unconstitutionally "commandeered" the legislative resources of the states. (*Id.* at 175–76.) Later, *Printz v. United States*, 521 U.S. 898, 933 (1997), relying upon *New York*, held that Congress may not commandeer state and local executives (to administer federal regulatory programs) either. Though the *New York* and *Printz* opinions do not purport to overrule *Garcia*, they certainly do articulate crucial situations in which the courts will enforce some limitations upon Congress' otherwise broad commerce clause powers.

Moreover, another aspect of federalism, state sovereign immunity (codified in part in the Eleventh Amendment), protects non-consenting states from being sued in federal or state courts for monetary relief in the absence of valid Congressional abrogation of sovereign immunity. Congress may not employ its powers under Article I of the U.S. Constitution (*e.g.*, the Commerce Clause) to abrogate state sovereign immunity in state or federal courts. (*See Federal Maritime Comm'n v. South Carolina State*

Ports Authority, 535 U.S. 743 (2002) (state consent required for federal agencies to award damages in administrative proceedings); *Board of Trustees of the Univ. of Alabama v. Garrett,* 531 U.S. 356 (2001) (state employees may not recover money damages for violation of the Americans with Disabilities Act (ADA); *Kimel v. Florida Board of Regents,* 528 U.S. 62 (2000) (ADA did not validly abrogate state sovereign immunity); *Alden v. Maine,* 527 U.S. 706 (1999); *College Savings Bank v. Florida Prepaid Postsecondary Educ. Expense Bd.,* 527 U.S. 666 (1999). *See also Seminole Tribe v. Florida,* 517 U.S. 44 (1996).) Thus, as a practical matter, certain federal statutory rights will be extremely difficult for private parties to enforce against the states. However, these cases also acknowledged that Congress, when adopting "appropriate" remedial or preventive legislation under § 5 of the Fourteenth Amendment could abrogate state sovereign immunity. (*See Board of Trustees*; *Alden*; *College Savings*. *See also Fitzpatrick v. Bitzer,* 427 U.S. 445 (1976).) Furthermore, local governments are not protected by Eleventh Amendment immunity unless acting as an "arm of the State." *Northern Insurance Co. of New York v. Chatham County, Georgia,* 126 S.Ct. 1689, 1694 (2006) (admiralty case).

These modern state sovereignty and state sovereign immunity cases have direct implications for state and local taxation and finance. Even before *Garcia, Massachusetts v. United States,* 435 U.S. 444 (1978), had held that state sovereignty did not forbid the imposition of an annual federal registration tax on all civil aircraft to be applied to state-owned police helicopters. Though the Court had difficulty agreeing upon a rationale, *Massachusetts* seems to hold that federal user fees (and possibly some taxes) which apply equally to the private sector and to state (or local) governments are constitutionally allowable. Later (after *Garcia* but before *New York*), *South Carolina v. Baker*, 485 U.S. 505 (1988), upheld a federal statute that required bonds issued by state or local governments to be issued in registered form in order to qualify for tax-exempt status under the Internal Revenue Code. The *Baker* Court also stated, in dicta, that neither the Tenth Amendment nor the doctrine of intergovernmental tax immunity prevents Congress from taxing the interest paid to the holders of state and local government bonds. (See IV G(2), below.) Although *New York v. United States*, as noted above, ruled that Congress may not commandeer state legislative resources, *New York* reaffirmed that Congress may attach conditions to the receipt of federal funds by a state, even though these conditions may influence that state's legislative choices. (See II K(1), below.)

Once a court has determined that the federal regulation is within Congress' commerce clause or taxing and spending clause powers and is not blocked by federalism constraints, then the court must decide whether the federal regulation preempts the state tax. If the state statute directly conflicts with the federal act, it usually will be preempted. Alternatively, the reviewing court might determine that the federal regulation of the relevant subject matter is so extensive that it occupies the field, preempting any state regulation or taxation in that field. These questions will often require the court to engage in careful statutory interpretation.

Cipollone v. Liggett Group, 505 U.S. 504 (1992), articulates several general principles of federal preemption analysis. While there is a presumption against pre-emption of state police power regulations, Congressional intent to pre-empt governs. State laws in conflict with federal laws are preempted. Federal laws that "occupy a legislative field" pre-empt state laws. *Id.* at 516–520. Helpful cases dealing specifically with federal preemption of state taxes include: *Cotton Petroleum Corp. v. New Mexico,* 490 U.S. 163 (1989), applied in *Montana v. Crow Tribe of Indians*, 523 U.S. 696, 713–715 (1998) (federal statute "did not] categorically pre-empt" nondiscriminatory state severance taxes on production of oil and gas on Indian reservation); *Aloha Airlines, Inc. v. Director of Taxation of Hawaii*, 464 U.S. 7, 12 (1983) ("plain language" of federal statute pre-empted state head tax on airline passengers); and *Maryland v. Louisiana*, 451 U.S. 725 (1981) (Louisiana's first Use Tax, imposed on natural gas imported into Louisiana from the federal Outer Continental Shelf for transmission to other states, invalidated on Supremacy Clause and interference with interstate commerce grounds).

Subsubsection ii. Dormant Commerce Clause as a Limitation on State Power. Even if Congress has not acted, the Commerce Clause has been held to prohibit certain state actions that interfere with interstate commerce. *South Carolina State Highway Dept. v. Barnwell Brothers, Inc.*, 303 U.S. 177, 185 (1938). Commentators attribute this "dormant" concept to the supreme court's decision in *Cooley v. Bd. of Wardens,* 53 U.S. 299, 317–320 (1851). *See* LAURENCE H. TRIBE 1 AMERICAN CONSTITUTIONAL LAW 1030 (3d ed. 2000). As initially interpreted, the dormant commerce clause rendered states powerless to tax goods and services in interstate commerce. The history of the so called "tax immunity rule," as established by Supreme court decisions, is summarized by Professor David Shores in *State Taxation of Interstate Commerce—Quiet Revolution or Much Ado About Nothing?* 38 TAX LAW REVIEW 127 (1983), and Herman C. McCloud in *Sales Tax and Use Tax: Historical Developments and Differing Features*, 22 DUQUESNE LAW REVIEW 823 (1984).

In 1872, the United States Supreme Court invalidated a Pennsylvania tax imposed on the transportation of goods. That tax was based on weight rather than distance traveled and was applied equally to intrastate and interstate transportation. The Court concluded that the tax was similar to a tariff on goods entering the state rather than a tax on the conduct of business within the state. Fifteen years later, the Court invalidated a Tennessee tax imposed on out-of-state firms for the privilege of selling goods within the state, ruling that "interstate commerce cannot be taxed at all." In effect, interstate commerce enjoyed immunity from state taxation even though such commerce might have significant effects on the facilities and institutions of a particular state.

The tax immunity rule, though severely criticized, remained in effect for approximately 100 years. The rule was inadequate, because it failed to recognize that the evil of state taxation of interstate activity is not taxation *per se* but rather the potential for multiple taxation by several states through improperly apportioned taxes. A complicated body of rules developed, based on finely tuned distinctions and subtleties in legislative drafting. The rules distinguished among such varied factors as: local or national subjects of taxation; direct or indirect burdens on interstate commerce; use of property in interstate commerce rather than interstate commerce itself; type of business license held; and the form of the tax (*e.g.*, privilege of exercising local franchise) instead of its measure (*e.g.*, gross receipts derived from out-of-state business).

Finally, in 1940, the Court recognized that interstate commerce should "bear its fair share of the state tax burden," so long as the tax involved was nondiscriminatory. *McCloud,* at 826, quoting *McGoldrick v. Berwind–White Coal Mining Co.,* 309 U.S. 33, 49 (1940). However, in subsequent cases, the Court continued for a time to insist that direct taxes on interstate sales were unconstitutional, even taxes that were nondiscriminatory and fairly apportioned. The tax immunity rule gradually gave way, as the Court shifted its focus to an emphasis upon and concern for multiple taxation. Eventually, the tax immunity rule was abandoned in *Complete Auto Transit, Inc. v. Brady*, 430 U.S. 274 (1977).

Complete Auto Transit involved a gross receipts tax assessed by the State of Mississippi against a Michigan corporation that transported cars by rail from an out-of-state assembly plant to Jackson, Mississippi .where they were transported by truck to dealers throughout the state. After reviewing the development of the law and the general dissatisfaction with the formalistic tax immunity rule, the Court abandoned that rule in favor of a four-prong test that considers the practical effect of the tax.

Under the *Complete Auto Transit* test, state taxation of interstate commerce is not prohibited by the commerce clause if: "[1] The tax is applied to an activity with a substantial nexus with the taxing state, [2] is fairly apportioned, [3] does not discriminate against interstate commerce, and [4] is fairly related to the services provided by the State." The Court held that interstate commerce may be made to "pay its way" and, therefore, a state tax that burdens interstate commerce is not per se invalid.

Commentators had long argued that a tax that was nondiscriminatory and fairly apportioned to business done within the state should not be treated as an infringement on interstate commerce because it would fall evenly on both interstate and intrastate commerce. Thus, the Court's decision in *Complete Auto Transit* was generally welcomed as establishing a framework for a more rational approach to a difficult problem of federalism.

Moreover, the United States Supreme Court has had several opportunities to apply the *Complete Auto Transit* framework to dormant Commerce Clause tax cases. The enormous complexity and diversity of interstate commerce and the increased pressures upon state and local governments to finance services through sources other than the property tax have led states to probe the outer limits of the dormant Commerce Clause with a variety of tax schemes.

Several cases have sought to flesh out aspects of the *Complete Auto Transit* four-part test, but a case decided in 1981 deserves special attention. In *Commonwealth Edison Co. v. Montana*, 453 U.S. 609 (1981), the Supreme Court sustained a state severance tax of up to thirty percent on coal mined within the state of Montana. The Court reemphasized its view that the focus of judicial review should be on "the practical effect of a challenged tax" rather than on the characteristics of the tax. The Court had little difficulty concluding that the thirty percent severance tax met the substantial nexus and fair apportionment prongs of the *Complete Auto Transit* test, because the tax applied only to coal mining activity within Montana, and there was no potential for multiple taxation because "the severance can occur in no other state." With respect to the nondiscrimination prong of the test, the *Commonwealth Edison* Court reasoned that although ninety percent of Montana's coal was shipped to other states under contracts that shifted the tax burden primarily to non-Montana utility companies, there was no discriminatory tax treatment of interstate commerce. This conclusion was based upon the fact that the severance tax was computed at the same rate regardless of the final destination of the coal.

In analyzing the fourth prong of the *Complete Auto Transit* test, the *Commonwealth Edison* Court ruled that a tax is fairly related to services provided by the taxing state if the measure of the tax (the basis upon which it is calculated) is reasonably related to the contacts the taxpayer has with the state. Because the Montana severance tax was based upon activity that occurred entirely within the state and was measured as a percentage of the value of the coal extracted, the Court concluded that the tax was in "proper proportion" to the taxpayers' "consequent enjoyment of the opportunities and protections which the State has afforded." The Court refused to accept the argument that the fair relationship prong of the *Complete Auto Transit* test required a factual inquiry into the costs and benefits of state services provided to the taxpayer. Characterizing the question of the appropriate level or rate of taxation as a legislative matter, the Court refused to second guess the Montana Legislature's decision to raise the coal severance tax to a maximum of 30 percent of the coal's "contract sales price."

Strong dissenting opinions argued that the coal severance tax singled out interstate commerce and that careful judicial scrutiny was needed to determine whether the tax was fairly related to services provided by the State. The dissenters contended that the proper approach was to develop a factual cost-benefit analysis of the tax through a trial. (Due process aspects of *Commonwealth Edison* are analyzed in II A(2)(e), above, and severance taxes are discussed in II F(3), below.)

The four-prong test of *Complete Auto Transit* remains the standard for testing state and local taxes under the dormant Commerce Clause. *See, e.g., American Trucking Associations, Inc. v. Michigan Public Service Comm'n,* 545 U.S. 429, 438 (2005) (applying *Complete Auto* factors in upholding flat fee imposed on trucks engaging in intrastate business, even though trucks might also be used in interstate business). Applications of each prong can be summarized as follows:

(a) Substantial Nexus. Most of the cases concerning this prong of the test have been challenges to state and local sales and uses taxes brought by mail order companies. The Supreme Court has ruled that such taxes cannot be imposed upon a company whose only contacts with the taxing state are by mail or common carrier, but that a use tax can be imposed upon catalogue sales from a store which has retail outlets in the taxing state. Therefore, lower court decisions on this subject have turned on the particular facts regarding the company and transactions involved. For example, the Supreme Court of Appeal of West Virginia has ruled that the Supreme Court's physical presence requirement for nexus articulated in *Quill Corp. v. North Dakota,* 504 U.S. 298, 317 (1992) was applicable "only to use and sales taxes and not to business franchise and corporation net income taxes." *Tax Commissioner v. MBNA America Bank, N.A.,* 640 S.E.2d 226, 232 (W.Va. 2006). If Congress lifts the current moratorium on state and local taxation of Internet sales, interesting questions are likely to arise concerning whether electronic commerce firms and transactions have a sufficient nexus with the taxing state or local government. (See II E(3)(b), below.)

(b) Fair Apportionment. In the context of the dormant commerce clause, fair apportionment refers to the extent to which an interstate (or international) business can be taxed, by a particular state, on its nationwide (or worldwide) income. This often involves the question whether a parent company operating within the taxing state is part of a "unitary business" that includes the parent and several subsidiaries operating outside the state. A commonly used apportionment formula incorporates the relative proportion of payroll, property, and sales receipts of the company for its in-state operations compared to the total of these three factors for its business as a whole (worldwide, if it is a unitary business). For example, if the corporation does one percent of its "business," as computed by this multi-factor formula, within the taxing state, then one percent of its total income may be used in computing the state's corporate income tax.

In two 1980 cases, the Court upheld state apportionment schemes. In *Mobil Oil Corp. v. Commissioner of Taxes*, 445 U.S. 425 (1980), the Court held that the vertically integrated oil company challenging the tax was a unitary business. The Court observed that it would be "misleading" to assign the income of such a company to a single geographical situs, because this would "fail to account for contributions to income resulting from functional integration, centralization of management, and economies of scale." Three months later, in *Exxon Corp. v. Wisconsin Department of Revenue*, 447 U.S. 207 (1980), the Court held that not even a separation of the parent company into quasi-competitive divisions, with distinct accounting, would serve as a constitutional barrier to state taxation of a fair proportion of the company's *total* business income.

After a two year hiatus, the Court returned to the unitary business issue and refined its analysis somewhat. It was not persuaded, even after close examinations of actual operations, that a unitary business existed in either *ASARCO Inc. v. Idaho State Tax Commission*, 458 U.S. 307 (1982), or in *F. W. Woolworth Co. v. Taxation and Revenue Department of New Mexico*, 458 U.S. 354 (1982). In *ASARCO*, the Court found that even though the mineral company challenging the tax potentially had the power to control its subsidiary, there was no evidence that it actually had done so. The Court held that an insufficient nexus precluded Idaho from taxing the subsidiary's income. (A strong dissent deplored the Court's approach to the unitary business and fair apportionment issues.) In *Woolworth*, the Court concluded that dividend income received from foreign subsidiaries was not properly taxed by the state of New Mexico. Woolworth and its foreign subsidiaries did not constitute a unitary business because each subsidiary was autonomous and independent from the parent company. The Court easily distinguished these multi-national retail merchandising companies from the vertically integrated businesses previously examined in *Mobil* and *Exxon*.

The Court later attempted to synthesize these cases, in *Container Corp. of America v. Franchise Tax Bd.*, 463 U.S. 159 (1983). There, the Court explained that a unitary business must have "some sharing or exchange of value not capable of precise identification or measurement—beyond the mere flow of funds arising out of a passive investment or a distinct business operation—which renders formula apportionment a reasonable method of taxation." (*Id.* at 169.) The *Container Corporation* Court also examined the type of formula to be applied to such a business. The Court explained that a fair apportionment formula must be both internally and externally consistent. That is, the allocation must be such that: (1) if applied by every jurisdiction, it would result in no more than all of the unitary business' income (or gross receipts or sales) being taxed (internal consistency); and (2) it would reflect a reasonable sense of how that income is generated (external consistency).

The *Container Corporation* Court found that the common three-factor formula described above, though imperfect, was constitutionally acceptable. The Court also reaffirmed that the challenging taxpayer has the " 'distinct burden of showing ... that [the scheme] results in extraterritorial values being taxed'." (quoting *Exxon*) Moreover, the Court suggested that in subsequent cases dealing with these issues, it would defer to lower court fact-finding rather than immerse itself in the financial minutiae of a business' operations. However, in *Hunt-Wesson, Inc. v. Franchise Tax Board of California,* 528 U.S. 458 (2000), the court invalidated a California statute that had the effect of authorizing the state to tax "nonunitary" income that 'derive[s] from unrelated business activity which constitutes a discrete business enterprise.' " *Id.* at 461.

(c) Nondiscrimination. This third prong of the *Complete Auto Transit* test may be the most significant. The Supreme Court has a long—and continuing—history of invalidating state and local taxes that facially discriminate against interstate commerce, especially if the tax provides a commercial advantage for businesses within the state imposing it.

In *Maryland v. Louisiana*, 451 U.S. 725 (1981), the Court invalidated Louisiana's First Use Tax, which was imposed on natural gas imported into Louisiana from the federal Outer Continental Shelf (OCS). The gas subject to the tax had not previously been taxed by Louisiana, by any other state, or by the United States, and it was processed in Louisiana for ultimate distribution to consumers in over thirty states. The Court found that the local nexus prong of the *Complete Auto Transit* test was met, but it concluded that the tax discriminated against interstate commerce because of the numerous tax credits and exclusions Louisiana granted to local users of offshore gas. Even though the First Use Tax was imposed at the same rate as the severance tax, it did not qualify as a compensatory tax. The Court reasoned that the gas was being extracted from federally owned lands and, therefore, did not constitute a loss of Louisiana natural resources. Because severance and first use (processing) were not "substantially equivalent events," the first-use tax did not complement the Louisiana severance tax the way a use tax complements a sales tax (by attempting to ensure uniform treatment of goods and materials consumed in the state). The Court found no such equality of treatment between local and interstate commerce in the Louisiana tax scheme. (Portions of the First Use Tax were also invalidated on supremacy clause grounds, see II A(2)(g), below.)

In 1984, the Court invalidated three separate taxes under the nondiscrimination prong of *Complete Auto Transit*:

(1) A New York franchise tax on the accumulated income of subsidiaries, which allowed a credit for gross receipts attributable to export shipments originating in New York, was invalidated in *Westinghouse Electric Corp. v. Tully*, 466 U.S. 388 (1984). There, the Court ruled that the credit discriminated against shipping originating in other states. The majority of the Court was not

persuaded that there was a significant difference between giving a credit for in-state business activity and imposing a higher tax on out-of-state business activity.

(2) In *Armco Inc. v. Hardesty*, 467 U.S. 638 (1984), the Court ruled that a West Virginia gross receipts tax on businesses selling tangible property at wholesale discriminated against interstate commerce because of an exemption granted to local manufacturers. Even though these local manufacturers were subject to a higher manufacturing tax, the Court ruled that the gross receipts tax imposed on interstate wholesalers could not be viewed as a "compensating tax" for the local manufacturing tax, because manufacturing and wholesaling are not "substantially equivalent events." (*See also Container Corp.*, discussed above.)

(3) In *Bacchus Imports, Ltd. v. Dias*, 468 U.S. 263 (1984), the Court held that an Hawaii tax on sales of liquor at wholesale discriminated against interstate commerce because of an exemption granted to local producers of fruit wine and brandy (from an indigenous Hawaiian shrub). Neither the ability of wholesalers to pass on the tax to consumers nor the fact that very little local liquor was produced under the exemption could save the tax, because "discrimination between in-state and out-of-state goods is as offensive to the Commerce Clause as discrimination between in-state and out-of-state taxpayers." *Bacchus* is further discussed in section II E(4)(c), below.

The Court has continued its pattern of invalidating state laws that discriminate against interstate commerce. For example, *American Trucking Ass'ns, Inc. v. Scheiner*, 483 U.S. 266 (1987), invalidated a flat highway tax on trucks. The Supreme Court insisted: "[I]mposition of the flat taxes for a privilege [using the state's highways] that is several times more valuable to a local business than to its out-of-state competitors is unquestionably discriminatory and thus offends the Commerce Clause." *Id.* at 296. In a significant decision, *Camps Newfound/Owatonna, Inc. v. Town of Harrison*, 520 U.S. 564 (1997), held that Maine could not deny a real property tax exemption to non-profit camps that catered to non-residents while granting such an exemption to non-profit camps that primarily served residents. Similarly, the Court recently invalidated Alabama's franchise tax scheme, which facially discriminated against foreign corporations and effectively taxed them at five times the rate of domestic corporations. *South Central Bell Tele. Co. v. Alabama*, 526 U.S. 160 (1999).

(d) Fair Relationship to Services. This fourth prong of the test has very little, if any, bite after *Commonwealth Edison* (discussed above). So long as the state provides some services, such as police protection or even "the benefits which it [confers] by the fact of being an orderly civilized society," (453 U.S. at 625), its taxes should be able to satisfy the fair relationship prong of the dormant commerce clause test.

Because the Commerce Clause is a grant of plenary power, Congress can choose to grant states the power to impose a tax that otherwise would violate the dormant Commerce Clause. For example, the Supreme Court of Wisconsin, applying a "reverse-preemption" analysis, concluded that amendments to the Federal Aviation Act of 1958, 49 U.S.C.A. § 40116 (2000 and West Supp. 2006), which "prohibit eight tax practices with regard to air carriers ... [b] clearly authorizes state taxes, including property taxes, except those proscribed," evidenced an intent to "authorize[] the states to create property tax exemptions for transportation property without exposing these exemptions to challenge under the dormant Commerce Clause." *Northwest Airlines, Inc. v. Wisconsin Dept. of Revenue,* 717 N.W.2d 280, 289–293 (Wis. 2006), applying *Department of Revenue of Oregon v. ACF Industries, Inc.,* 510 U.S. 332 (1994).

As tax laws have become more complex, the economy moves into a global phase and information technology matures, the elements of dormant Commerce Clause jurisprudence are tested. For an excellent article advocating a rethinking of this jurisprudence, particularly the nexus requirement, see Bradley W. Joondeph, *Rethinking the Role of the Dormant commerce Clause in State Tax Jurisdiction,* 24 VA. TAX REV. 109 (2004).

Subsection iii. The Indian tax immunity rule. As noted above, the same constitutional provision that contains the Commerce Clause contains the clause giving the Federal Government exclusive authority over relations with the Indian Nations. *Oneida Indian Nation v. County of Oneida,* 414 U.S. 661, 670 (1974). This has produced a complex body of law affecting states' ability to tax activities engaged in by Indians and/or taking place on Indian lands. States "are categorically barred from placing the legal incidence of an excise tax '*on a tribe or on tribal members* for sales made *inside Indian country*' without congressional authorization." *Wagnon v. Prairie Band Potawatomi Nation,* 546 U.S. 95, 101–102 (2005), quoting *Oklahoma Tax Comm'n v. Chickasaw Nation,* 515 U.S. 450, 459 (1995) (emphasis in original). On the other hand, a balancing test evaluating federal, state and Indian interests is used when activities of non-Indians on Indian land are scrutinized. *White Mountain Apache Tribe v. Bracker,* 448 U.S. 136, 144 (1980). Applying these tests, the Supreme Court refused to apply the balancing test to a Kansas motor fuel tax that was imposed on motor fuel received by non-Indian fuel distributors who later delivered the fuel to a to a gas station owned by and located on the Prairie bend Reservation and concluded that the tax could be imposed despite the fact that the fuel later was delivered to the Reservation. *Wagnon,* 546 U.S. at 110–115.

    Subsection g.   *Supremacy Clause.*

The Supremacy Clause, article VI, cl. 2 of the United States Constitution, provides: "This Constitution, and the Laws of the United States which shall be made in Pursuance thereof ... shall be the supreme Law of the Land ... any Thing in the Constitution or Laws of any State to the Contrary notwithstanding." Its principal application in this field involves claims that state or local tax statutes conflict with federal regulations, especially congressional acts passed pursuant to the commerce clause or the taxing and spending clause. (*See Maryland v. Louisiana*, 451 U.S. 725, 749–52 (1981).) In the case of such a conflict, the supremacy clause dictates that the "supreme" federal law shall prevail. (See II A(2)(f)(i), above.) Many preemption cases involve state taxes that conflict with federal statutes designed to protect Native American tribes.

The supremacy clause also protects the federal government from taxation by the states. (*See McCulloch v. Maryland*, 17 U.S. (4 Wheat.) 316 (1819).) The Supreme Court has explained that federal tax immunity is appropriate "when the levy falls on the United States itself, or on an agency or instrumentality so closely connected to the Government that the two cannot realistically be viewed as separate entities, at least insofar as the activity being taxed is concerned." The Court will, therefore, closely examine the entity being taxed to determine its relationship to the federal government. In *United States v. New Mexico*, 455 U.S. 720 (1982), a unanimous Court held that contractors managing federally owned atomic laboratories within the State were not such closely connected instrumentalities. Therefore, the State's sales and gross receipts taxes, could validly be applied to the contractors.

Subsection   h.   Privileges   and   Immunities Clause.

Article IV, section 2 of the U. S. Constitution provides: "The Citizens of each State shall be entitled to all Privileges and Immunities of Citizens in the several states." In *Austin v. New Hampshire*, 420 U.S. 656 (1975), the Court relied upon the privileges and immunities clause to invalidate the New Hampshire Commuters Income Tax, because it effectively exempted all of the State's own citizens. Reviewing the genesis of the clause in the Articles of Confederation, the Court concluded that this taxing scheme would offend "the structural balance essential to the concept of federalism" because it might invite retaliation by other states. In *Lunding v. New York Tax Appeals Tribunal*, 522 U.S. 287 (1998), the Court held that a New York income tax provision that allowed New York residents, but not nonresidents, to deduct alimony payments violated the privileges and immunities clause.

Subsection i.   The First Amendment.

The First Amendment's guarantee of freedom of religion, speech and assembly, as well as a free press has led courts to scrutinize carefully state and local taxes affecting those freedoms. Nondiscriminatory sales and use taxes on receipts from sales of newspapers and religious publications have been approved by the Supreme Court, *Arkansas Writers'*

Project, Inc. v. Ragland, 481 U.S. 221 (1987) (newspapers) and *Jimmy Swaggart Ministries v. Board of Equalization,* 493 U.S. 378 (1990) (religious publications), but discriminatory use taxes on ink and paper products used by publishers, as well as sales tax exemptions for religious publications have been disapproved. *Minneapolis Star and Tribune Co. v. Minnesota Com'r of Revenue,* 460 U.S. 575 (1983) (use tax on ink and paper) and *Texas Monthly, Inc. v. Bullock,* 489 U.S. 1 (1989). The Court refused to hear an argument that a content-neutral admissions tax, focusing on crowd control and other secondary effects, that was imposed on movie theatres and other recreational facilities violated the First Amendment. *Regal Cinemas, Inc. v. Mayfield Heights,* 738 N.E.2d 42 (Ohio App. 2000), *cert. den.,* 531 U.S. 1125 (2001).

PART B.   REAL PROPERTY (AD VALOREM) TAXES

Section 1.   General Characteristics

Historically, local governments have relied heavily upon the ad valorem property tax, which is a tax upon the value of real property located within the local government's borders. Several large American cities have begun to reduce their dependence upon real property taxes by adding (or increasing) their use of sales, income, and other taxes, and by imposing various types of fees and charges (*see* II F, G & H below). However, many smaller local government entities, especially school districts, still employ the real property tax as their principal revenue source.

Determination whether a particular charge is a property tax can be problematic. Property taxes generally are defined as charges "imposed by a governmental unit upon property or upon a property owner as a direct consequence of ownership of that property except incurred charges and assessments for local improvements." Oregon Const. Art. XI, § 11b(2)(b); *Roseburg School Dist. v. City of Roseburg,* 851 P.2d 595 (Or. 1993). Applying that definition, the Supreme Court of Oregon concluded that a $15.00 per unit "public safety surcharge" on persons responsible for paying water and sewer bills was not a property tax because there was no provision for the imposition of a lien on the property. *Knapp v. City of Jacksonville,* 151 P.3d 143, 144 (Or. 2007).

Though there has been substantial debate among commentators, most agree that the ad valorem tax tends to be "regressive," that is, its burden is greater on lower-income persons than higher-income ones (*see* II A(1), above). Its regressivity is somewhat mitigated in some jurisdictions by the assessment of residential property at a lower level than commercial property (*see* II B(4), below), homestead exemptions, and/or circuit breakers (*see* II B(5), below). Initially, these devices shift the tax burden from residential property owners to owners of rental, industrial, and commercial property. Where economic conditions permit, however, owners of rental property increase rents to reflect their higher property taxes, and industrial and commercial property owners pass on their property taxes to consumers in the form of higher product prices.

Real property taxes also tend to be "income inelastic" and "non-cyclical" (*see* II A(1), above). There is not a direct and immediate relationship between typical increases and decreases in a taxpayer's income and his or her real estate purchases, sales, or improvements. For example, an individual who obtains a pay raise of $1,000 usually will not purchase a new home within the same jurisdiction. Similarly, a small decrease in income will not necessarily result in the sale of his or her home. Instead, residential real property purchases and sales tend to reflect the family life cycle rather than immediate changes in income.

Furthermore, even if a taxpayer does spend all of his or her increased income on property improvements, the increase in property value may not be reflected for some time on the tax rolls because of the delays inherent in reassessments in most jurisdictions. A few state and local governments have computerized the assessment process to reduce these delays.

Section 2. Rate Limitations and Other Restrictions Upon the Level of Real Property Taxes

The property tax levied upon a particular piece of real property equals: (1) the *tax rate* multiplied by (2) the *value of the property* multiplied by (3) the *assessment ratio*. (Factors (2) and (3) are sometimes combined and referred to as the "property tax base.") Property tax limits, levy limits, and full value assessment requirements each restrict different factors in this three-part equation.

Property tax limitations, which restrict factor (1) in the above equation, are the most common form of restriction and have the longest history. They first appeared in state statutes in the 1870s and 1880s and were later incorporated into many state constitutions. These early tax limitations were designed to restrain local government debt (by preventing tax increases to pay debt service on capital projects), to control then-current governmental expenditures, and to protect property owners from undue increases in their tax burdens.

The second round of constitutional tax limitations appeared during the Depression of the 1930s. They were aimed at forcing tax reductions, thereby stemming the tide of tax delinquencies and tax foreclosures of residential property.

The next round of tax limitations was sparked by Proposition 13 (the Jarvis–Gann initiative), adopted in June 1978 and now codified as article XIII A of California's Constitution. It drastically reduced the level of state and local property taxes in California by: (a) setting a maximum rate of one per cent of the tax base; (b) initially rolling back the tax base to 1975–76 assessment levels for landowners with continuous tenure; (c) severely restricting annual increases in the tax base; (d) preventing other forms of property taxation and requiring a two-thirds majority for state statutes or local referenda to increase other types of taxes. Several constitutional attacks upon the basic structure of Proposition 13 have been rejected by the California courts. These courts, however, have generally approved efforts by local governments to preserve flexibility through imaginative tax provisions designed to operate beyond the confines of Proposition 13. Sales taxes imposed by transportation special districts, new fees for processing subdivision and other land applications, increased payroll and gross receipts taxes for general revenue purposes, and special assessments to service and redeem assessment bonds for local improvements all have been held to be outside the purview of, and therefore unrestricted by, Proposition 13. Several studies indicate that Proposition 13 has benefited commercial property owners as much as or more than homeowners. In *Nordlinger v. Hahn*, 505 U.S. 1 (1992), the United States Supreme Court rejected a variety of constitutional challenges to Proposition 13.

Similar constitutional and statutory provisions were considered in several other states after California's adoption of Proposition 13 in 1978. One of the most publicized was "Proposition 2½," a statutory initiative which reduced real estate taxes in Massachusetts to 2.5% of real property values.

Levy limits, which first emerged in state statutes in the 1970s, represent a different approach to tax relief for homeowners faced with inflation-induced increases in their property assessments. Unlike traditional tax rate limits, which restrict factor (1) in the above equation, levy limits restrict the product of the equation, allowing the total property tax levy to rise by only a specified percentage each year. For example, the final amount to be raised from regular property taxes by a taxing district in the state of Washington may not exceed by more than 6% "the amount ... levied ... in the highest of the three most recent years." (Certain additions, however, are authorized.) Thus, if assessments rise substantially, the rate must be reduced in order to stay within the levy limit. State-mandated increases are typically excluded from levy limits. Generally, levy limit statutes allow for increases which are approved by local voters in referenda or by the appropriate state agency.

Section 3. Devices Used to Avoid or Evade Property Tax Limitations

Property tax limitations contain a number of exemptions, which allow government officials to avoid the limits legally. Also, devices have been developed for illegal evasion of these limitations.

Nearly all property tax limitations contain a broad general exemption for taxes imposed by the governmental entity to pay debt service. A notable exception to this pattern was California's Proposition 13, which allowed taxes above its one percent limit only for the payment of debt service on indebtedness that a local government incurred prior to 1978, but not for subsequently incurred debt. Massachusetts' tax limit was even more restrictive. It allowed taxes to be raised above its 2.5% limit to pay debt service (periodic principal and interest payments) on outstanding debt only when the increase had been approved by the local voters. (*See also* IV A–B, below.)

Many state and local governments can increase their property tax revenues without violating the restrictions upon their tax rates simply by increasing their property assessments. This approach is not available, however, in states which have levy limits, states which restrict reassessment levels (like California), or localities that are already at full value assessment. (See II B(4), below.)

A particularly dangerous—and usually illegal—device sometimes used to evade tax limits is "capitalizing of expense items," *i.e.*, transferring operating expenses (such as salaries and pension payments) from the Expense Budget to the Capital Budget. This approach involves borrowing money to pay for current expenses that would ordinarily be financed from current taxes. By using this device, local government officials can increase property taxes above the limitation (because of the above-described exemption for tax increases used to pay debt service), and they can shift part of the cost of these current expenses to future generations of taxpayers (who must pay the debt service). New York City capitalized expense items on a massive scale prior to its fiscal crisis, and other cities subsequently have employed this device on a smaller scale.

Section 4. Full Value Assessment and Other Approaches

Historically, commercial and industrial property was assessed at higher levels than residential property. That is, the assessment ratio, factor (2) in the real estate tax levy equation stated in II B(2), above, has been higher for commercial and industrial property. In several states, these differential levels were used by assessors or tax commissioners without statutory authority or even in contravention of statutory mandates. The process was maintained largely because it benefited homeowners.

During the last 30 years, however, there has been a trend toward voluntary or court-ordered "full value assessment," which requires that all property in the jurisdiction be assessed at its full market value, *i.e.*, that the assessment ratio be 1.0 for all property in the jurisdiction. The catalyst for this trend was *Hellerstein v. Assessor of Islip*, 37 N.Y.2d 1, 371 N.Y.S.2d 388, 332 N.E.2d 279 (1975), a case brought by a law professor on behalf of his wife and himself. In *Hellerstein*, the New York Court of Appeals ordered local governments to end their long-standing practice of disregarding the state statute that mandated full-value assessment.

The New York Legislature later eliminated the statutory mandate underlying the *Hellerstein* court's decision, but several New York counties had already voluntarily adopted full value assessment. Also, some other states have followed the *Hellerstein* reasoning, by insisting that "full value" means exactly what it says and nothing less. Other states,

however, have followed the California model of setting an artificial property value for longstanding
owners, based upon market value several years earlier. (See II B(2), above).

Compliance with a full value requirement does
not, in and of itself, solve all assessment problems.
Questions remain as to what exactly constitutes full
value. Market value is persuasive, but not determi-
native. Other factors to be considered are income
potential, location, historical cost, and construction
costs. Comparisons to the market values of other
property may be necessary, particularly when the
property has not changed hands for many years, as
is often true of commercial property. It is, however,
difficult to determine which property to use for
comparative purposes. For an analysis of the "true
cash value" issue in large commercial property assessments, see Samuel J. McKim, *Is Michigan's Ad
Valorem Property Tax Becoming Obsolete?* 77 U.
DET. MERCY L.REV. 655 (2000). Furthermore, it is
often difficult to keep pace with rapid changes in
property values throughout a large city. Computeri-
zation of the assessment process has been beneficial
in responding to this problem.

Section 5. Exempt Property and Other Tax Collection Problems

Over the years, nearly every state has developed a
large body of property tax exemptions, which have
the effect of reducing the revenues that can be
collected from the real property tax. The exemptions can be classified as charitable (*e.g.*, non-profit

medical care providers), religious, intergovernmental (*e.g.*, state and federal property exempted from local taxes), educational (*e.g.*, private universities), homeowner, and incentive (*e.g.*, to encourage business expansion). The United States Supreme Court has made it clear that real property tax exemptions are subject to constitutional constraints.

Some commentators have criticized the religious and educational exemptions because they often extend not only to sanctuary and classroom buildings but also to land owned by religious or educational institutions but used for other purposes. Other commentators have warned that too-heavy reliance on economic development incentive ("EDI") programs that include tax abatements and exemptions raises dormant Commerce Clause issues because of fierce interstate competition to lure new business and risks serious harm to programs relying on traditional state and local funding assistance. While a Commerce Clause challenge to state and local tax incentives to encourage an automobile manufacturer to expand its operations in Toledo, Ohio was dismissed in 2006 by the United States Supreme Court for lack of standing, *DaimlerChrysler Corp. v. Cuno*, 126 S.Ct. 1854 (2006), the issue is not likely to go away.

General homestead exemptions for residential property exist in the majority of the states. Typically, they exclude from real property taxes a specified dollar value of property owned by permanent residents, *e.g.*, the first $5,000 of assessed value. The amount of property value exempted and the additional requirements for eligibility vary somewhat from state to state.

Additional exemptions are sometimes granted to elderly persons, widows, or veterans. The United States Supreme Court, in *Kahn v. Shevin*, 416 U.S. 351 (1974), held that Florida's grant of a $500 exemption to widows, without allowing a comparable exemption for widowers, did not violate the equal protection clause of the Fourteenth Amendment, because it was a form of benign discrimination to compensate women who had suffered from various forms of economic discrimination in the past. Other Supreme Court cases have held that exemptions for veterans cannot be restricted to veterans who lived in the state prior to their time in the military.

Another method of providing property tax relief is the "circuit breaker," which is more narrowly tailored to benefit low-income homeowners. Its relief provisions are usually triggered when the homeowner's property tax bill exceeds a specified portion of his or her household income. Some states, however, grant relief in the form of a percentage of the owner's property tax bill, with the percentage declining as the household income increases (often with a cap at a specified income level). Alternatively, circuit-breaker relief may be provided in the form of a credit against the property owner's state income taxes or as a direct cash refund. Massachusetts and New Jersey have even provided relief for renters in their income tax systems.

Property owners who believe they qualify for tax exempt status must apply for and receive a designation of such status from the applicable state revenue agency. Maintenance of tax exempt status requires property owners to comply with applicable state laws granting that status. Failure to comply can lead to revocation of the tax exemption. Some property owners who are not entitled to an exemption are, nevertheless, unable or unwilling to pay their property taxes. Though there are procedures for imposing a tax lien on such property and forcing a tax sale to satisfy the lien (see II L(1), below), complying with these procedures is often a long, laborious process. As a result, at any particular time, the tax rolls generally contain some property upon which the taxes are uncollectible.

PART C.   PERSONAL PROPERTY TAXES

Though most states and some local governments tax personal property in one form or another, personal property taxation declined steadily as a revenue source during the Twentieth Century. Instead, state and local governments have come to rely more heavily upon real property, sales, and income taxes. Personal property tax systems are riddled with even more exemptions than real property tax systems (see II B(5), above). Indeed, some states have totally exempted personal property from taxation.

The decline in personal property taxation has generally been attributed to administrative difficulties with this form of taxation. These difficulties include: (a) personalty, being more mobile than realty, can be hidden within the taxing jurisdiction or moved to another jurisdiction; (b) effective discovery of household personalty might involve serious violations of privacy; (c) once discovered, personal property presents greater valuation problems than does real estate. States have attempted to respond to these administrative problems by imposing lower tax rates for personalty than for real property, by assessing personal property at the state rather than at the local level, and by linking their personal property taxes to other registration systems (*e.g.*, state automobile registration).

There are three general classes of personal property: business tangibles, household tangibles, and intangibles. "Business tangibles" are machinery, equipment, and inventory. They are taxed, at least to some extent, in most states. Classification of property as "tangible" can become a source of dispute between tax payer and tax collector. Computer software is a case in point. The Ohio Supreme Court has ruled that canned application software is taxable as tangible business property because it is "always stored on a tangible medium [disc or tape] that has physical existence." *Andrew Jergens Co. v. Wilkins,* 848 N.E.2d 499, 502–503 (Ohio 2006). Fewer states tax household tangibles, and most of those taxing states allow many exemptions. "Intangibles" include stocks, bonds, and bank deposits. They are taxed in very few states, but income from these sources will be reached by state income taxes (see II

D (1), below). In general, personal property taxes have the same economic characteristics as real property taxes (see II B(1), above). The lower cost of most personalty, however, can make personal property taxes somewhat more cyclical and income elastic than real property taxes if reassessments are performed regularly. Taxation of household personalty can be fairly regressive, though the regressivity is generally mitigated by the many exemptions. Initially, the taxation of business intangibles and tangibles (like the taxation of commercial real property) also mitigates the regressivity of personal property taxes; however, the businesses involved may be able to pass on the cost of these taxes to their customers in the form of higher prices.

In addition to the practical problems listed above, taxation of certain forms of personalty raise special policy questions. Taxation of inventories has been criticized as placing a burden on businesses during recessionary periods, when they are generally forced to maintain large inventories but have less income to pay tax bills. Also, taxation of intangibles is often criticized as a form of "double taxation" when the intangibles are corporate securities or mortgages that represent investments in real estate that is already subject to real property taxes.

PART D.   PERSONAL AND CORPORATE INCOME TAXES

Section 1.   General Characteristics and Rates

The vast majority of states levy some form of personal income tax and impose corporate income taxes, but only a few (15) authorize municipalities to impose local income taxes. D. BERMAN, STATE-LOCAL RELATIONS: PARTNERSHIPS, CONFLICT, AND AUTONOMY 53 (ICMA Municipal Yearbook, 2005). Most of the municipalities with income taxes are in Ohio and Pennsylvania; very few are in the South or the West. Large cities using the local income tax include Kansas City, New York, Philadelphia and St. Louis. Cities with a personal income tax also typically levy a corporate income tax, though some states preempt this form of taxation. Cities employing a personal and/or corporate income tax have found it to be an important source of revenue.

Compared to other forms of taxation, state and local income taxes are income elastic and cyclical, and state income taxes are relatively progressive (see II A(1), above). They are inherently income elastic, because they are a function of income. They tend to be cyclical, because increases (or decreases) in personal or corporate incomes are recorded regularly and taxes are withheld monthly or quarterly by employers, corporate treasurers, and self-employed taxpayers. As a result, the time lags which make property taxes non-cyclical (see II B(1), above) generally do not affect income taxes.

State income taxes are fairly progressive, but
their marginal rates are not as high as the federal
income tax system. Though the income tax rates
vary from time to time and from state to state, the
highest state marginal rate has rarely exceeded 15%
in recent years. Furthermore, several states have
"indexed" their personal income tax brackets to
expand with the consumer price index or other
measure of inflation. Indexation is designed to reduce "bracket creep," the process by which inflation-induced salary increases can pull taxpayers
into higher marginal tax brackets under inflexible,
progressive income tax systems.

Most cities that impose personal income taxes
employ a flat or very slightly graduated rate of 1%
to 3% of personal income. A notable exception is the
District of Columbia, whose highest marginal rate is
approximately 10.7%. Some cities tax only "earnings" or "wages," thereby excluding other forms of
income (*e.g.*, interest, dividends, capital gains) from
their personal income tax systems.

The highest marginal rate for state corporate
income taxes rarely exceeds 10 per cent. Municipal
corporate income tax rates are even lower. About
half of the states participate in the Multistate Tax
Compact, under which business income is apportioned to participating states based on the amount
of property, personnel and sales within a particular
state. Business income is defined as "income arising
from transactions and activity in the regular course
of the taxpayer's trade or business." *See, e.g.*, RSMo
§ 32.200, art. IV(1). Courts have used a two-part

test, evaluating whether income is derived from a transaction "in which the taxpayer regularly engages" and whether the income also comes from an "activity [function] that is an integral part of the taxpayer's regular business." Under this standard, the Missouri Supreme Court held that income from the sale and liquidation of a business was not taxable business income because it was a "one-time, extraordinary event." *Abb C–E Nuclear Power Inc. v. Director of Revenue*, 215 S.W.3d 85 (Mo. 2007) But administrative dissolution of a corporation by its state of domicile did not prevent the Supreme Court of Alaska from concluding that the corporation was liable for corporate income taxes in Alaska because it continued to do business in that state. *Northwest Medical Imaging, Inc. v. Dept. of Revenue*, 151 P.3d 434 (Alaska 2006).

Section 2.   Authorization and Administration

Generally, specific legislative authorization has been deemed necessary for municipal income taxes, but the Michigan and Ohio Supreme Courts have held that broad home rule grants constitute sufficient authorization for a municipal income tax. Even in these two states, however, subsequent legislation restricts the rate structure and many administrative details of municipal income tax systems. Several states, by statute or constitutional provision, prohibit municipal income taxes.

Income tax systems are relatively inexpensive to administer. Interestingly, attempts to make them more equitable or progressive tend to increase costs.

For example, taxing income that is not subject to payroll withholding (*e.g.*, dividends and interest) increases enforcement expenses, and allowing deductions or credits (*e.g.*, for taxes paid to other state or local governments) increases the cost of making refunds.

Section 3. Taxation of Nonresidents

Income taxes allow a city, especially a central city, to expand substantially its tax base without altering its boundaries, by taxing persons who earn income within the city but live elsewhere. Attempts by such nonresident taxpayers to attack uniform, neutral state and local income taxes on constitutional grounds have failed. The United States Supreme Court has held, however, that a state or local income tax system that applies solely to nonresidents, or which denies nonresidents certain deductions that it allows for residents, violates the privileges and immunities clause (article IV, § 2, cl. 1, of the United States Constitution). (See II A(2)(h), above.)

PART E. SALES AND OTHER CONSUMPTION TAXES

Section 1. General Characteristics and Definitions

Most states and many local governments levy a tax on the production, use or consumption of goods and services. Such taxes take a variety of forms, including the general retail sales tax (the most common), the special sales (or excise) tax, the use tax, and the gross receipts tax. General sales and gross receipts taxes were products of the Great Depression, being first introduced at the state level in Mississippi in 1932 and at the local level in New York City and New Orleans at about the same time. Special sales (or excise) taxes, however, are of much earlier origin. They were known to the philosopher Hobbes, in 1651, and were imposed in this country as early as 1790, in the form of the whiskey tax.

From the inception of general sales, use and gross receipts taxes, states have embraced them as major alternatives to income and property taxes. In fact, the U.S. Bureau of the Census has reported that sales and gross receipts taxes are the largest source of total state revenues; and some forty-five states, as well as the District of Columbia, now impose a sales tax.

Local governments were slower to utilize sales taxes, mainly because states, which must delegate taxing authority to local governments (see II A(2)(a), above), have tended to guard consumption taxes as a source of revenue. The sales tax is, however, an important local revenue source in states where local property tax rates are severely limited; and local governments in two thirds of the states now levy sales taxes.

Sales and gross receipts taxes have increased in popularity because of strong public pressure to reduce income and property taxes without a corresponding decrease in public services. The principle of taxation based on benefits received makes consumption taxes attractive because of their potential for taxing nonresidents and the greater sense of control taxpayers may have over the incidence of taxation (by reducing their purchases of taxable goods and services).

The general sales tax is imposed on sellers at the time of retail sale to a customer of tangible personal property and/or tangible services. The use tax, which is complementary to the sales tax, is imposed upon the privilege of using, storing, or consuming personal property within the taxing jurisdiction (especially property purchased in another jurisdiction). Excises are special sales taxes targeted at the sale of specific items, such as alcohol, tobacco, and motor fuel. Both the general sales tax and excises are imposed on the seller, but the economic burden is immediately passed on to the purchaser as a specific percentage of the sales price of the good or service being taxed. The gross receipts tax, by contrast, is imposed on manufacturers or sellers on a periodic basis as a percentage of a business' total revenue.

Although sales taxes have some characteristics that resemble property and income taxes, their distinguishing characteristics predominate. Unlike property taxes, which are levied on the basis of the assessed value of property owned by the taxpayer (see II B, above), sales taxes are generally measured by the amount of business done or the extent to which products or services have been used by the purchaser. The gross receipts tax, in particular, resembles the income tax (see II D, above), because it is measured by money received. It is not, however, considered to be an income tax, because its levy does not depend upon the taxpayer actually realizing any income after expenses are deducted.

Sales taxes are often referred to as consumption taxes, because they tax items that are used or consumed by the public. General sales and use taxes are based upon the retail price of the goods or services being taxed. These taxes vary with price differentials and, therefore, are said to be "unit elastic". Because sales and use taxes are passed on to the purchaser or user without regard to his or her income, changes in personal income do not affect the tax rate. Therefore, these taxes are not directly income elastic. Changes in income do, however, affect the taxpayer's ability or willingness to purchase goods and services. Thus, the tax varies somewhat with the taxpayer's income and, therefore, is, indirectly somewhat income elastic (see II A(1), above).

On the other hand, because sales and use taxes are tied to the price of goods and services, rather than to the taxpayer's income, the burden of these consumption taxes increases in inverse proportion to the taxpayer's income; the lower the income, the greater the tax burden. This regressivity, which has made the sales tax controversial, often is reduced by exempting from the tax items viewed as necessities, such as food and medicine. As of March, 2006, 29 states and the District of Columbia exempted food, and an even larger number of states exempted medicine. A few other states have attempted to introduce greater progressivity by imposing special excise taxes on luxury items.

Section 2.   General Sales Taxes

Subsection a.   Characteristics.

The general retail sales tax is a tax imposed on all sellers for the privilege of engaging in the business of selling tangible services within the taxing jurisdiction. It is imposed at the final stage of the production and distribution process, the sale to the consumer. Although the definitions of "tangible personal property," "sale at retail" and "taxable services" may vary from state to state, these terms generally include consumer goods, admission charges for recreational and entertainment activities, payments for public accommodations (*e.g.*, hotels, restaurants), utility and telephone charges, payments for commercial transportation (*e.g.*, airlines, railroads), and rental fees for tangible personal property (under certain circumstances).

The term "sale" includes installment and credit sales, exchanges of property, and the transfer of tangible personal property for a valuable consideration, as well as the furnishing of certain services denominated as taxable under the statute authorizing the levy of a sales tax. "Sale at retail" usually is defined to include the transfer for a valuable consideration, by a person engaged in business, of the ownership of tangible personal property to a purchaser for his or her use or consumption, *i.e.*, not for the purchaser's subsequent resale as tangible personal property. Transfers of property in connection with corporate reorganizations, contributions of capital to corporations and partnerships, distributions, dividends and returns of capital, and business liquidations generally are not considered sales at retail.

In addition to taxing retail sales, some states impose sales taxes on transactions at the intermediate or wholesale stage (see II E(5), below). Special sales or excise taxes frequently are imposed on the retail sale of specific items, such as alcohol, cigarettes and gasoline (see II E(4), below).

Early versions of the sales tax were essentially taxes on the privilege of doing business. In most states, the sales tax was later changed to a form of transaction tax imposed on the purchaser, with the seller being required to serve as the primary collection agent for the state. (See II E(2)(b), below.) In either case, the ultimate economic burden of the tax is passed on to the purchasers as a specific percentage of the purchase price of the tangible goods or services sold to them.

Subsection b. Authorization and Administration.

In many states, both the state and local governments impose a sales tax. In a few states, local governments (usually cities and counties) are authorized to levy the tax by virtue of a generous delegation of home rule powers. More commonly, specific state legislative authorization is necessary.

The typical statute authorizing local sales taxes is enabling rather than mandatory, thus permitting local governments to exercise discretion with respect to the imposition of the tax. The rates of local government general sales taxes are frequently restricted by state statutes. On the other hand, home rule municipalities often may impose special excises without express statutory authorization; and local government special excises (such as taxes on alcohol or gasoline) are usually collected directly by larger local governments.

Statutes authorizing general retail sales taxes contain detailed provisions concerning the imposition and administration of the tax. They place the burden of collecting the tax on the seller. In general, two different theories regarding the seller's legal liability are reflected in those statutes. Under the privilege tax theory, the tax is imposed on the retail seller's gross receipts as a charge for the privilege of doing business within the state. These statutes permit the seller to pass the tax on to purchasers, but the seller remains primarily liable for the tax. Under the transaction theory, the sales tax is imposed on the purchaser and the purchaser is primarily liable for payment of the tax. The seller is required to collect the tax from the purchaser, but the seller is not primarily liable.

The main effect of the difference between the two approaches emerged with the introduction of the bracket system (described below). Typically, purchasers do not pay sales taxes on the first 15 to 25 cents of a purchase under a bracket system. If the sales tax is viewed as a privilege tax, the seller still has to pay tax on that amount. If, however, the tax is viewed as a transaction tax, then no tax is due on the exempt portion of the sales price.

Many states have gone to great lengths in their statutes to characterize the tax as a privilege tax. Generally, this characterization has been upheld against equal protection and uniformity attacks (see II A(2)(c)-(d), above), with courts ruling that it reflects a reasonable balance of the fractional charges between seller and purchaser in a situation where perfect uniformity is not possible.

One study has classified state sales taxes into three types: (1) a privilege tax on the seller, with varying provisions for shifting the tax to the consumer; (2) a transaction tax on the purchaser; and (3) a hybrid containing elements of both types. In the hybrid states, the courts determine the legal status, with the majority favoring privilege taxes with the law's mandatory shifting of the burden. Though all three types of taxes operate satisfactorily, statutes imposing liability for the tax on the seller have several advantages, which flow from the greater clarity of responsibility for payment.

Collection of the sales tax is the administrative responsibility of a state (and, sometimes, local) government agency, with the retail sellers serving as the primary tax collectors. State statutes provide detailed instructions regarding the imposition of the tax, in most cases using a bracket system, which identifies the amount of tax to be collected on sales of specified amounts. The purposes of the bracket system are to ease the burden of calculating the tax due by sellers of large volumes of varied, low-price items and to allocate fractional amounts. Typical brackets for a three and one-eighth percent tax are as follows:

Sale Price	Tax Due
$0.00—$0.14	None
.15—.47	$.01
.48—.79	$.02
.80—1.11	$.03

For larger amounts, the tax will increase $.01 for each addition $.32 of sales. Many states set forth the specific bracket calculations within their statutes, thus necessitating a revision of the calculations whenever the tax rate is changed, but the trend is toward delegating to the relevant administrative agency the responsibility for establishing the specific brackets. These statutes typically also authorize vendors to make their own calculations based on the applicable tax rate so long as the formula used is uniformly and consistently applied to all similarly situated purchases.

Sellers are required to remit the taxes collected on a periodic basis, usually quarterly. Monthly returns are required if the tax to be remitted exceeds a certain amount. Sellers are not permitted to absorb the tax but must pass it on to the purchaser by separately stating it and adding it to the purchase price.

Most states permit retail sellers to retain a small portion of the tax collected (two or three per cent of the tax) to help defray their costs of collection. There is, however, no constitutional obligation upon states to allow such a collection deduction. Courts that have examined the question have had little difficulty rejecting sellers' claims that the imposition of the burden of collection constitutes either an unconstitutional taking of property, a deprivation of due process, or involuntary servitude. Though the collection deduction may encourage prompt payment, it is not designed for that purpose but only to compensate the seller for recordkeeping and other costs of collection.

Subsection c.   Transactions Subject to the Tax.

Subsection i.   Traditional Sales.   Perhaps the most controversial aspect of sales tax administration is determining which transactions are subject to the tax. Though most statutes contain broad language purporting to cover "any retail sale" and "any transfer," they also contain many specific exclusions and exemptions. Thus, states often expressly exclude sales of intangible personal property, sales of personal property for the purpose of resale, purchases of materials and/or machinery for use in manufacturing or fabricating tangible personal property for sale, sales of personal property to charitable organizations, and sales of containers and packaging materials.

The exemption categories are quite detailed and vary considerably from state to state, but, in general, they are designed to exempt from taxation sales of goods intended for resale, equipment and machinery used to produce goods for retail sales, sales in interstate commerce (including funds for vessels engaged in interstate commerce), and sales to tax-exempt organizations and governmental entities. Analysts have identified three basic reasons for granting a sales tax exemption: (1) difficulty in determining who bears the ultimate tax burden, (2) concern that production of goods not be discouraged by taxation, and (3) avoidance of tax discrimination among certain types of industries. In addition, goods used in production are often excluded to prevent multiple taxation, and certain exemptions, especially the common ones for food and drugs, are designed to lessen the regressivity of the sales tax.

As statutory exclusions and exemptions increase, state courts are called upon to construe the meaning of such exemptions. For example, an Ohio statute exempts from sales tax items purchased to be used or consumed "directly in the rendition of a public utility service." Construing that statute, the Ohio Supreme Court held that income received by a cable television company from the rental of cable converter boxes to its customers was not exempt from sales taxation and that the company "should have collected sales tax for the rental of the converter boxes." *Time Warner Operations, Inc. v. Wilkins,* 857 N.E.2d 590 (Ohio 2006).

Another common exemption is for machinery and equipment used in manufacturing. Judicial decisions construing this exemption in Missouri have concluded that equipment used to produce basic telephone service and vertical telephone products such as Caller ID and Call Forwarding are products used in manufacturing because telephone service requires that "the voice be 'manufactured' into electronic impulses that can be transmitted and reproduced into an understandable replica;" *Southwestern Bell v. Director of Revenue,* 78 S.W.3d 763, 768 (Mo. banc 2002), that replacement parts for hydraulic pumps and liquid-dispensing machines may qualify as exempt machinery but only when the replacements are "combinations of parts that work together as a functioning unit;" *Lincoln Industrial, Inc. v. Director of Revenue,* 51 S.W.3d 462, 466 (Mo. banc 2001) that fuel oil mixed with clay in the process of manufacturing clay pots was a "component part or ingredient" of the final product and, therefore, exempt under the component part exemption, but that fuel oil used to heat ovens for baking charcoal briquettes did not become a component part of the charcoal and was, therefore, subject to the tax; that dirt bikes were "motor vehicles" primarily designed for use on highways even though they were not equipped with lights and, therefore, the seller of such bikes was exempted from collecting the sales tax because the sales tax statute required purchasers of a "motor vehicle" to pay the tax directly to the state; and that sales of time share interests in a resort under a vacation lease guaranteeing the purchaser a certain type of accommodation for one or two weeks per year for thirty years were not "fees for public accommodation or recreation" and, therefore, were not subject to the tax.

In the hydraulic pumps and charcoal briquette cases, as well as a companion case involving aluminum manufacturing, the Missouri Supreme Court adopted a "high tech" integrated plant concept, first articulated in New York, to determine when the manufacturing process begins and ends. Under this approach, machinery and equipment used in the several stages of a manufacturing process are exempt from sales tax if they are necessary to the production and form a part of "an integrated and synchronized system," regardless of whether they perform the direct manufacturing function of changing raw material into a finished product.

Subsection ii. Internet Sales. As noted above (II A(2)(e) & (f)), due process and commerce clause issues are triggered by state taxation of interstate sales. Such sales are not subject to sales taxes unless the seller had some physical presence in the state where buyer was located. This creates a particular problem with respect to the increasingly popular use of the Internet for electronic commerce. As the U. S. Treasury has noted, "electronic commerce doesn't seem to occur in any physical location but instead takes place in the nebulous world of cyberspace. Persons engaged in electronic commerce could be located anywhere in the world and their customers will be ignorant of, or indifferent to their location." OFF. OF TAX POL'Y, U. S. DEP'T OF THE TREASURY, SELECTED TAX POLICY IMPLICATIONS OF GLOB-AL ELECTRONIC COMMERCE, § 7.2.3.1., at 25, *available at* www.ustreas.gov/taxpolicy/library/internet.pdf (quoted in Arthur J. Cockfield, *Designing Tax Policy for the Digital Biosphere: How the Internet is Changing Tax Laws*, 34 CONN. L. REV. 333, 338 (2002)).

In such an environment, traditional rules regarding imposition of sales taxes, by whom and against whom, don't work particularly well. For example, a California appellate court used the *Quill* nexus rule in concluding that Borders Online, a subsidiary of Borders Group, had sufficient contacts with the state of California to subject its online sales to California taxation. But the court made this finding because of a "cross-promotional" relationship with Borders' other subsidiary, Borders Book and Music, that enable persons who purchased items on the Internet to return or exchange them at a retail store. *Borders Online, LLC v. State Bd. of Equalization,* 29 Cal.Rptr.3d 176, 187–188 (Ct. App. 2005). A student commentary on the case argues that guidelines are less clear about states' ability to reach internet sales of companies that do not permit exchanges or returns at physical locations or companies such as Amazon.com that may have a physical location in only one state through a headquarters/warehouse. Walter J. Baudier, *Internet Sales*

Taxes from Borders to Amazon: How Long Before All of Your Purchases Are Taxed? 2006 DUKE L. & TECH. REV. 5, 11 (2006).

States have been attempting to resolve internet taxation issues in two ways: 1) promulgation by the National Conference of State Legislatures (NCSL) of a model state sales tax law and 2) promotion of a Streamlined Sales and Use Tax Agreement drafted by the Streamlined Sales Tax Project (SSTP). Forty of the forty-five states imposing sales and use taxes had signed on to the Agreement as of April 2005. A book by Professors Hellerstein and Swain, STREAM-LINED SALES AND USE TAX (2004) discusses the project. Congress has assisted the effort by imposing a moratorium on e-commerce taxation at least through 2007. Pub. L. No. 108–435, 118 Stat. 2615 (2004).

Subsection d.   Taxes on Services.

Some states impose sales taxes on a variety of services. However, most states have chosen to exempt professional, personal, and other services from their sales taxes, so long as a significant portion of these services does not involve tangible property.

Controversies have sometimes arisen as to the applicability of that exemption to payments for commercial artwork and related advertising materials. Judicial resolution of these disputes has not been consistent.

In one case, for example, a Florida court held that a telephone company was not subject to a state sales tax on transactions between it and artists who produced "speculative" and "finished" art work used in advertisements that appeared in the company's yellow pages telephone books. The court opined that in this case the company was actually purchasing the artists' ideas, and the fact that the ideas were transmitted on tangible personal property was an inconsequential element of the transaction.

By contrast, an Ohio court held that the sale of advertising materials that included radio and TV commercials, as well as artists' sketches used in newspaper and magazine compositions, were not exempt from the state's sales tax. Applying the "true object" test that has been adopted by a number of state courts, it ruled that the advertisers' true or "real object," in the transactions in question, was to acquire possession of the advertising materials rather than to purchase the service performed in producing them. Thus the transactions constituted taxable sales of tangible property.

In 1987, Florida generated substantial controversy by extending its sales (and use) taxes to all retail services delivered within the state (including nearly all professional services). These taxes were challenged, on First Amendment grounds, by advertising executives and national broadcasting networks. They were also the subject of a suit by members of the Florida Bar, who contended that the taxes violated the equal protection clause and impermissibly burdened access to the courts and the right to legal counsel.

The Florida Supreme Court issued an advisory opinion rejecting those facial challenges to the taxes premised upon provisions of the Florida Constitution. Nonetheless, in response to substantial public opposition, as well as the economic pressure imposed by national advertisers (who protested the taxes by diverting convention business to other states), the Florida Legislature repealed the newly adopted taxes later in 1987.

The Commonwealth of Massachusetts had a similar, abortive experience with the taxation of services. Massachusetts' broad-based tax on services lasted for only two days before it was repealed by the state legislature. That state tax on services had been challenged in lawsuits instituted by, among others, the Massachusetts Bar Association.

Subsection e.   Local Sales Taxes.

Administration of local sales taxes is similar to that of state sales taxes. Imposition of the tax by an eligible city or other local government usually is discretionary. Authorization is a two-part process in many states, with both the governing body and the electorate of the city being required to approve it (see II E(2)(b), above). The tax is added to the purchase price and collected by the seller from the purchaser. Generally, the same exclusions and exemptions present in the state sales tax system are recognized for local sales taxes, though some states permit local governments to authorize their own exemptions.

Local governments, like their state counterparts, frequently exempt the provision of services from their sales taxes, as long as those provisions of services do not involve transfers of tangible property in significant amounts. These exemptions sometimes require state courts to consider whether a particular transaction constitutes a non-taxable sale of intangible property or a taxable sale of personal property.

This precise issue was confronted by the United States Court of Appeals for the D.C. Circuit, in construing a provision of the District of Columbia Use Tax Act that exempted, from local sales and use taxes, "professional insurance, or personal service transactions which involve sales as inconsequential elements for which no separate charges are made."

The Court reviewed the tax consequences of contracts between a newspaper publishing company and several syndicates that supplied fiber mats, bearing impressions of sequences of comic strips, that the newspaper used to produce metal plates from which it printed its comics page. Noting that the value of the mats in question was less than 10% of the amount charged by the syndicates for the services they provided to the newspaper, the court held that the property sales in question were "inconsequential elements" of the transactions in question, and thus exempt from the local sales tax.

In most states, the local collection process is piggy backed onto the state sales tax process in order to ease collection burdens on sellers and to take advantage of economies of scale in the administration of the tax. The funds remitted to the state by retail sellers are deposited in an earmarked fund and later transmitted to the appropriate local government by the state. The state deducts a fee (usually one per cent of the amount collected) for the collection service it provides for the local governments.

Because many businesses subject to the sales tax operate within more than one local jurisdiction imposing the tax, questions concerning multiple taxation and locus of responsibility often arise. States have responded to this problem by providing, in the sales tax enabling legislation, that the tax is to be imposed at the place of business of the seller. In most states, if there is more than one place of business, the tax is imposed at the place where the initial order was taken, even if the order must be forwarded elsewhere for acceptance, shipment, or billing. If the order was taken by an employee, for example as a phone order, the tax is imposed at the employee's place of work.

In addition to the multiple taxation problem, imposition of local sales taxes by a number of municipalities within a single metropolitan area can raise serious questions regarding fair allocation of tax revenues. For example, a suburban town that happens to be fortunate enough to be the site of a regional shopping center might be accused by the officials of surrounding local governments of reaping a windfall if it imposes a sales tax, because many of the shoppers who pay the tax will not be residents of that suburb.

To remedy this problem, several states have devised methods of sharing the local sales tax revenue. For example, cities in St. Louis County, Missouri which have enacted sales taxes have a choice of becoming a "point-of-sale" city or a "pool" city. Cities that opt for point-of-sale designation retain all of their sales tax collections. Pool cities share their sales tax collections with other pool cities and with St. Louis County, but not with point-of-sale cities. The system, though imperfect, does give the cities some degree of choice and some possibility of sharing benefits derived from increased commercial activity in the metropolitan area.

Section 3.   Use Taxes

Subsection a.   Characteristics.

The use tax, or compensating use tax as it is sometimes labeled in state statutes, is a tax imposed upon the privilege of using, storing, or consuming tangible personal property within the state or local government boundaries. It is not a property tax but rather an excise tax imposed upon the enjoyment of personal property, such as automobiles or boats purchased in one state and brought into another state or local jurisdiction by the purchasers. The use tax is complementary and supplementary to the sales tax. It is designed to protect the sales tax base by offsetting purchasers' attempts to buy outside the jurisdiction to avoid the state or local sales tax. In addition, the use tax ordinarily compensates for revenue that would otherwise be lost because of commerce clause limitations on the taxation of sales of goods purchased outside the state but used in the state. (See II A(2)(f)(ii), above.)

Use taxes are usually imposed as a percentage of the retail sales price, generally at the same rate as the sales tax. If sales tax has been paid on a particular item in another jurisdiction, a credit will usually be allowed, or the item may be exempted from the state or local use tax (see II E(3)(b), below). Liability for the tax is imposed on the person using, storing or consuming the property, but responsibility for actually collecting the tax and remitting it to the state often may be imposed on the seller of the goods, even if the seller is located outside the state boundaries (see II E(3)(b), below).

Subsection b.   Authorization and Administration.

In most states, both the state and local governments impose use taxes as a supplement to their sales taxes. Local governments are authorized to levy the tax either through their home rule powers or by special legislation (see II A(2)(a), above). But, like the sales tax, the use tax is generally collected by the state (see II E(2)(e), above). To reduce the potential for multiple taxation, most state and local governments provide for a credit or exemption from their use tax if the out-of-state purchase of goods was subject to a sales tax in the state of purchase.

In 1985, without reaching the question whether such a credit is a constitutional requirement in all circumstances, the U.S. Supreme Court struck down a special Vermont motor vehicle purchase and use tax. The tax granted a credit to residents who purchased automobiles outside the state and paid a sales tax to the state of purchase, but it denied the credit to nonresident purchasers who subsequently became residents. The Court regarded this as "an arbitrary distinction that violates the equal protection clause." The Court did not reach commerce clause, privileges and immunities clause and right to travel questions because the statute "on its face" presented a question of "unconstitutional discrimination."

In 1994, the U.S. Supreme Court considered the constitutionality of a flat 1.5% state use tax imposed by Missouri on the privilege of storing, using, or consuming, within that state, tangible personal property that had been purchased outside the state. Although Missouri did not impose a corresponding state sales tax upon goods purchased in-state, many Missouri local governments had established their own sales taxes. Reversing a decision of the Missouri Supreme Court, the U.S. Supreme Court held that in those localities where the state use tax exceeded the local sales tax, the taxation scheme—as a whole—constituted invalid facial discrimination against interstate commerce.

Several years later, however, the U.S. Supreme Court upheld a use tax that Ohio had imposed upon industrial gas consumers who purchased natural gas from suppliers other than a local monopoly. The Court reasoned that there were, in fact, two distinct markets for natural gas sales in Ohio. Thus, the use tax in question was not a tax that afforded different treatment to similarly situated in-state and out-of-state entities.

With the enactment of sales taxes in most states, the incentive to buy out-of-state to avoid a sales tax is greatly diminished. However, some states do not impose sales taxes at either the state or local levels, and there often are differences in rates within a metropolitan area.

To survive lawsuits based upon the dormant commerce clause, state and local use taxes on mail order companies that ship from out-of-state must demonstrate, *inter alia*, that the challenged tax is being applied to an activity with a "substantial nexus" with the taxing state. This requirement has sometimes been difficult for state and local governments to satisfy, with the result turning on factual distinctions.

For example, in *National Bellas Hess, Inc. v. Department of Revenue of Illinois*, 386 U.S. 753 (1967) the U.S. Supreme Court held that a company engaged in the interstate sale of mail order goods, that did not maintain an office in the taxing state, lacked a sufficient nexus to allow the state to impose a use tax collection obligation. In contrast, in 1988, the Court determined that a department store that had contracted with an out-of-state printer to print and mail catalogues to customers in a state where the store had established retail outlets *did* have a sufficient nexus to support a use tax on the distribution of those catalogues. In 1992, however, the Supreme Court reaffirmed the *Bellas Hess* "substantial nexus" test. It ruled that the imposition of a use tax upon a company, whose only contacts with the taxing state were by mail or common carrier, violated the dormant commerce clause.

In the future, the limits placed by the federal Constitution upon the power of state and local governments to impose use taxes may be tested in the context of a state or local tax imposed on interstate electronic commerce. (*See* II B(2)(c)(ii).) Congress has imposed a temporary moratorium on state and local taxation of Internet sales. However, Congress seems likely to be pressured by state governors (concerned about potential losses of state tax revenues from increasing interstate electronic commerce) to end that moratorium.

In any event, at present purchasers of goods are usually ignorant of their liability for the use tax, and their out-of-state purchases are hard for officials to discover. As a result, the use tax is difficult to collect unless the seller is required to pay (as discussed above) or the purchased item is subject to a separate registration requirement (*e.g.*, an automobile purchased outside the state but operated within it). New Jersey has acknowledged these problems; it informed its residents of their potential liability for use taxes on goods purchased out-of-state and requested that they make voluntary use tax payments along with their state income tax returns. Other states have also sought such voluntary payments, but with only limited success.

Section 4.   Special Sales (Excise) Taxes

Subsection a.   Characteristics.

In addition to broadly applicable general retail sales taxes, most states levy special sales taxes, also known as "excise taxes," targeted at purchases of specific items. The most common excises are the cigarette or tobacco tax, the motor fuel tax, and the alcoholic beverages tax. The items subject to these excises are not taxed as a part of the general sales tax. Like the general sales tax, however, these excises are generally imposed on the seller, with the economic burden passed on to the consumer as a specific percentage of the item's purchase price (see II E(2)(b), above).

The cigarette tax is a tax imposed on the sale, use, or consumption of cigarette and/or tobacco products. Depending upon the state, the tax may be imposed on cigarettes only or may include other tobacco products such as cigars, snuff, and chewing tobacco. The tax is imposed as a flat amount per cigarette or per given number of cigarettes (or specified amount of other tobacco products). Payment of the tax by the seller is evidenced by the issuance of stamps, which then are usually attached to the package containing the tobacco product that has been taxed.

The motor fuel tax is imposed on the storage, distribution, sale and use of gasoline and other motor vehicle fuels. Separate taxes might be imposed on special fuels such as jet fuel, diesel fuel, and liquified petroleum gas. Though the method of taxation varies somewhat from state to state, the tax is generally imposed on each gallon of fuel purchased, and on the distributor who first receives the motor fuel. The motor fuel tax, however, is not treated as a consumption tax, but rather as a tax on the privilege of using the highways or airports. Proceeds generally are spent by the state for construction and maintenance of public roads and highways, though the funds are not always dedicated to these purposes. When they are so dedicated, taxpayers have been held to have standing to challenge diversions of such funds to other state projects or to state general revenue accounts.

The tax on alcoholic beverages is an excise tax assessed on a per gallon basis, and it varies with regard to volume and/or alcoholic content. Generally any alcoholic beverages manufactured or sold in the state are subject to taxation.

Subsection b.   Authorization and Administration.

Special sales taxes usually are imposed only by state governments, which either preempt these taxes or specifically prohibit local governments to impose them. Some state statutes, however, allow one or more of these taxes to be imposed at the local level, and some home rule municipalities can impose them without special authorization. For instance, New York has special legislation authorizing New York City to levy a cigarette tax (*see also* II A(2)(a), above). These authorized local excise taxes are usually collected directly by larger local governments.

Subsection c.   Legal Constraints.

Tobacco, alcoholic beverage, and motor fuel taxes are subject to the same general public purpose, uniformity, equal protection, commerce clause and rate limitations applicable to other taxes (see II A(2), above).

A 1984 United States Supreme Court decision concerning an Hawaiian alcoholic beverages tax exemplifies the situation most likely to provoke a challenge to the validity of these taxes. In *Bacchus Imports, Ltd. v. Dias*, 468 U.S. 263 (1984), the Court invalidated that liquor tax, because it exempted fruit wine and brandy produced locally from an indigenous Hawaiian scrub. The Court found that the state's purpose for excluding the local wine and brandy from taxation was to stimulate the production and marketing of these local products, thus aiding Hawaiian industry.

Proponents of the tax and its exemption claimed that the local products were produced in such small quantities that they did not compete with other alcoholic beverages sold in either interstate or intrastate commerce. The Court rejected this argument, asking only if "any" competition existed, not the extent of it. The Court held that the tax amounted to economic protectionism for the exempted local products. Because both the purpose and effect of the tax were to discriminate against out-of-state producers in favor of local producers, the Court invalidated the tax under the dormant commerce clause. (See *generally* II A(2)(f)(ii), above.)

Another issue in the *Bacchus* case, one peculiar to alcoholic beverage taxes, was the extent to which the Twenty–First Amendment affects regulation by Congress and the states of the sale of alcoholic beverages. The Twenty–First Amendment provides: "The transportation or importation into any state, territory, or possession of the United States for delivery or use therein of intoxicating liquors, *in violation of the laws thereof*, is hereby prohibited." (Emphasis added.)

The *Bacchus* Court acknowledged that it had, at times, been argued that the Twenty–First Amendment "confers power upon the states to regulate commerce in intoxicating liquors unconfined by ordinary limitations imposed on state regulation of interstate goods by the commerce clause." The Court ruled, however, that the Amendment does not entirely preclude congressional regulation of alcoholic beverages. The Court then articulated a balancing test to determine the extent to which authority granted by the commerce clause or by the Twenty–First Amendment should prevail. Under the facts before the Court, the balance tipped against state regulation. The Court reaffirmed the *Bacchus* test, in a regulatory context, in 2005 when it struck down discriminatory regulatory systems in Michigan and New York that favored in-state wine producers over out-of-state wine producers by permitting in-state wineries to obtain licenses for direct sale to consumers but denying that privilege to out-of-state wineries. *Granholm v. Heald,* 544 U.S. 460 (2005).

Section 5.   Gross Receipts Taxes

Subsection a.   Characteristics and Distinguishing Features.

Gross receipts taxes are levied upon the total revenues of a business on an annual or other periodic basis. A typical example of a gross receipts tax is the occupational license tax, which is imposed on foreign and domestic corporations for the right to do business in the state. That tax is measured as a percentage of the total gross revenues of such a corporation during a given period, usually set by state statute.

The gross receipts tax differs from the corporate income tax (see II D(1), above) because the gross receipts tax is levied on the total revenues received by the business rather than on its profits (revenues minus expenses). Though the general retail sales tax could technically be considered a type of gross receipts tax, it is usually distinguishable because it taxes retail sales and is intended to reach only the consumption of goods and services produced by particular business activities (see II E(2)(a), above). By contrast, the gross receipts tax is a tax on the business activity itself and, therefore, is sometimes treated as a license tax (see II G, below). Furthermore, the gross receipts tax is assessed as a percentage of the revenues received, regardless of the source of the revenue. For example, a merchant selling an item for $1.00 who adds 3 cents to the sales price to pass on to the purchaser the cost of his or her gross receipts tax payment will have gross receipts of $1.03. Therefore, the merchant must pay a gross receipts tax on $1.03 rather than on $1.00. The sales tax, by contrast, is assessed as a percentage of the price paid by the purchaser for the item prior to the tax ($1.00 in this example).

Subsection b.   Legal Constraints.

Though the economic impact of a sales tax and of a gross receipts tax (if pro-rated and itemized by consumer) may not be materially different, the characterization of a tax as one or the other can be important in states that require a favorable vote by the electorate before a local sales tax can be implemented or its rate increased. In most states, gross receipts taxes do not require such voter approval. An important exception is Missouri, whose levy limitation requires voter approval before raising "any tax, license or fees."

Gross receipts taxes are subject to the same legal constraints as other taxes. Several dormant commerce clause cases discussed in II A(2)(f)(ii), above, involve the imposition of gross receipts taxes upon multistate businesses and activities.

PART F. OTHER STATE AND LOCAL TAXES

Section 1. Entertainment Taxes

The growth of tourism as a key industry has spawned a wide range of state and local entertainment taxes. Many are special sales taxes (see II E(4), above). Others are gross receipts taxes (see II E(5), above) or license taxes (see II G, below). The tax usually is calculated as a percentage of the admission price for the entertainment activity. Courts have upheld the separate classification of the entertainment industry for tax purposes and the imposition of rates higher than those paid by other industries so long as the rates are not confiscatory. For financially distressed cities, these taxes are sometimes the only available revenue source that requires neither a vote of local residents nor state legislative approval. They may also be a means of obtaining revenue from nonresidents, who cannot vote in local elections.

A variation of the entertainment tax is the hotel/motel room tax, which is a special sales tax paid on the rental of hotel and motel rooms. Funds derived from this tax often are earmarked for the support of cultural and performing arts attractions, as well as the promotion of local tourism efforts. The hotel/motel room tax has special appeal because of its potential for tax exportation. Apart from an occasional "getaway weekend" or second honeymoon, residents of the taxing jurisdiction rarely pay this tax, but their local government is able to reap its benefits.

As with general sales taxes, the determination of what types of activities are subject to an entertainment tax has occupied many courts and tax administrators. For example, a Missouri court upheld the state Administrative Hearing Commission's conclusion that a train taking tourists in the Branson, Missouri recreation area on scenic excursions through the Ozark Mountains in southwestern Missouri and northern Arkansas was not entitled to a statutory exemption from an entertainment sales tax for sales made in interstate commerce. Likening the excursion train to miniature trains employed at zoos and amusement parks, the court concluded that the trains was in the entertainment business rather that the transportations business and the short trips into Arkansas did not rise to the level of interstate commerce.

In another Missouri case, the State Administrative Hearing Commission was asked to decide whether sales of resort time shares were subject either to the state amusement tax or to a hotel room tax. In concluding that time share sales were not subject to either tax, the Commission observed first that the amusement tax is payable on receipts associated with amusement, entertainment or recreation, but not on receipts derived from lodging. Though resort time shares may provide amusement, entertainment or recreation, their primary purpose is to guarantee a certain type of accommodation on a regular, recurring basis. The Commission further noted that the hotel room tax is based on the relationship of innkeeper and guests. Although time share purchasers are seeking lodging, their relationship with the owner of the property under a time share vacation lease is not that of innkeeper and guest, but is more like that of landlord and tenant.

Section 2.   New York City Stock Transfer Tax

Since the turn of the century, New York has imposed a tax on securities transactions. The tax is imposed on the transfer of shares or certificates of stock. For transfers involving sales, the rate is graduated according to the selling price per share. When the transfer is by gift, a constant rate per share, approximately one-half the highest rate for sale transactions, is imposed. A 25% surcharge was added to all transfer taxes in 1976.

The basic tax has withstood challenges under the Fourteenth Amendment as well as the commerce clause. However, a 1968 amendment reducing the rate for in-state transactions, in order to relieve what was thought to be a competitive disadvantage of the New York Stock Exchange (compared to out-of-state exchanges), was invalidated by the U.S. Supreme Court. The Court ruled that the provision violated the commerce clause, because it discriminated against interstate commerce.

A 1975 amendment to the Securities Exchange Act of 1934 prohibits states from taxing stock transfers unless activities besides mere delivery or transfer by a registered clearing agency or transfer agent take place within the state.

Section 3. Severance Taxes

Severance taxes, which sometimes are also referred to as conservation or privilege taxes, are imposed on the extraction or severance of natural resources from the land. Resource-rich states have turned to severance taxes as a means of shifting or exporting the tax burden to nonresidents. States imposing them assert that severance taxes are a necessary reimbursement for the costs of exploitation of depletable natural resources, including increased demands for roads, schools, and other capital infrastructure.

In addition to the better known energy sources such as coal, oil and gas, severance taxes are imposed on a wide variety of resources such as fish (Washington), clams and oysters (Maryland), iron (Minnesota), salt (Mississippi), sulphur (Texas), timber (Mississippi, Oregon and Virginia) and uranium (Nebraska). Severance taxes, often set at high rates, are important sources of revenue in some of those jurisdictions.

Subsection a.   Coal Severance Taxes.

Coal severance taxes, now imposed in at least twenty-four states, have withstood two major attacks by coal producers and energy-consuming states, one in 1922 and the other in 1981. In both challenges, the decision of the U.S. Supreme Court turned on the then-prevailing doctrine concerning state taxation of interstate commerce. In 1922, the theory was that the commerce clause made interstate commerce absolutely immune from state taxation but allowed local activities to be taxed by the states. (See II A(2)(f)(ii), above). Under that now-defunct theory, a Pennsylvania coal severance tax was upheld because it was imposed on the coal before it entered the stream of interstate commerce.

In 1981, the Supreme Court, in *Commonwealth Edison Company v. Montana*, 453 U.S. 609, upheld Montana's severance tax, which could be as high as 30% of the price of the coal extracted. The Court relied upon the four-prong test of *Complete Auto Transit* (see II A(2)(f)(ii), above). The *Commonwealth Edison* Court had little difficulty finding that the Montana tax met the sufficient nexus and fair apportionment prongs of the *Complete Auto Transit* test, because the severance tax was levied only by the taxing state and was based only upon activities which occurred there—extraction of coal. Even though 90% of the coal was exported to other states, the Court found no discrimination against interstate commerce because the tax was imposed whether the coal was consumed in-state or out-of-state. A potentially serious problem was the fourth prong, which required that the tax be "fairly related to the services provided by the State." The 30% level of the tax, coupled with the many services the coal company provided for itself, cast serious doubt on this point. The Court, however, resolved the case in favor of Montana by, in one commentator's view, repudiating the "fairly related to services" test in favor of a requirement that companies bear a "just share of state tax burden." (*Commonwealth Edison* is further discussed in II A(2)(f)(ii), above.)

Subsection b.   Oil and Gas Severance Taxes.

At least thirty states impose a severance tax on the production of oil and gas. The tax usually is levied on oil and gas producers in proportion to their ownership interests at the time of severance. The tax, which is based on the fair market value, as defined by statute or administrative regulation, of oil and gas produced in the taxing state, is paid by the person in charge of production operations, who then deducts the appropriate percentage of the tax from the proceeds paid to the persons sharing in the production activities.

As states in recent years have increased the oil and gas severance tax, they have sought to soften the blow by exempting royalty owners (landowners leasing mineral rights to oil producers) from the increases and prohibiting producers from passing on the increases to consumers. The Supreme Court found both a royalty-owner exemption and a pass-through prohibition enacted by the State of Alabama to be rational classifications under the equal protection clause, but it concluded that federal law regulating the sale of natural gas in interstate commerce preempted the pass-through provision, because it applied to sales of gas in interstate commerce.

Subsection c.   Louisiana's First Use Tax.

In a variation on the severance tax approach, the State of Louisiana attempted to tax the "first use" of natural gas coming into the State from the federally owned Outer Continental Shelf. Numerous tax credits and exclusions had the effect of exempting Louisiana gas producers from the tax and of forcing pipeline companies, which brought the gas into Louisiana for "drying" before shipping it to producers and nonresident consumers, to absorb the tax themselves or pass it on to the nonresident consumers. These features caused the Supreme Court to conclude that the tax violated the dormant commerce clause because it discriminated against interstate commerce. (*See* II A(2)(f)(ii), above.)

Section 4.   Estate and Gift Taxes

All states impose some form of taxes on the occasion of death. Three basic types of these death taxes are levied: inheritance taxes, estate taxes, and "pick up" taxes.

The most common tax is the inheritance tax, which is imposed on the transfer of property following the death of the property owner. It is a tax upon the privilege of succeeding to property, rather than one on property ownership as such. The person responsible for paying the tax is the recipient of the property. Numerous exemptions designed to cushion the impact of the tax are contained in the state statutes imposing inheritance taxes.

A few states impose an estate tax instead of an inheritance tax. The estate tax is levied upon the estate of the deceased person. It is a debt due the state and must be paid prior to distribution of the estate, usually nine months to a year after death. As with the inheritance tax, numerous deductions and exemptions are applied before the tax is imposed.

A third form of death tax, the so-called "pick up" tax, is levied by all states, either in conjunction with inheritance or estate taxes or by itself. The "pick up" tax is related to the credit for state death taxes permitted under the federal estate tax. If a state inheritance or estate tax is not payable because of exemptions, or is less than the maximum state tax credit which a federal taxpayer can claim, a special state tax is imposed to take advantage of the federal estate tax credit, by "picking-up" the difference between the inheritance or estate tax and the maximum tax credit. When the decedent's estate contains property in more than one state, the calculation of the "maximum state tax credit" is limited to that portion of the estate attributable to the taxing state.

Gift taxes are levied by only a handful of states. These taxes are assessed in conjunction with death tax systems and designed to prevent the avoidance of death taxes through inter vivos transfers.

PART G. LICENSE FEES (OR TAXES)

State and local governments often impose a charge or fee on businesses, professions, and certain activities, particularly those believed to have an impact on the health, safety or general welfare of the people in the community. Authority to impose such fees must be granted by statute or home rule provision (see II A(2)(a), above). In some older statutes, local governments are authorized to license a plethora of activities extending over several statutory pages, which provide a fascinating look into a by-gone era of hansom cabs, livery stables and public masquerade balls.

A variety of names are used to describe these fees, such as franchise taxes, license taxes, occupation taxes and privilege taxes. Their common denominator is that they are charges for the privilege of conducting the particular business, profession or activity. State and local governments impose these license fees for two basic reasons: (1) to recover the costs associated with regulation of the activity subject to the charge, and (2) to generate additional revenue for governmental purposes.

The person paying the fee is issued a license, which grants him or her permission to engage in the particular business, profession or activity. When the purpose of the licensing scheme is primarily regulation, other requirements are usually imposed on the licensee in addition to the license fee, such as a particular level of education or experience or a standard of conduct. The regulation of otherwise lawful activity through licensing is upheld where the regulation bears a reasonable relationship to the health, safety or general welfare of the people in the regulating community. The charge in these situations is imposed to recover the direct and indirect costs of the regulatory system, and is called a "license fee."

State and local governments have attempted to derive extra revenues from the licensing process. Typically, some of these revenues are used to cover the administrative expenses connected with issuing the license and regulating the activity. These revenues, however, may also be earmarked to provide certain services related to the activity (*e.g.*, fees from hunting and fishing licenses are sometimes used solely for fish and wildlife conservation management).

Charges of this type, unaccompanied by other regulatory standards and imposed primarily for revenue purposes, are more properly referred to as "license taxes." A popular approach, particularly in states like California, which have enacted severe limitations on state and local taxing powers (see II B(2), above), is to increase sharply the cost of various building and development permits to help finance the parks, roads, sewers, and other public facilities needed for a new development. These impact taxes are discussed in II H(3), below.

Because of the general requirement that taxes be levied only in accordance with state enabling legislation, courts will scrutinize license taxes carefully and will invalidate those that appear to be disguised attempts to circumvent the requirements of the tax statutes. However, where the taxing entity does have specific legislative authority to impose license taxes, certain types of taxes, such as a residential development tax of $150.00 per unit imposed on builders, have been sustained as reasonable.

License taxes and fees must conform to applicable state law, as well as state and federal constitutional provisions (see II A(2), above). In interpreting the extent of the power to impose such taxes and fees, state and local officials typically have faced the problem of determining whether a particular activity may be subjected to the licensing process, and of deciding whether the revenues derived from the process can be used to fund general governmental services.

The answer to both questions depends upon the enabling legislation. Older legislation, containing a lengthy list of activities subject to licensing, has often been interpreted by the courts to mean that the legislature intended that only those activities on the list could be subjected to local licensing procedures. As a result, communities operating under such narrowly interpreted enabling legislation have had to obtain separate state legislative approval to license and regulate new activities, such as cable television and video arcades. More modern state legislation attempts to eliminate the need for local government officials to make annual pilgrimages to the state capitol to obtain permission to license the latest activities, by giving municipalities general power to regulate and impose license fees to cover the cost of regulation. Indeed, the modern legislation generally gives municipalities discretion to determine by ordinance those businesses and activities within their territory which should be subjected to regulation.

Whether license fees and occupation charges can be pegged at rates higher than the costs of regulation, with the excess proceeds going into the general revenue fund, is also a matter of statutory interpretation. Such charges really are taxes and, like other taxes, must be authorized by statute or general home rule power. When found to be authorized, they generally will be upheld provided the rates are viewed as reasonable and not discriminatory or excessive. If not authorized as taxes, however, the charges will usually be invalidated by the courts as attempts to disguise a tax as a license fee and to circumvent the legal or political constraints upon taxation.

The growth of interstate business and the pressure on governmental officials to avoid increases in income and property taxes have led to sharp increases in the number and amount of privilege taxes on businesses. The principal federal constitutional constraints upon the operation of these taxes are the commerce clause and due process clause (see II A(2)(e)-(f), above). But excise taxes for the privilege of engaging in an occupation, such as a $7.00 per ton charge on waste haulers imposed by a municipality in Nebraska, have been upheld so long as the tax met the dormant Commerce Clause standards. *Waste Connections of Nebraska, Inc. v. City of Lincoln,* 697 N.W.2d 256 (Neb. 2005). Also, some aspects of these taxes are preempted by federal statutes, such as the 1973 statute prohibiting states from taxing air transportation. In *Aloha Airlines, Inc. v. Director of Taxation of Hawaii,* 464 U.S. 7

(1983), the Supreme Court held that that statute preempted taxes measured by the amount of air transportation business done, such as gross receipts taxes and head taxes, but did not preempt franchise taxes imposed for the privilege of conducting the air transportation business within the state.

A California appellate court enjoined, on First Amendment grounds, a municipality's business license tax as applied to a television subscription service. The tax was imposed on many businesses under a variety of methods, such as flat fees, per unit fees, flat fees plus sums based on the number of employees, and fees tied to gross receipts. It was imposed solely as a revenue-raising device. Only two of 87 businesses subject to the tax were required to pay a pure gross receipts tax without exemption or other qualifications. The television subscription service, which sold subscriptions for cable and satellite dish television service and leased antennas that permitted subscribers to receive the television services, faced a gross receipts tax that for one year could be as high as $6,300, while most other businesses were permitted to pay under an alternative method that would have yielded a tax on the same level of receipts of only $472.50. Finding no justification for the differential treatment other than raising of more revenue, the court invalidated the tax as it was applied to the television subscription service company because it placed an impermissible burden on the company's First Amendment rights. (*See City of Alameda v. Premier Communications*

Network, Inc., 202 Cal.Rptr. 684 (Ct. App. 1984), *cert. denied*, 469 U.S. 1073 (1984).)

A Tennessee bank excise tax that taxed bank earnings on obligations of the United States and its instrumentalities and on obligations of other states, but not interest earned on obligations of Tennessee and its political subdivisions, was invalidated by the U.S. Supreme Court as a violation of the principle of intergovernmental tax immunity. The immunity rule prohibits state and local governments from imposing the legal incidence of taxation on the federal government. (See II A (2) (g), above.)

Numerous cases have upheld state taxes where the economic but not the legal incidence of the tax fell upon the federal government, provided the taxes were not discriminatory. The fatal flaw in the Tennessee bank excise tax, however, was the fact that it discriminated in favor of securities issued by Tennessee and its political subdivisions and against federal obligations. (*See Memphis Bank & Trust Co. v. Garner*, 459 U.S. 392 (1983)).

PART H.   SPECIAL ASSESSMENTS AND SERVICE CHARGES (USER FEES)

Numerous local governments assess property owners for special benefits received and charge the public for services provided. These assessments are generally treated as charges for the special benefits provided to property owners and others, rather than as taxes. For this reason, courts generally require a correlation between the amount of the assessment and the value of the benefit conferred.

Section 1.   Real Estate Special Assessments and the "Special Benefit" Principle

The real estate special assessment and its more sophisticated offspring, the special benefit exaction, are variations of the property tax, which are designed to raise revenue for local public improvements said to provide "special benefits" to owners of adjacent or neighboring property. Special assessments are not employed to raise revenue for general governmental purposes, but rather to reimburse municipalities for particular expenditures which have enhanced the value of the property subject to the assessment. They have been used to finance such improvements as curbs, gutters, sidewalks and streets, drains, ditches, levees and sewers, off-street parking facilities, public parks and street lights.

Subsection a.   General Characteristics.

Although special assessments are levied as an exercise of the taxing power, and are part of the system of taxation, they are not "taxes" in the strictest sense of the term. The characteristics that distinguish special assessments from taxes are the one-time nature of the assessments, their application only to specially benefited property, and the requirement that their level be correlated with the benefit received. By contrast, real estate taxes are imposed throughout the jurisdiction on a recurring basis for general governmental purposes, regardless of whether expenditure of the tax revenues produces a direct benefit to the persons or property taxed (see II B(1), above). Special assessments generally are not subject to the rate and levy limitations imposed on real estate taxes (see II B(2), above), unless they are specifically included in those laws. Furthermore, the equality and uniformity provisions (see II A(2)(c)-(d), above), only require that the rate of assessment must be uniform for all property within a particular special benefit classification or district.

Special assessments are not voluntary in the sense that user charges are (see II H(2)(a), below). Although an individual can avoid a user charge for a bridge by not using the bridge, a property owner cannot avoid an assessment for sidewalks abutting his property by not using the sidewalks.

The key characteristics of the special assessment are the imposition of the assessment on a relatively small number of property owners, the requirement that the assessment finance improvements that will be of particular benefit to the property being assessed, and the fact that the assessment is against the land rather than the improvements. This latter feature has led to the general rule that "future uses of the land may be taken into account in justifying the assessment."

Subsection b.   Authorization.

Municipalities must be authorized by state legislation or by local charter, if the home rule delegation is broad enough to encompass the taxing power, to raise revenue through special assessments. As with general taxation and debt-financing, the particulars of the authorizing legislation must be observed. Failure to do so can result in invalidation of the special assessment. Strict observation of statutory procedures is required, and doubtful cases are construed against the municipality and in favor of the taxpayer.

Subsection c.   Application of the Special Benefit Principle.

Determination of the number of property owners to be assessed is a frequent cause of controversy. The special benefit is an "enhancement more localized than a general improvement in community welfare, but not necessarily unique to a given piece of property." The most clear-cut case involves assessment of the cost of a new sidewalk to the owners of property abutting that sidewalk. The theory for such an assessment is that the sidewalk provides a measurable "special benefit" to the abutting property. The property is said to increase in value because of the enhanced convenience, safety and other advantages the sidewalk provides.

The extent of benefit is a factual question which is answered, in the main, by a comparison of property values before and after the improvement. The requirement that the persons who reap the benefits of this increase in value should reimburse the municipality for the sidewalk expenditures generally is viewed as a reasonable allocation of costs rather than an unlawful non-uniform tax.

Oakland, Missouri, in the suburbs of St. Louis, is striking testimony to the fact that property owners do not always agree with the special benefit/reasonable allocation theory of assessments. Oakland was born out of a controversy over sidewalks in the 1920s. The City of Glendale decided to build sidewalks throughout the community and finance the cost via special assessments. Dissenting property owners at the southern end of the community broke away and incorporated Oakland, a community of 1,700 persons with an area of six-tenths of a square mile, as a non-sidewalk municipality.

Despite the history of Oakland, Missouri, the test of special benefit is the "value of the land in the marketplace, not in the minds of the present owners." Nonetheless, to justify a special assessment, the municipality must establish that the property to be assessed will be specifically benefited "in an amount equal to or greater than the amount of the assessment." This latter requirement is constitutional in origin. Assessment in the absence of such a special benefit would amount to a deprivation of property without due process of law, in violation of the Fourteenth Amendment, and a taking of private property for public use without just compensation, in violation of the Fifth Amendment as applied to the states through the due process clause of the Fourteenth Amendment. Such an assessment-without-benefit may also violate state constitutional provisions.

The standards for judicial review of municipal determinations of special benefit vary, depending upon the court's perception of the degree of legislative policy making involved in the special assessment decision. Many courts will look quite closely at these special assessment determinations on the theory that they constitute quasi-judicial decisions that, therefore, do not carry the usual presumption of validity. A number of courts, however, have articulated a policy of judicial restraint. The Oregon Supreme Court has characterized special assessments as forms of taxation, noting that "[t]he decision to tax is not subject to judicial review." The Kentucky Supreme Court views the special assessment as a legislative act that will not be disturbed "unless there is an abuse of discretion or a showing of fraud or illegality." The Texas Supreme Court requires that assessment decisions be affirmed "unless reasonable minds could not have reached the conclusion the Council reached in justifying its action." In Missouri, judicial review is limited to whether the legislative determination was: (1) arbitrary; (2) induced by fraud, collusion or bad faith; or (3) in excess of city powers. Florida courts will uphold legislative determinations concerning the "existence of special benefits and ... the apportionment of the cost of those benefits...unless the determination is arbitrary." *City of Winter Springs v. State,* 776 So.2d 255, 257 (Fla. 2001).

As noted above, the fact of a special benefit in an amount equal to or greater than the assessment must be established. The burden of proof in such

cases is generally borne by the complaining landowner. The court, however, is not a rubber stamp
for the assessing municipality and it is not required
to accept the city's evidence uncritically. There is no
presumption of special benefit simply because of a
public improvement, such as street widening; but a
disagreement between experts concerning the
amount of benefit will be resolved in favor of the
municipality.

The landowners' procedural due process rights
are satisfied by notice reasonably calculated to ap-
prise them of the proposed assessment, such as
mailing of individual notices to the owners of record
and a public hearing prior to the special assessment
decision. A trial-type hearing is not required, so
long as all benefited property owners are given an
opportunity to be heard in a meaningful time and
manner. The public hearing must be held before the
assessment liability is fixed for particular parcels of
property. It can be held anytime after liability attaches, whether or not the exact assessment for the
landowner has been determined.

Most special assessments are imposed upon property that abuts the particular improvement and,
therefore, identification of the special benefit ordinarily presents little difficulty. Occasionally, however, courts have invalidated a special assessment
because they were unable to find a special benefit
for the assessed property. Examples of such cases
include a storm water drainage project to solve a
traffic problem caused by the flooding of streets in
low-lying areas, the addition of curbs and gutters

and repairing of a street to which abutting landowners had no access, road widening to reduce
traffic congestion, and the construction of a library
building to serve a rural area.

When cities have attempted to assess non-abutting property for construction of public improvements, problems of identification of the requisite
special benefit are compounded. For example, a
sidewalk assessment district in which only some of
the streets in the district received the sidewalks but
all property within the district was assessed was
invalidated because the scheme did not provide a
"substantially equal" benefit for the abutting and
non-abutting property. Likewise, street widenings
to improve traffic and reduce the time for delivery
of emergency services have not been perceived as
conferring an identifiable special benefit to justify
an assessment on non-abutting property owners.

Not all assessments on non-abutting property,
however, have been invalidated, because some special benefits do extend more widely. For example,
downtown parking districts in which only a very
small percentage of the assessed property abutted
the parking lot or garage to be financed have been
upheld because they conferred recognizable benefits
on all property in the area. So also, a special assessment program designed to fund an integrated fire
rescue program has been upheld, but its companion
piece funding an emergency medical services program was invalidated. The Florida Supreme Court,
in distinguishing the two programs, found a "logical
relationship" between fire rescue services and bene-

fit to real property, but concluded that emergency medical services "provide a personal benefit to individuals" rather than to property. *City of North Lauderdale v. SMM Properties, Inc.,* 825 So.2d 343, 349–350 (Fla. 2002).

When the special assessment district format is used, a key question involves the drawing of the district boundaries. No set formula exists for answering that question. Courts generally approach the issue by examining the particular improvement contemplated and then determining whether the benefit to the land within the district will be "actual, physical and material and not merely speculative or conjectural."

One approach receiving favorable consideration is the "zoned district," in which the assessments are reduced as the distance between the improvement and the assessed property increases. Of course, if the assessment district becomes so large as to encompass most or all of the area of the general taxing jurisdiction, the scheme is likely to be invalidated as one conferring a general benefit that should be financed through the general taxing power.

Subsection d.   Assessment Methods.

Since the amount of a special assessment must be related to the benefit conferred in order to comply with constitutional mandates for equality of treatment and avoidance of confiscation (see II H(1)(c), above), the method of assessment is an important consideration. The three most common methods of assessment are the "cost per front-foot method," the "appraisal method," and the "area method."

Under the cost per front-foot approach, the total cost of the improvement is divided by the total feet of assessable land abutting the improvement. The resulting figure is the cost per front-foot. This figure is multiplied by the total frontage (number of front feet) owned to determine a particular property owner's assessment. For example, if a 1,000 foot sidewalk costs $4,000, the front-foot cost is $4.00. The special assessment for a person owning a lot with 100 feet of frontage on the sidewalk, therefore, would be $400.00. The cost per front-foot basis has the advantage of simplicity, but it has been criticized because it ignores factors such as the area and shape of the lots involved.

In a leading New Jersey decision, *McNally v. Township of Teaneck,* 379 A.2d 446 (N.J. 1977) landowners challenged special assessments that had been levied, on a front-footage basis, for the purpose of obtaining reimbursement of the costs of paving streets and installing curbs. The court noted that, under New Jersey law, a municipality's total assessments may not exceed its total costs, and individual assessments must not be in excess of the enhanced value to each property that results from the improvement in question. Nonetheless, the *McNally* court upheld the cost per front-foot basis, when employed in conjunction with visual observations and examinations of property by qualified officials, as a presumptively appropriate method of fixing assessments. Taxpayers challenging such assessments have the burden of overcoming that presumption by clear and convincing evidence.

The "appraisal method," in which property is formally appraised before and after the improvement, has the advantage of flexibility, by permitting adjustments to be made for peculiar situations such as corner or irregularly shaped lots or hilly terrain. Given the subjective nature of all appraisals, however, this method can result in more protests from owners who are dissatisfied with their assessments.

Under the "area method," properties with a larger area pay a larger special assessment. This method is particularly well-suited to localized utility improvements, where the demand placed upon the utility is more closely correlated with a property's area than with its front footage.

In a number of instances, all three methods (or some combination of them) have been utilized to determine an appropriate assessment rate.

Section 2. Service Charges and Pricing of Public Services

Subsection a.   General Characteristics.

One of the most significant changes in the financing patterns of local governments during the 1980s and early 1990s was the growth in the practice of charging for public services. That development has been significant enough to spawn conferences and reports on the "privatization" of public services.

As budgetary pressures during that period increased, more and more local governments responded to the continual demand for services by imposing charges for what had been free services or contracting with private firms to deliver the service for a fee. The most common services for which charges have been imposed are water supply and waste disposal, but other traditional public services such as parks and recreation, public transportation and health care are now funded, at least in part, through such charges.

User fees or service charges are not considered taxes but are said to be the "price" for the goods or services being sold by the government imposing the charges, or "rents" for the facilities being used. Such charges have been defined as "payments imposed on a benefit or quid pro quo principle provided the payee acquiesces in the payment of the levy." The definition identifies a major distinction between service charges and taxes: the voluntary nature of a service charge compared to the compulsory nature of a tax. The definition also points to the essential limitation on the use of service charges by government, namely that charges be imposed only for those types of services from which non-payers can be excluded without serious harm to themselves or significant impact upon others. Basic police services could not be sold under this definition because all members of the community share in the security provided by the police force, but around-the-clock guard service for a particular area could be sold because persons who do not desire that service can be excluded.

Two arguments often given by supporters of service charges are: (1) service charges are fairer than general taxes because the only persons who must pay are the ones receiving the benefit of the service, and (2) service charges are more efficient because they permit the government to allocate its resources in line with consumer preferences, as measured by the willingness to pay. In addition, the services paid for by service charges should be divisible to priceable units (e.g. gallons of water, trips across a bridge, etc.).

Subsection b. Pricing Policies for Service Charges.

The monopoly position that municipalities generally occupy when they provide services minimizes market pressures that influence private pricing policies; as a result, judicial and legislative regulation of municipal pricing decisions is very common. The general rule is that prices must be "fair, reasonable and just, uniform and nondiscriminatory." Municipal suppliers are not required to provide goods and services at cost; they may make a "fair profit," which may be transferred to the general fund to be used for other general governmental purposes. Use of funds in this manner does not, in and of itself, convert a service charge into a tax subject to the usual constitutional and statutory limitations applicable to taxation. The amount of revenue generated by the charge and allocated to general governmental purposes may, however, have a bearing on whether the charge is deemed fair and reasonable.

As in other areas of the law where a standard of reasonableness is employed, analysis of user charge rates must be based on the circumstances of the particular case. In evaluating the reasonableness of service charges, courts consider such factors as employee wages, costs of operation, expense of installation of new facilities, and assumption of new responsibilities, as well as evidence regarding similar services under similar circumstances. Municipalities also have been permitted to take into account the purpose for which the services are received, particularly in distinguishing residential from agricultural, commercial or industrial uses.

Municipalities imposing user charges for public services often are said to be acting in a business or proprietary capacity rather than in a governmental capacity and, as such, have been compared to private utility companies. In a bit of circular reasoning, the business capacity characterization is sometimes used as the basis for concluding that a service charge is not a tax. A better test to determine whether the municipality's charges are reasonable is to compare the charges with rates received by private utility companies. If the comparison is favorable, the charges most likely will be declared to be reasonable.

Because of the monopoly status that municipal suppliers enjoy, municipal service charges are governed by the common law rule forbidding unreasonable discrimination unless legislative authority to charge discriminatory rates is granted. Municipalities are not required to charge the same rate in all cases, but if they establish different rates, they must be able to show a reasonable relationship between those rates and the cost of providing the service.

Constitutional provisions requiring uniformity of taxation do not prevent municipalities from establishing different rates for service charges because of the almost universal conclusion that service charges (or user fees) do not constitute taxes. Most courts examining the question have upheld different rates for nonresidents where the nonresidents are treated as a separate class of users and the classification has a reasonable basis, such as distance from the service facility or cost of extending service lines. But if residents and nonresidents are treated as part of the same class or unit by the municipality for other purposes, a rate differential based solely on nonresidency is likely to be disapproved as unreasonably discriminatory unless it has been specifically authorized by statute. Claims of unconstitutional denial of equal protection because of higher rate charges are likely to fail unless the complaining parties can establish that the municipality has engaged in intentional discrimination against racial or other minorities in the provision of services. (*See also* II A(2)(d), above.)

Despite the tendency to characterize municipal service activities as business or proprietary rather than governmental in nature, most courts treat the ratemaking function as legislative and accord it the familiar presumption of validity. Judicial review is thus limited to consideration whether a particular charge is unauthorized, discriminatory, excessive or arbitrary, and the burden of proof is on the complaining party.

Section 3. Impact Taxes

A close relative of both the special assessment and the service charge is the impact fee or tax, imposed by an increasing number of local governments as a condition to granting land use approval for the construction of new residential or commercial developments. Impact fees might be assessed for any number of reasons, including concern that internal improvements (such as street grading, sidewalks, water mains and sewers) be provided, that external effects (such as additional strain on parks and roads) be alleviated, and that additional revenue be raised for general municipal purposes. In those cases where revenue generation is the prime motivation for the impact fees, they are more properly referred to as "taxes."

An impact fee usually is assessed as a per-unit charge and is payable upon issuance of the building permit for the construction project. The funds generated may or may not be earmarked for a particular expenditure, such as water or sewer services. Impact fees have become popular because they offer a way of passing on to new arrivals the public costs associated with growth. They raise the fundamental question, however, whether it is fair to transfer all the public costs of a new development to the individuals who will occupy that development.

The special benefit theory behind real estate special assessments (see II H(1), above) is often used to justify the full-scale transfer of costs through impact fees. Under this theory, the sub-divider of land creates a need for local improvements which are of special benefit to the subdivision. In addition, the increase in density occasioned by the development means that more persons will be using the public improvements. When these arguments are taken together, the conclusion is reached that the owners of the private development should pay for the new public improvements. This approach wears thin, however, if the funds are deposited in the municipality's general account and spent for regular governmental services.

State courts generally have been willing to uphold impact fees if a sufficient "nexus" exists between the community needs for which the funds would be spent and the new development upon which the fees were being imposed. This "nexus test" took on federal constitutional dimensions in two U.S. Supreme Court decisions. In *Nollan v. California Coastal Commission*, 483 U.S. 825 (1987), the Court held that conditioning approval of a permit for the rebuilding of a beachfront home upon a grant by the owners of a public easement across a part of their land violated the takings clause of the Fifth Amendment, as applied by the Fourteenth Amendment. The Court ruled that there had to be a nexus between the underlying permit condition and the purpose for which the building permit was imposed. Absent such a logical link, the owners' land had been unconstitutionally taken.

Several years later, in *Dolan v. City of Tigard*, 512 U.S. 374 (1994), the Court resolved a question it had not reached in the *Nollan* case: how specific a connection must there be between a mandatory exaction imposed by a local government and the likely impact of a landowner's proposed development, for the requirement to pass constitutional muster? In *Dolan*, the city had conditioned a permit (that allowed for the expansion of a downtown plumbing and electric supply store) on the public dedication of land for drainage improvements and for a pedestrian/bicycle path. The Supreme Court struck down this permit under the takings clause. It established the rule that an exaction will not constitute a taking if there is an "essential nexus" between a legitimate state interest and the potential impact of the proposed development *and* there is "rough proportionality" between the exaction and the projected impacts of the proposed development. In *Dolan*, however, the city had failed to meet its burden of showing such a rough proportionality. The *Nollan/Dolan* "nexus" test was later limited to the type of land-use exaction that "conditions[] approval of development on the dedication of property to public use" and thus is not applicable to impact fees. *City of Monterey v. Del Monte Dunes*, 526 U.S. 687, 702 (1999). However, some state courts may continue to apply a nexus standard to impact fees pursuant to state law.

One of the most difficult questions raised by impact fees is whether an acceptable line can be drawn between new users and prior users of public facilities. For example, should the cost of a new park or a new sewage treatment plant be borne solely by new residents of the community through impact fees, or should the cost be spread throughout the community over the traditional tax base? Courts have attempted to draw the line between expansion and replacement of capital improvements. The costs of new facilities designed to expand services to reach a new development can be imposed on that development, but new facilities designed to replace existing facilities should be paid for by the entire community. Extremely difficult questions are posed when the capital improvement is being proposed for both reasons, especially after *Dolan*.

In addition to the basic fairness issue, impact fees raise questions of proper authorization and of taxation in disguise. If they are viewed as taxes, they face serious questions regarding equality and uniformity.

Section 4. Revenue Sources for Special Districts

A form of local government, called the special district because it generally performs one function (or a small number of functions) instead of the wide range of functions performed by a general purpose municipality, draws heavily upon both special assessments and service charges as its revenue sources. The use of special districts to circumvent municipal debt limitations is discussed more fully in IV I(6)(b), below.

In the typical situation, a special district is formed under state enabling legislation or local home rule powers to carry out a particular activity such as water and sewer service, fire protection, parking lot operation, neighborhood schools and libraries, or trash collection. District boundaries drawn by the district organizers typically are for a service area smaller than the general purpose government in which the district is to be located, though district boundaries may be coterminous or even extended beyond the parent government if properly authorized by state law.

Special districts may or may not have the power to impose property taxes. Those that do not may be almost completely dependent upon special assessments and service charges to finance their activities. Some districts are formed solely to administer a finite special assessment program, such as a sidewalk district composed of the property that will be specifically benefited by the sidewalk installation. Most districts, though, have a governmental form and identity that continues indefinitely. These districts impose special assessments or service charges to finance the functions they perform. For example, transportation districts generally rely upon bridge and tunnel tolls as their revenue source.

The determination that a special assessment or a service charge is not a tax can have significant consequences for the special district. Specific limitations, such as the amount that can be raised by taxation or the requirement that a popular election be held to authorize a tax increase, are not applicable to special assessments and service charges unless the state constitutional or statutory provision contains language broad enough to encompass even non-tax revenue sources.

The traditional tax limitation provisions, designed to restrict the ability of state and local governments to impose ad valorem property taxes for general governmental purposes (see II A(2)(a) and II B(2), above), have been held not to apply to special assessments imposed by special districts (or by municipalities) for local improvements. Nor do these limitations apply to service charges that do not exceed the reasonable costs of the services and are not used for unrelated revenue purposes. On the other hand, some spending limitations have been held to apply to service charges.

Section 5.   The Treatment of Special Assessments and Service Charges in Federal Law

Subsection a.   Internal Revenue Code.

A significant, but often misunderstood, consequence of the state law determination that a special assessment or a user charge is not a local tax is that the assessment or charge will not be deductible for federal income tax purposes. Section 164 of the Internal Revenue Code authorizes taxpayers, in calculating their federal income tax liability, to deduct from their income the payments they have made for state and local property, income and sales taxes, as well as taxes incurred in carrying on a trade or business or in conducting income-producing activities. (*See also* IRC §§ 162, 212). Deductions, however, are not allowed under Section 164 for "taxes assessed against local benefits of a kind tending to increase the value of the property assessed." (The taxpayer can, nevertheless, add the assessments to the adjusted basis of his or her property, thereby lowering the taxable gain if and when the property is sold.)

The determination of what constitutes a state or local tax for purposes of Section 164 is based primarily on the law of the applicable state. If the state law does not consider special assessments or service charges to be taxes (or if it justifies their imposition on a benefit theory), such payments may not be deducted by the taxpayer in computing his or her federal income tax liability. This non-deductibility may come as a distinct shock to the taxpayer, particularly in the case of special assessments, which can be quite high and often are beyond the control of the taxpayer.

Subsection b.   Federal Bankruptcy Code.

The federal Bankruptcy Code contains a separate provision for special assessments in cases of municipal bankruptcy. A particular category of interested persons, called "special taxpayers," is given access to bankruptcy court proceedings in cases where the governmental entity that has imposed a special assessment has filed a petition for adjustment of its debts.

"Special taxpayers" are defined as property owners whose property is subject to an outstanding assessment or special tax "the proceeds of which are the sole source of payment of an obligation issued by the debtor to defray the cost of an improvement relating to such real property." 11 U.S.C.A. § 902(3). They are entitled to examine any plan developed by an insolvent municipality for adjustment of its debts and may participate in the negotiations involving debt adjustment in the same general manner as other creditors of the municipality. They may object to confirmation by the court of a debt adjustment plan. The reason for this special treatment is that the revenues from special assessments are designed to provide a particular benefit to the property of the special taxpayer, and thus he or she has an interest in how the plan affects those assessments. Municipal bankruptcy is treated more fully in IV G(3), below.

PART I.   LOTTERIES AND LEGALIZED GAMBLING ("GAMING")

Many states have turned to state lotteries as a means of finding new revenues while avoiding unpopular tax increases. Under recent counts, 40 states and the District of Columbia now authorize official state lotteries. Typically a state commission administers these lotteries; and it is responsible for the disbursement of lottery proceeds.

Generally, the net profits produced by a lottery go directly into the state's general fund. A number of states, however, devote the profits (or a portion of the profits) to special funds, the most common being a fund for the support of education. Other programs directly subsidized by lottery profits include transportation, aid to local governments, outdoor recreation and capital improvements, and college athletics.

Though lotteries provide an additional revenue source for state governments, they also present policy problems. There is a continuing debate over whether or not lottery fees are a regressive form of "taxation" rather than a type of "service charge." Some commentators believe that the poor spend a larger proportion of their income on lottery tickets than do members of higher income groups, while others argue that it is middle class ticket purchasers who spend the most. Critics of lotteries maintain that lotteries target poor persons by advertising mainly in low-income areas. Supporters, however, counter that lottery proceeds are frequently used to fund programs that help the poor. There is also some concern about the danger of possible corruption in the administration of lotteries. Though lotteries produce a large total number of dollars, they actually account for only a fairly small (though increasing) proportion of their states' total general revenues.

Other, even more controversial, sources of revenue are legalized casinos and other forms of gambling (also called "gaming"), such as video poker machines in bars and other entertainment locations. Many states have long allowed legalized gambling on certain sporting events, such as horse racing and jai alai, but Nevada is the only state with a long history of large-scale, casino gambling as well as many other forms of gaming. Also, Atlantic City, New Jersey has nearly twenty years of experience with multiple casinos.

Many states have legalized riverboat casinos, which have had explosive growth along the Mississippi Gulf Coast. The Louisiana Legislature approved a single land-based casino, located in New Orleans. Casinos for other cities have been repeatedly proposed in recent years.

Proponents of casinos contend that they raise a large amount of revenue for the state from casino taxes and license fees. They also point to the opportunity that casinos provide to share the economic benefits of a casino's construction and operation throughout the community.

On the other hand, some groups and commentators are wary of the possibility of increased crime associated with legalized gambling, potential negative effects upon recruitment of other new businesses, possible administrative and law enforcement costs, encouragement of gambling addiction, and the danger of disruption or distortion of local housing, land and job markets. Critics of casinos also argue that casinos siphon consumer dollars away from other portions of the entertainment industry, including movie theatres and sporting arenas.

PART J.　FINES

Fines are monetary penalties imposed upon persons who violate state statutes or local ordinances. They may be imposed in conjunction with or as alternatives to other penalties, *e.g.*, imprisonment. Unlike taxes, fines are only imposed upon those who have violated the law (as determined by the appropriate judicial or administrative officials). Just as service charges (user fees) can be avoided by persons who do not use the service (see II H(2), above), fines can be avoided by abiding by the relevant laws, for example by not speeding or double parking.

Like the power to tax (see II A(2)(a), above), the authority to impose fines must be granted by statute or home rule provision. The level of the fine for a particular violation may be set specifically by statute or ordinance or may be left to the discretion of the court, within the bounds of reasonableness.

Fines are a fairly insignificant source of revenue for state governments. They can, however, be of some importance to certain small towns. Most people probably can identify one or two municipalities having reputations for closely monitoring automobile speeds on major community thoroughfares and/or parking meters near popular sites such as colleges and universities.

PART K. INTERGOVERNMENTAL AID

Intergovernmental aid remains an important source of funds for state and local governments. Though federal aid does not constitute as substantial a portion of state and local revenue as it once did, federal aid is still significant, and state aid to localities (in most states) remains at a fairly high level.

Section 1. Federal Aid

Today, federal aid is distributed to state and local governments in the form grants, loans or tax subsidies. Intergovernmental grants tend to be categorical grants or block grants. Although each type of federal aid has its own set of requirements and restrictions, some requirements apply to all forms of federal intergovernmental aid.

Most of federal intergovernmental aid has been, and continues to be, distributed through intergovernmental grants, either unconditional or conditional, for specified program categories such as health, income security, education and training, and transportation. These categorical programs contain very detailed controls over spending purposes, administrative procedures, and the level of matching funds to be supplied by recipient state or local governments.

A smaller portion of federal assistance to state and local governments comes through so-called block grants, in which "certain specific grant programs—encompassing a wide range of domestic functions—were consolidated into a smaller number of more broadly defined block grants." Block grants offer greater flexibility for recipient governments, by allowing discretion in spending and administrative decisions within broadly defined program purposes (*e.g.*, community development). Block grants first appeared in the late 1960s in the fields of health, law enforcement and housing. In 1974 and again in 1981, Congress combined a number of preexisting categorical grant-in-aid programs into a small number of block grants. The new, broader block grants, however, were funded at a lower overall level than the categorical programs they replaced. In 1993, there were fifteen federal block grant programs, and approximately 10% of all federal grant funds were paid in the form of block grants. The Temporary Assistance for Needy Families (TANF) block grant program approved in 1996 and reauthorized in 2003 replaced a long-standing public welfare categorical grant program, Aid to Families with Dependent Children (AFDC).

During its fourteen years of existence, the general revenue sharing program provided the broadest spending discretion for its state and local government recipients. Though the original State and Local Fiscal Assistance Act of 1972 contained various spending restrictions and priorities, amendments in 1976 eliminated those provisions. Therefore, after the 1976 amendments, recipients could spend federal revenue sharing funds for virtually any public purpose. The 1972 Act allocated $2.2 billion per year to states and $4.6 billion per year to local

governments, distributed on the basis of fixed formulas that balanced population, revenue effort, and
relative income of the recipient governments. The
allocation to the states was effectively eliminated in
1980, but the federal revenue sharing program continued to allocate $4.6 billion to local governments
through fiscal year 1985–86. That $4.6 billion con-
stituted approximately 4% of federal intergovernmental aid and provided an average of 2.1% of
municipal budgets in that year. In October 1986,
the federal revenue sharing program was eliminated
by Congress.

The specific spending and administrative requirements of current federal intergovernmental aid programs (categorical grants and block grants) vary
from program to program, but governmental recipients of any form of federal aid must comply with
various federal constitutional requirements (*e.g.*,
holding due process hearings in certain settings)
and statutory requirements (*e.g.*, prohibitions upon
discrimination on the basis of race or gender by
programs receiving federal funds). Failure to comply with these requirements can result in termi-
nation of funding and, in some cases, monetary
damage claims by aggrieved private parties. (However, recent cases have recognized Eleventh Amendment and state sovereignty barriers to private suits
against states based upon certain federal statutes.
See II A(2)(f)(i), above.)

State and local government challenges to the constitutionality of conditions attached to federal aid
programs have been largely unsuccessful. For exam-

ple, *South Dakota v. Dole*, 483 U.S. 203 (1987), held that the federal government could require the states, as a condition of continuing to receive federal highway funds, to adopt age 21 as their minimum drinking age. (*See also United States v. American Library Association, Inc.*, 539 U.S. 194 (2003) (upholding against First Amendment challenge a statutory requirement that public libraries install software to block obscene or child pornographic images in order to receive federal assistance to provide Internet access); *North Carolina v. Califano*, 445 F.Supp. 532 (E.D.N.C. 1977) (upholding condition attached to receipt of federal health care funds, even though the recipient state would have to amend its constitution to comply with the condition), *aff'd*, 435 U.S. 962 (1978).) These and other cases, however, do articulate certain requirements for federal aid programs adopted pursuant to the spending clause. Conditions attached to such a spending program must: further the general welfare, be reasonably related to the articulated goal, and be stated in clear and authoritative language. Furthermore, the conditions cannot authorize the state or local government recipient to violate other provisions of the Constitution, and the conditions must not be enforced in a coercive manner. (*See, e.g., Dole*, 483 U.S. at 210–11; *Pennhurst State School & Hospital v. Halderman*, 451 U.S. 1, 17 (1981).)

Section 2.   State Aid

State aid remains extremely important for most local governments. In 1982, state aid averaged

29.1% of total local government revenues. In 2002, that figure had increased to almost 37%. By far the greatest amount of aid was for public education and public welfare programs, but significant amounts also were received for support of health and hospital services, roads and highways, as well as general local government support. Also, in recent years, state tax expenditure programs, such as tax credits to encourage private investment in local affordable housing and economic development programs, have had significant impact on local government budgets. (See II M, below.)There are, however, wide variations from state to state. Furthermore, the proportion of local government revenue from the state varies from one local government to another within any particular state.

Though there are some differences among states, most state aid to local governments is of the categorical kind, with spending limited to the particular purposes of the assistance program. Illinois, however, is an example of a state that maintains a revenue sharing program, sharing one-tenth of the state income tax revenues monthly with counties and municipalities on a population ration basis, for use in furtherance of recipient local government priorities. 30 ILL. COMP. STAT. 115/1 to 115/11.

PART L.   STATE TAX ASSESSMENT AND COLLECTION PROCEDURES

Section 1.   Assessment and Collection

The procedures for the assessment of state and local taxes vary from state to state and from one type of tax to another. Most state and local taxes paid by individuals are self-assessed (*e.g.*, through the preparation of state income tax returns). The primary exception to this rule is the real property tax, which is generally imposed based upon an assessment by a taxing authority. Local government departments or separate local assessors usually take the lead in real property assessments, but in several states responsibility for such assessments is shared by state and local government taxing authorities. These authorities also often share the power to audit or reconsider any assessments to determine their accuracy. If a tax audit determines that an initial assessment was too low, the taxing authority can usually issue a "notice of deficiency."

Taxpayers seeking to challenge a tax assessment or a notice of deficiency generally can do so via an administrative proceeding. (See II L(2), below.) Often these administrative challenges are subject to short statutes of limitations or notice of claim requirements. Sometimes, a taxpayer is required to pay the assessed tax first and then file a claim for a refund with the relevant agencies.

Tax agencies must comply with federal and state due process requirements when making assessments (and issuing deficiency notices) and in setting the procedures for taxpayers to contest an assessment (or notice of deficiency). Due process requires adequate notice and the opportunity for a hearing. The threshold for compliance with due process norms in the tax assessment area is relatively low; an adequate hearing before an administrative agency is necessary, but judicial review of the assessment usually is not constitutionally required.

Once an assessment or notice of deficiency has been fully appealed under the applicable state procedures (see II L(2), below), the relevant state or local agency may begin collection proceedings. Such proceedings usually involve granting the taxpayer a brief time to pay, and penalizing any delay after that date. The taxing authorities may engage in enforced collection by whatever means are provided by state law.

Usually, unpaid property taxes are made a lien on the property, with collection authorized by warrant. For other taxes (see II C–G, above), the taxpayer is usually personally liable for payment (though garnishments or other actions may be taken against his or her property to enforce that personal liability). If state agencies have reason to fear that delay will jeopardize receipt of taxes owed (*e.g.*, if the taxpayer is close to bankruptcy), such agencies may order immediate payment. Taxpayers are provided certain means to challenge these "jeopardy assessments" and may also avoid immediate payment by filing a bond before assessment is completed.

Section 2. Challenges to Assessments and Suits to Recover Taxes Paid

Administrative challenges to assessments usually involve an initial, informal presentation by the challenging taxpayer to a representative of the tax agency, whose decision can then be the subject of a more formal appeal to an administrative appeals board. Where adequate administrative remedies are available to taxpayers, such remedies must usually be exhausted before a claim can be brought in the state courts. Exhaustion of administrative remedies is not required, however, when the administrative agency cannot provide adequate relief, *e.g.*, when the taxpayer is challenging the constitutionality of the tax statute itself. (*See generally* II A(2), above.)

After taxes have been assessed and collected, taxpayers may bring suits in state court to recover allegedly improper tax payments. Plaintiffs in such lawsuits usually will have no difficulty establishing standing to bring suit where they are suing to recover the taxes they have paid. However, taxpayers who challenge a tax paid by someone else which has only an indirect impact upon them will have more difficulty satisfying the standing requirements. The U.S. Supreme Court has ruled that to establish standing-to-sue (in these and other cases) the plaintiff must show: 1) a concrete and particularized "injury in fact," 2) a "fairly traceable" causal connection between that injury and the conduct complained of, and 3) a likelihood that the injury will be "redressed by a favorable decision." In addition the Court has held associations (of taxpayers and others) may establish "representational standing" if: a) the association's members would otherwise have standing to sue in their own right, b) the interests that the association seeks to protect in the lawsuit are germane to its organizational purpose, and c) neither the claim asserted nor the relief requested requires that the association's individual members participate in the lawsuit. States generally apply the same legal tests as the federal courts in this area.

The burden of proof to establish wrongful assessment or improper collection generally rests upon the challenging taxpayer. However, in cases where a state is a creditor, and the taxpayer/debtor has filed a timely claim in bankruptcy court, most courts that have considered the question have held that the state taxing authority must bear the burden of proving both the validity and the amount of its tax claim.

Section 3.   Remedies for Taxpayers Who Successfully Challenge Tax Assessment or Collection

Taxpayers' suits to challenge state or local tax assessments have sought a range of remedies, including injunctive relief and declaratory relief and (more rarely) mandamus. States generally have discretion regarding the method of providing relief to plaintiffs who successfully challenge the assessment or collection of taxes. State relief systems, however, must satisfy certain minimum constitutional requirements.

In *McKesson Corp. v. Division of Alcoholic Beverages and Tobacco*, 496 U.S. 18, 36 (1990), the United States Supreme Court explained: "Because exaction of a tax constitutes a deprivation of property, the State must provide procedural safeguards against unlawful exactions in order to satisfy the commands of the due process clause" of the Fourteenth Amendment. "Allowing taxpayers to litigate their tax liabilities prior to payments might threaten a government's financial security," so the *McKesson* Court did not require the usual due process pre-deprivation hearing for the tax collection process. (*Id*. at 37.) Therefore, a state can require taxpayers to pay the tax first and then raise their objections to it in a post-deprivation refund action. However, when a State "relegates" a taxpayer's constitutional challenge to a tax to such a "postpayment refund action," the due process clause "obligates the State to provide meaningful backward-looking relief to rectify any unconstitutional deprivation." (*Id*. at 31.) Providing "meaningful backward-looking relief" will usually require refunding the illegally collected tax (subject to a reasonable statute of limitations). Depending upon the nature of the constitutional violation, it might be possible instead to reformulate the tax scheme so as to extend the same burden to the taxpayer's competitors (subject, of course, to other constitutional constraints) or to combine a partial reassessment with a partial refund. (*See id*. at 39–41.)

Taxpayers are not likely to be able to obtain, in either state or federal court, an injunction against collection of a tax. Because of the availability of administrative remedies and other refund mechanisms, plaintiffs usually will have great difficulty satisfying the usual prerequisites for injunctive relief in state courts. Furthermore, many states have enacted legislation or developed case law that prevents judicial interference with tax collections. State courts are, however, more willing to render declaratory judgments regarding the constitutionality *vel non* of tax statutes, especially where no questions of fact are presented. In such cases, they might also award injunctive relief if it is necessary to avoid the imposition of penalties based upon erroneous statutory construction and/or to prevent a multiplicity of actions at law.

Only on rare occasions can tax officials be required to act by writ of mandamus. This extraordinary remedy will only be available when other remedies are not, and when the official act involved is ministerial (non-discretionary).

Both federal statutory law and federalism principles severely limit the authority of federal courts to interfere with state tax administration or collection. The Tax Injunction Act, 28 U.S.C. § 1341, forbids federal court injunctions against the "assessment, levy or collection of any tax under state law where a plain, speedy and efficient remedy may be had in the courts of such state." The United States Supreme Court has interpreted the "plain, speedy and efficient remedy" phrase in a lenient manner. For example, in *Tully v. Griffin, Inc.*, 429 U.S. 68 (1976), the Court held that the plaintiff had an adequate remedy under state law, even though invoking that remedy required him to travel outside his home state. Furthermore, *Rosewell v. LaSalle National Bank*, 450 U.S. 503 (1981), held that state procedures were "plain, speedy and efficient," even though the time between payment and refund (after successful protest) was customarily two years and the refunds were paid without interest.

Other cases have held that comity and equitable principles forbid federal declaratory judgments regarding the constitutionality of state tax laws. *Fair Assessment in Real Estate Association, Inc. v. McNary*, 454 U.S. 100, 116 (1981), added that comity also prevents federal court suits for damages under 42 U.S.C. § 1983, if the state provides alternative remedies that are "plain, adequate, and complete." As a result, most cases in which taxpayers seek to challenge state or local tax administration or collection must be brought in the state courts.

On the other hand, the United States Supreme Court has unanimously held that "the Tax Injunction Act, as indicated by its terms and purpose, does not bar collection suits, nor does it prevent taxpayers from urging defenses in such suits that the tax for which collection is sought is invalid," even if those defenses later result in removal of the case to federal court. *Jefferson County v. Acker*, 527 U.S. 423, 435 (1999). The Court did note, however, that "abstention and stay doctrines may counsel federal courts to withhold adjudication, according priority to state courts on questions concerning the meaning and proper application of a state tax law." (*Id.* at

435 n.5.) In a later case, the Court held that the Tax Injunction Act did not bar federal court

PART M.   TAX EXPENDITURES TO FOSTER PUBLIC POLICIES

Section 1.   Tax Expenditures

States and local governments increasingly are permitting taxpayers to claim deductions, exemptions or credits against tax liability in return for some act or failure to act that fosters a program or policy desired by the taxing jurisdiction. Such devices are called tax expenditures because they reduce, rather than increase, the amount of revenue generated by a particular tax. Tax credits in particular are popular with taxpayers because 100% of the credit amount can be subtracted from a taxpayer's tax liability. Examples include credits against state income taxes for investment in low and moderate income housing development or local economic development projects, as well as credits for donations to not-for-profit organizations that provide tuition assistance for children to attend private schools. Tax credits have become "useful state financing tools [because] they leverage the states' resources by encouraging the private sector to contribute to or invest in state-supported projects that promote the public welfare." Janette Lohman & Paul Tice, *Using Tax Credits to Implement Public Policy: the Missouri Experiment*, 8 J. AFF. HOUS. & COMM. DEV. L. 284, 284 (1999).

Tax expenditure programs are subject to the same type of constitutional and statutory authorization issues discussed in II A above. While courts usually will give broad deference to legislative policy decisions, the courts' response to the default of the Washington Public Power Supply System, discussed in IV H below, is a reminder that proper authorization for a tax expenditure program is critically important.

Section 2. Taxpayer Challenges to Tax Expenditures

As noted in II L above, standing can be a significant issue for taxpayers seeking to challenge tax expenditure programs because, by definition, they are not subject to a tax but rather are objecting to a credit, deduction or exemption given to some other taxpayer. For example, the Supreme Court held, in *DaimlerChrysler Corp. v. Cuno,* 126 S.Ct. 1854 (2006), that Ohio taxpayers did not have standing to challenge a state franchise credit and a local property tax exemption granted an automobile manufacturer for new investment in a Toledo, Ohio Jeep manufacturing plant. In rejecting standing, the Court emphasized the "conjectural or hypothetical nature" of the plaintiffs' alleged injury. The Court noted that tax expenditure programs are designed to "spur economic activity, which in turn *increases* government revenues. ... Establishing injury requires speculating that elected officials will increase a taxpayer-plaintiff's tax bill to make up a deficit; establishing redressability requires speculating that abolishing the challenged credit will redound to the benefit of the taxpayer because legislators will pass along the supposed increased revenue in the form of tax reduction. Neither sort of speculation suffices to support standing." *Id.,* at 1862–1863 (emphasis in original).

Assuming standing and other procedural issues can be overcome, the Supreme Court has held that the Tax Injunction Act, discussed in II L above, did not bar federal court suits challenging state income tax credits made available to organizations providing scholarships and tuition grants for attendance at private schools. *Hibbs v. Winn,* 542 U.S. 88 (2004).The Court majority stressed that the Tax Injunction Act has been applied "only in cases Congress wrote the Act to address, *i.e.,* cases in which state taxpayers seek federal-court orders enabling them to avoid paying state taxes." (*Id.,* at 107).

CHAPTER III

STATE AND LOCAL GOVERNMENT EXPENDITURE PATTERNS

PART A. BUDGETARY REQUIREMENTS

A tradition of strong fiscal controls on spending by state and local governments has existed in this country since the mid–1800s. All states except Vermont require their governments to operate under balanced budgets of one form or another. In most cases, budgets must be adopted on an annual basis, although some states still use a two-year cycle.

The actual process of achieving a balanced budget can be difficult. Revenues do not always match expenditures during or at the end of the fiscal year. Major administrative expenditures, such as employee salaries and building maintenance, occur regularly throughout the year. Program expenditures, such as public assistance payments, school aid and health care, also occur regularly. Other expenditures, such as street and highway repair, however, can vary with fluctuations in the severity of weather and the extent of road use.

On the revenue side, however, only part of state and local government revenues are received on a regular basis. For example, sales and use taxes, income tax withholdings and federal assistance payments usually are paid to the taxing government monthly or quarterly. Property taxes, on the other hand, typically are received only once per year. Because the time of payment usually is in the middle or toward the end of the fiscal year, a certain amount of financial juggling by governments that rely upon property taxes must take place to meet regular expenses incurred prior to the receipt of these property taxes.

One use of short-term borrowing power, discussed in IV D below, is to overcome cash flow problems that may occur when tax or other revenue collections cannot be synchronized with required expenditures.

An additional complication arises when revenue collections fall short of expectations. Cancellation of a major federal aid program or an unanticipated downturn in the economy can play havoc with revenue forecasts, especially for governments which rely upon cyclical taxes. (See II A(1), above.) Most states give their chief executive officer the power to reduce the level of spending through layoffs and other actions when revenues are less than anticipated.

Section 1. The Appropriations Process

State and local spending has three segments: budgeting, appropriation, and expenditure. States typically require all funds to be received by one office, usually the treasurer's office. A budget, which is "a complete and itemized plan of proposed expenditures," usually must be developed by the chief executive (the mayor or governor) and be presented to the legislative body (the city council or state legislature).

No funds may be spent unless the legislative body has enacted an appropriations law (or ordinance) specifying the amount and purpose of the appropriation; and the actions of a state legislature, in appropriating or refusing the appropriate funds, may not typically be redressed in the courts. Thus, legislatures have great discretion not to fund programs, to fund them partially, or to establish spending priorities within programs.

However, a legislature's failure to follow state laws (or local charter provisions) requiring the adoption of a single operating budget and a single appropriations bill has resulted in the judicial invalidation of subsequent piecemeal appropriation bills. The normal requirements for legislative action— formal introduction of bills, public hearings by legislative committees, public debate and legislative vote—apply to appropriations bills.

Public hearings can be an important source of information for interested citizens concerning proposed public expenditures. They are also the stage in the appropriations process at which the executive branch defends its spending plans to the legislature, which has the responsibility for raising the necessary funds through taxation or borrowing. Failure to conduct a public hearing or to take other essential steps in the legislative process can render an appropriations bill void and can result in personal liability under statutes imposing civil liability upon officials for unauthorized expenditures of public funds.

The chief executive has a degree of control over the appropriations process through the initial presentation of the recommended budget and his or her use of the veto power. All states except North Carolina give the state's chief executive the power to veto an entire appropriations bill. Many states give the chief executive greater flexibility through the line item veto, which allows the chief executive to delete one or more appropriations items without having to veto the entire appropriations bill. Some states also permit the chief executive to add expenditures that have been deleted by the legislature—a kind of reverse veto, which stands approved unless rejected by the legislature in a special veto-override session.

Actual expenditures are made by the executive branch once the legislature has appropriated the funds. In the typical case, the agency or department proposing to spend the money files a written request, usually called a requisition, with a central administrative office (controller, department of administration, etc.) where the request is checked against the approved budget and the appropriated funds. If the request is consistent with the budget and the appropriations, it is forwarded to the treasurer's office with a request that a check be drawn to make the payment. If all is in order, a "warrant" is drawn by the treasurer, which is an official order that a check be issued for payment.

As noted above, should the chief executive determine that spending must be slowed down or reduced because of lower than anticipated revenue collections, statutes or constitutional provisions usually permit the executive to stop or curtail spending during the expenditure process, even though funds have been appropriated by the legislature. This is usually accomplished through a directive to line agencies to reduce their planned spending or a directive to the central administrative agency that reviews spending requests.

As noted in II H–K, above, state and local governments receive a large percentage of their revenues from sources other than traditional taxes (*e.g.*, grants from higher levels of government, charges for services, and income from proprietary activities). This expansion of non-tax revenue sources has raised the question whether state constitutional and statutory provisions that require "all revenue collected and money received" to go to a central depository and be spent only through legislative appropriations should be applied to non-tax revenues, as well as traditional tax revenues. In general, the answer to this question is "yes," though courts have often gone to great lengths to sustain an expenditure that does not meet these requirements if other legislative support for the expenditure pattern can be found.

In most cases involving non-tax revenues generated by the activities of a state or local governmental department, the courts have concluded that the funds received are subject to the appropriations process before they can be spent. For example, "profits" generated by commissaries or canteens in a public building may not be segregated into a special account of the parent agency but must be deposited in the treasury and expended only after an appropriation. Likewise, revenues from service charges and special fees normally are subject to the appropriations process. Nonetheless they can be, and often are, deposited in special accounts from which appropriations may be made for particular purposes, such as street maintenance.

On the other hand, special authorities and special districts are often established under state law (or local charter provisions) as independent governmental entities not subject to formal supervision of their day-to-day activities by state or city governments. See II H(4), above. Courts often conclude that the independence conferred on such a special district or authority constitutes a decision to exclude the entity from the regular appropriations process. Thus, proceeds collected from the sale of tax-exempt revenue bonds by state housing, environmental improvement, and health and educational facility authorities (see IV C(2) and E, below) are not generally subject to state appropriations requirements. Nor is the service charge revenue collected by these special authorities usually subject to general appropriations requirements.

In addition to the general checks upon expenditures created by public hearing and public debate

requirements, specific appropriations laws and program enabling legislation impose limitations on
state and local government spending practices. Although courts are generally sympathetic to the
plight of harried state and local officials seeking to
discharge their day-to-day duties, they will not permit spending of public funds that is not authorized
by law. For example, if a state statute requires
substantial changes in urban renewal plans to be
formally approved through a public hearing process,
courts have ruled that spending funds for any purpose not approved at a formal hearing is unauthorized and that officials who approve such spending
are personally liable. Similarly, New Jersey statutes
providing for municipalities to receive a share of the
proceeds of several different taxes collected by the
State have been held to require specific appropriations by the legislature of the funds generated by
those taxes before the funds can be distributed to
eligible municipalities. In the New Jersey court's
view, the state constitutional requirement that a
single appropriations law be enacted to cover each
fiscal year made it impossible to regard the separate
taxing statutes as self-executing current appropriations.

The appropriations process can result in a loss of
efficiency because of the difficulty of amending appropriations laws when the legislature is not in
session. One approach to this problem is delegation
of authority to a legislative committee to make
spending decisions and to modify appropriations
laws during the periods between sessions. This pow-

er usually must be exercised with the concurrence of a senior executive officer. Courts in several states have accepted this process, or have ruled that challenges to it are not justiciable, but the Missouri Supreme Court has ruled that it is an unlawful attempt to delegate the constitutionally mandated legislative function of appropriating public funds.

Section 2. Auditing and Other Accounting Requirements

Statutes in many states now authorize citizens to request an audit of a local government's expenditures by the state auditor. Missouri, for example, requires the state auditor to conduct an audit if a specified number of qualified voters (calculated on a sliding scale based upon voter turnout in the most recent gubernatorial election) sign petitions seeking the audit. The affected local government is required to cooperate in the audit and must pay for its cost. No local government may be audited in this manner more than once every three calendar or fiscal years.

A number of commentators and organizations, including the Government Finance Officers Association, have recommended that local governments develop financial accounting systems that comply with generally accepted accounting principles (GAAP). The Accounting Principles Board defines GAAP as follows:

> Generally accepted accounting principles incorporate the consensus at a particular time as to which economic resources and obligations should be recorded as assets and liabilities by financial

accounting, which changes in assets and liabilities should be recorded, when these changes should be recorded, how the assets and liabilities and changes in them should be measured, what information should be disclosed and how it should be disclosed, and what financial statements should be prepared.

In 1984, a Government Accounting Standards Board was organized by the National Council on Governmental Accounting (NGCA), and the American Institute of Certified Public Accountants (AICPA), with the participation of state and local governments and the accounting profession. This Board has issued a set of Statements and Interpretations that represent advances in the development of generally accepted accounting principles for governmental financial reporting.

At the present time, however, Securities and Exchange Commission (SEC) rules regarding offerings of municipal securities do not specify any particular set of accounting requirements. Nonetheless, issuers of municipal bonds are required by the SEC to specify the type of financial information and operating data that they will provide annually, the accounting principles that will be used with regard to financial statements, and an indication whether such statements will be audited.

Section 3. Spending Priorities Imposed by Intergovernmental Aid Programs

Attempts by states to assert greater control over federal intergovernmental aid funds (see II K, above) by subjecting them to the state appropriations process have proven controversial. A few state courts have concluded that federal funds may be received and spent by state or local officials without legislative appropriations. Courts adopting this approach have reasoned that the executive branch, or one of its officials or agencies, is receiving the federal funds as custodian and administrator, with responsibility for expending the funds in accordance with the dictates of the federal legislation establishing the particular program. Under this theory, the traditional legislative oversight function designed to assure that public funds are expended for the benefit of the public has already been performed by Congress. Therefore, the state legislature has little or no role in the process.

When federal funds were a relatively insignificant part of the states' budgets, state legislators made few objections to this exclusion of federal funds from the legislative process. Many states included a routine statement in their appropriations bills simply declaring that federal funds received by a particular state agency were deemed to be appropriated when received.

When federal funds became a more significant portion of a state's budget, however, state legislators were faced with a substantial loss of control over a major part of state finances. In response to this development, a number of states enacted laws requiring that all federal funds be deposited in the general revenue fund, without designation as a restricted or separate account, and that they be spent only after the legislature made a specific appropriation.

The Pennsylvania Supreme Court, over a strong dissent, upheld such a law. (*See Shapp v. Sloan*, 391 A.2d 595 (Pa. 1978), *appeal dismissed sub nom.*, *Thornburgh v. Casey*, 440 U.S. 942 (1979).) The Court reasoned that funds received from the federal government belonged to the state, not to its officers or agencies, because the federal laws establishing the programs clearly provided that grants were to be made to "state and local governments." The state officials authorized to apply for the federal funds did so on behalf of the state. As such, the funds, and the persons administering them, had to comply with existing laws regarding expenditures of state funds.

In reaching its decision, the Pennsylvania Supreme Court was influenced by a report of the United States Advisory Commission on Intergovernmental Relations (ACIR), which concluded that decisions whether to participate in federal programs can have long-term budgetary and policy implications for the state because of the increasing impact of federal funds on state budgets and the potentially severe consequences of a congressional decision to alter radically or terminate a particular program. In addition, the ACIR noted the substantial increase in professionalism in state government and concluded that the legislative oversight function could be performed effectively, and perhaps more efficiently, by the states.

A dissenting opinion in the Pennsylvania case argued that requiring state appropriation of federal funds prior to their distribution violated both the supremacy clause of the United States Constitution and the separation of powers doctrine.

In some states, the question of whether federally granted money is to be controlled by state legislatures or state executive branch officials turns on whether such funds meet a statutory definition of "custodial funds," i.e. funds as to which the state is deemed a custodian or trustee of funds, not generated by tax revenues, that were given to the state for particular purposes. With regard to such funds, the executive, not the legislative, branch retains control over the money in question. The legislature, in contrast, has plenary power in those jurisdictions with regard to the expenditure of tax-generated "state monies."

The federal supremacy issue is raised whenever the state appropriations requirement is said to conflict with the mandates of the federal legislation providing the intergovernmental aid funds. Analysts have noted that very few of the federal statutes provide a role for state legislatures, and most require that federal programs be administered by a state agency, usually designated by the governor; therefore, the potential for conflict is present.

Courts will invalidate a state law that directly conflicts with federal grant legislation. (See II A(2)(g), above.) If there is no direct conflict, however, the supremacy clause issue can be, and often is, avoided.

Courts seeking to avoid the issue reason that no conflict exists between a state appropriations requirement and the federal grant legislation because congressional silence on the appropriations question represents a desire not to dictate the precise form of state administration.

The separation of powers issue was raised in the Pennsylvania case because the federal money that became embroiled in the dispute was to be used to fund a special prosecutor investigating allegations of corruption in Philadelphia. Legislative withholding of such funds, the dissent argued, constituted an impermissible legislative interference with the executive and judicial function of enforcing the laws and combating official corruption. Other separation of powers arguments, often political rather than constitutional in nature, tend to reflect the executive prerogative to formulate and carry out programs and the legislative prerogative to control the budgetary process.

Section 4.   Spending Exclusively for "Public Purposes"

Just as the powers to tax and to borrow may be used only for public purposes (see II A(2)(b), above, and IV C(1)(b) and IV F(2), below), state and local governments may spend money only for public purposes. The same basic tests used to review taxing and borrowing for public purposes are also applied to spending decisions.

Courts have tended to defer to legislative determinations of public purpose, applying the oft-quoted standard that "determination of what constitutes a public purpose is primarily for the legislative department and it will not be overturned unless found to be arbitrary and unreasonable." Under this standard, spending for both traditional and non-traditional state and local government activities, such as housing for low and moderate-income persons, economic development, public power generation, higher education buildings, health care facilities and pollution control, have been upheld. Furthermore, the fact that funds will be distributed to private individuals is not, in itself, fatal to a public spending program.

In some jurisdictions, courts employ a "primary effect" test to determine whether there is a sufficient public purpose behind a grant of public money. Under that approach, if the "primary object" of a public expenditure is to promote some private purpose the expense is unlawful, even where it may incidentally serve a public purpose. On the other hand however, public funds may be legally expended where they are primarily spent for public municipal purposes, even if the expenditure in question involves an incidental expense which serves a private interest.

PART B.   COLLECTIVE BARGAINING AND EMPLOYEE SALARIES

State and local government employees have a First Amendment right to form and join unions. Nonetheless, the courts have upheld state restrictions upon certain activities of public sector unions, such as attempts to compel collective bargaining, withholding of union dues from paychecks, and striking, especially by police.

The daily operations of public sector unions are governed by state law because the National Labor Relations Act exempts state and local governments from its coverage. Most states have, however, enacted laws patterned after this federal legislation, thereby authorizing state and local government employees to engage in traditional collective bargaining activities, except the right to strike. To compensate for the strike prohibition, many states authorize resort to alternative dispute resolution techniques such as mediation, fact-finding (also known as advisory arbitration), and binding arbitration.

Employee salaries make up a large portion of governmental budgets, particularly at the local level. An impasse over salaries, therefore, can have a substantial effect upon local budgets, as well as the conduct of public affairs and the allocation of public funds. As a result, the resolution of impasses through resort to mediation, fact-finding and binding arbitration has gained wide popularity in recent years.

The form of binding arbitration generally used in public salary disputes is known as "final offer" interest arbitration, in which each party submits its best offer to the arbitrator. The arbitrator is not permitted to develop a compromise award but must select whichever final offer appears more reasonable. Moreover, in making that decision, in some states, the arbitrator must take account of municipal budget caps. It is believed that this process encourages voluntary settlements, because the parties are forced to develop their proposals with an eye toward the arbitrator's view of reasonableness.

Overly generous settlements or arbitrator's awards obtained through the impasse resolution process can produce conflicts with budgetary regulations prohibiting deficit operations and imposing limits on taxation and expenditures. When salary increases result in deficits and the appropriate taxing authorities fail to raise taxes to cover these deficits, courts have sometimes refused to enforce the salary agreement. They rely upon one of two rationales: (1) the contract is subject to an implied condition precedent that it will be funded by the independent legislative body having taxation power (or the electorate, if a vote is required) and failure of this implied condition renders the contract unenforceable; or (2) the contract is void because the government has no power to enter into an agreement that requires deficit financing.

Two related problems associated with the budget process can occur as a result of state-mandated impasse resolution procedures. The first springs from the typical requirement that governments adopt a budget by a particular date. If the impasse resolution procedures have not succeeded in producing a settlement by that date, officials charged with the responsibility for preparing the budget must estimate the likely costs to be incurred by the eventual salary agreement. Some courts have held, on statutory interpretation grounds, that mandatory impasse resolution procedures could and should use the budget date as the final date for completing the procedures. That view, however, has not been adopted universally by the judiciary, particularly where statutory amendments set a cut off date for negotiations that is contrary to a court's previous statutory interpretation.

If the government engaged in the dispute is subject to a tax or expenditure limitation (see II B(2), above, and III C, below), the costs of any settlement negotiated or imposed by arbitration must be included in the budgetary calculations made to determine compliance with the limitation. This requirement can cause substantial readjustments to other parts of the budget, particularly if the dispute is not resolved until late in the budgetary process.

PART C.   SPENDING LIMITS

Several states and some local governments are subject to statutes that limit their annual expenditures. The first such statutory spending limit was imposed upon Arizona counties and municipalities in 1921. (The Arizona Supreme Court had previously developed a local spending limit, which it saw as the logical corollary to the state's local levy limits (see II B(2), above).)

The contemporary version of Arizona's local expenditure limit, which is now part of the state's constitution, mandates that a state "economic estimates commission" compute and publish the limits for each county and municipality. Excluded from "revenues" are tax collections to pay debt service on long-term debt, federal aid, and payments made in lieu of taxes by tax-exempt institutions. These and other exclusions serve to allow local governments additional expenditures over and above the constitutional limits. Also allowed are excess direct expenditures for disasters declared by the Governor, but such expenditures must occur in the fiscal year of the disaster or during the next fiscal year. In addition, a majority of local voters can approve spending in excess of the mandated limit for a specific year. However, this excess level of spending is not included in the base for calculating the following year's spending limit.

In 1976, New Jersey adopted fairly simple local government expenditure limits, as well as the nation's first state spending limit. These new spending limits were a concession to the voters because the same session of the Legislature adopted New Jersey's first income tax (see II D(2), above). Both expenditure limits were allowed to expire, however, without being renewed.

Several other states (including Arizona and Michigan) also added state government spending limits to their constitutions; and California voters adopted a constitutional limit on state and local government spending (Article 13B). The rate of adoption of state government spending limits, however, has slowed in recent years.

The advocates of state spending limits contend that the limits will restrict the capacity of government officials to expand their budgets in response to interest group pressures. As a result, they argue, spending limits will ultimately be more effective than either tax rate limits or levy limits (which generally apply only to real estate taxes, see II B(2), above) in lowering the overall level of taxes.

Most current state expenditure limits do, however, allow for some expansion of governmental budgets. Several of them include measures of inflation, population expansion, or per capita income growth in their formulas, thereby allowing increased government spending in response to one or more of these growth indices. Also, certain categories of expenditure or sources of revenue are excluded from some of the spending limits.

PART D.   SCHOOL FINANCE REQUIREMENTS

One of the major uses of public funds by state and local governments is the support of public elementary and secondary schools. In most states, this support comes in three forms: (1) use of property tax revenues, collected at the local level, for school operational expenses; (2) use of funds produced by tax-exempt bonds, issued by local school districts, to pay for the capital costs of construction and repair of school buildings; and (3) direct state aid to local school districts. State aid, in turn, usually has two components: (a) a flat grant to districts paid on a per pupil basis, and (b) an "equalization grant" to help provide greater equality in educational spending throughout the state.

In virtually all the states, free public education to all persons through the age of at least sixteen is a state guarantee and often a state constitutional requirement. Almost all states have delegated the task of providing public education to local special purpose districts that usually function independently of the general purpose county and city governments within whose territory they operate. A few large cities, however, have dependent school districts.

Public school districts receive the tax dollars generated locally (usually from the real property tax) and the grants distributed by the state, along with any federal grants that may be available, and the districts make many of the educational decisions regarding how those funds should be spent. Aside from a requirement in many states that a fixed percentage—often between 70% and 80%—of the total amount of state aid received be allocated to pay teachers' salaries, the local school districts generally are free from state restrictions upon the manner in which the educational budget is drawn.

They, however, are often subject to severe administrative regulations, imposed by the state department of education or comparable state body, concerning teacher qualifications, course requirements, and other subjects.

Over the past sixty years, state aid as a percentage of local public school revenue has increased from less than 20% to almost 50%, while local property taxes have declined from more than 80% of the total to just over 40%. Federal aid has increased from less than 1% to approximately 7% of local public school revenues.

Because of the traditional reliance on the local property tax as a source of funds for public education, shifts in population and wealth resulted in a serious fiscal imbalance among local school districts in many states by the mid to late 1960s. The severity of the problem was clear when the finances of inner city school districts and rural districts were compared to wealthy suburban districts (often within the same metropolitan area). Indeed, in the 1960s, it was not unusual for neighboring districts to differ by as much as $500 per pupil in the amount of tax dollars that could be generated for schools by imposing the same rate of taxation. Because state aid was distributed under formulas that guaranteed a minimum amount to all schools and placed particular emphasis on average per pupil daily attendance, the rich districts in many states got richer and the poor districts got poorer.

Since 1968, the vast majority of states have had their locally based systems for financing public education challenged on federal and/or state constitutional grounds. In many cases, changes in state aid patterns have followed.

Section 1.   Federal Constitutional Challenges

The main federal court challenges to school financing have centered on the equal protection and due process clauses of the Fourteenth Amendment. In *McInnis v. Shapiro*, 293 F.Supp. 327 (N.D. Ill. 1968), *aff'd sub nom., McInnis v. Ogilvie*, 394 U.S. 322 (1969), the federal district court concluded that the Illinois public school finance system, which fit the pattern described above and which produced variations in per pupil expenditure of $480 and $1,000, did not violate the federal constitutional rights of students. The district court refused to accept the argument that the Fourteenth Amendment required states to distribute school aid funds according to the educational needs of the students. The district court concluded that the question whether educational needs should form the basis for allocation of funds was a policy decision for the legislature rather than the courts and that the Illinois system, which depended on variable property values and local tax rates, was a rational one that did not reflect invidious discrimination.

The question whether heavy reliance on local property tax revenues (which varied widely) violated federal equal protection standards was answered in the negative by the United States Supreme

Court in *San Antonio Independent School District v. Rodriguez*, 411 U.S. 1 (1973). In concluding that substantial interdistrict disparities in school expenditures existing in Texas did not violate the Fourteenth Amendment, the Court reasoned that none of the three possible groups that could claim discrimination—"poor" persons as such, persons "relatively poorer" than others, or persons residing in "relatively poorer school districts"—constituted a suspect category entitled to strict judicial scrutiny. Furthermore, the Court found no denial of a fundamental right that justified subjecting the state financing scheme to strict judicial scrutiny, because no pupils were totally deprived of a basic education. In the Court's view, plaintiffs had not established that the two main results of interdistrict disparities—lower pupil-teacher ratios and higher teacher salaries—correlated directly with the quality of classroom instruction. Over strong dissents, a majority of the United States Supreme Court upheld the Texas system as a rational effort at balancing the desire for basic education for all children in the state with local control of that education, and it observed that basic reform must come through the legislative process.

Given the extremely deferential approach taken by the *Rodriguez* Court (evaluating the federal equal protection clause challenge under the rational basis test), it is not surprising that parents subsequently challenging locally based public school financing have premised their claims upon state constitutional grounds. (See III D(2), below.) One important exception is *Plyler v. Doe*, 457 U.S. 202 (1982), in which the United States Supreme Court ruled that Texas had violated the equal protection clause by denying free public education to "undocumented" alien children, while providing it to other children (American citizens and legally admitted aliens). The majority employed the intermediate scrutiny standard, because of the interest being denied (access to free public education) and the persons being denied that interest (children who were not responsible for their undocumented status). That standard required the State to prove that the challenged laws substantially furthered a substantial state interest, and the Court ruled that none of the State's asserted justifications was sufficient to satisfy this standard of judicial scrutiny. Justice Powell, who wrote the majority opinion in *Rodriguez*, distinguished *Plyler* as follows:

> [I]n *Rodriguez* no group of children was singled out by the State and then penalized because of their parents' status. Rather, funding for education varied across the State because of the tradition of local control. Nor, in that case, was any group of children totally deprived of all education as [occurred in *Plyler*].

Id. at 239 n.3 (Powell, J., concurring).

Other federal constitutional cases regarding school finance involve challenges, under the equal protection clause of the Fourteenth Amendment or the establishment clause of the First Amendment, to the provision of financial or other assistance to private and parochial schools. Other types of school cases involve challenges under federal statutes to a school's treatment of students with disabilities.

Section 2.   State Constitutional Challenges

Lawsuits challenging school finance which are premised upon state constitutional provisions have fared better than their federal counterparts. The California Supreme Court twice invalidated the California school financing system on equal protection grounds—prior to *Rodriguez* under the Fourteenth Amendment of the U.S. Constitution and after *Rodriguez* under the equal protection clause of California's Constitution. In the second opinion, the Court repeated its basic conclusions: "(1) discrimination in education opportunity on the basis of district wealth involves a suspect classification, and (2) education is a fundamental interest."

In New Jersey, a slightly different approach was used. The New Jersey Constitution requires that the Legislature provide for the "maintenance and support of a thorough and efficient system of free public schools for the instruction of all the children in the State." While rejecting an equal protection claim, the New Jersey Supreme Court held that the State's school financing system, which was similar to those described above, did not satisfy the state constitutional requirement of a "thorough and efficient" system of public education. For the next three years, the Court and the Legislature engaged in a difficult struggle to define an approach that would satisfy the Court's interpretation of the New Jersey Constitution, yet preserve legislative control over taxing and spending decisions. After a Court order closing all the public schools in the state, the Legislature finally enacted New Jersey's first state income tax to fund an education finance reform package. These reforms were subsequently upheld on judicial review.

Results of similar state court litigation—based upon state equal protection clauses or education clauses (similar to New Jersey's) have been mixed. Such state constitutional challenges have been successful in several states, including Arizona, Connecticut, Ohio, Texas, Vermont, West Virginia, and Wyoming. On the other hand, several school financing systems (so far) have survived such state court challenges, including those in Colorado, Georgia, Idaho, Minnesota, New York, Wisconsin and North Carolina. However, in some of the latter states, litigation over the constitutional acceptability of the state's school financing system remains ongoing.

In the wake of all the litigation and public controversy, many state legislatures have substantially modified the basic school financing system to redress the imbalances caused by heavy reliance on local property taxes for the funding of public schools. Alternative tax sources have been sought, with a state sales tax increment for education gaining favor in several states.

PART E.   STATE AND LOCAL GOVERNMENT RESPONSES TO FISCAL CRISES

Officials of state or local governments facing fiscal crises must make difficult decisions about the best use of scarce resources. Analysts have noted that such officials respond by seeking to establish a balance between revenues and expenditures that meets the minimum expectations of both their employees (keeping layoffs to a minimum) and their constituents (minimizing service reductions).

Governments typically act like any other human organization when confronted with unpleasant budgetary decisions. The first tendency is to delay the impact of the problem by drawing upon surpluses and other "rainy day" funds. Studies have documented that in a number of states, such as California and Michigan, the impact of "tax revolt" tax and expenditure limitations (*see* II B(2), above) was cushioned initially by use of substantial state surpluses to substitute for the suddenly declining local property tax revenues. Other delaying tactics include selling assets—such as hospitals, transit systems and utilities—to obtain one-time-only revenue increases; manipulating accounting devices—such as shifting from accrual to cash basis accounting or vice versa, changing fiscal years (*see* IV I(6)(d), below), or borrowing to support operating deficits; and seeking to maximize untapped, ever-declining federal and state aid sources (*see* II K, above).

When a reduction in expenditures finally becomes necessary, governments usually have attempted to cut their costs without reducing services. Thus, the first cuts typically involve expenditures that are not directly related to service delivery, such as building maintenance and repair, administrative costs, and "frills." Attempts to define the last category, however, can spark lively debate.

An increasingly popular method of reducing expenditures without appearing to decrease services is to transfer the service function involved to another level of government that is not experiencing the same fiscal pressures. Many public assistance and social service programs, as well as courts and penal institutions, have been transferred from cities to states. Increasingly, hospitals and related health care services are being transferred from cities to counties or regional authorities.

"Privatization" of traditional public services— such as trash collection, sewerage disposal, health care, and even penal institutions—has gained favor as another means of reducing (or appearing to reduce) government expenditures. Such a move may, however, face substantial opposition from public sector unions fearing the loss of union jobs.

Improved cost control through more efficient management of social programs and modernization of record keeping practices is often high on reformers' agendas. The results have been mixed, however, partially because of human inertia and partially because of the substantial cost and complexity of the necessary computer and organizational systems.

CHAPTER IV

STATE AND LOCAL GOVERNMENT DEBT FINANCING AND CAPITAL EXPENDITURES

PART A. INTRODUCTION

Debt-financing plays an important role in state and local government efforts to provide public services. Since the early 1800s, governments have borrowed money to pave roads, build schools, lay sewers and finance other public works. In recent years, public debt-financing has been employed to raise capital to finance a myriad of services including economic development programs, housing for low and moderate-income families, hospital construction, sports stadiums, pollution control facilities, and student loans.

Public debt-financing is accomplished through the issuance and sale of tax-exempt bonds (long-term obligations) and notes (short-term obligations), often referred to as "municipals" because of their historical origins as debt securities of general purpose municipal governments. Today, "municipals" are issued by all sorts of public entities for a variety of traditional and innovative purposes.

Purchasers of municipal bonds and notes, in effect, lend money to the issuing municipality for a price (the interest rate) established through a public bidding process or private negotiations. The interest rate is lower than that demanded for comparable quality corporate bonds and notes because interest income from state and local government obligations is exempt from federal income taxation, see I.R.C. § 103, and from income taxes imposed by the state in which the issuing government is located. Periodic interest payments are made by the issuing government to bondholders or noteholders, but the principal is generally not paid to the holders until the end of the bond's or note's term.

Municipal bonds and notes are categorized in a number of ways. A common categorization, and one that will be followed in this discussion, is:

1. Long–Term Bonds

a. General Obligation Bonds

b. Revenue Bonds

c. "Moral Obligation" Bonds

d. Industrial Development Bonds (now usually referred to as "Private Activity Bonds")

(Though moral obligation bonds and industrial development bonds are forms of revenue bonds, they are categorized separately here because of their special features.)

2. Short–Term Notes

a. Tax Anticipation Notes

b. Revenue Anticipation Notes

c.   Bond Anticipation Notes

d.   Tax Exempt Commercial Paper

Although the state, as sovereign, has inherent power to borrow money, a number of specific limitations have been placed on that power by federal and state constitutions. Local governments may borrow only if they have been delegated this authority by state constitutional or statutory provisions because they usually have no inherent borrowing power. Both authorization to borrow and limitations on that power are expressed in a variety of constitutional and statutory provisions, most of which contain highly technical language.

To assist the reader confronting for the first time the technical language associated with public debt-financing, the next section of this chapter contains definitions of certain key words and phrases. The definitions are taken from several different sources, including law dictionaries, statutes and judicial opinions. Because the terms often are used in different ways in particular constitutional and statutory provisions, and because reported cases do not always employ precise terminology, these definitions should be viewed only as attempts to provide basic, working concepts to aid the reader.

Following the definitions, the chapter describes each form of public indebtedness. It concludes with discussions of federal constitutional issues and recent federal statutory developments.

PART B.   DEFINITIONS

AD VALOREM TAX—The English translation of the Latin term, "ad valorem," is "according to value." Therefore, this term describes a tax levied as a percentage of the value of property located within the boundaries of the taxing governmental unit and is often used in constitutional and statutory provisions affecting public debt-financing. Ad valorem taxes are further discussed in II B above.

ARBITRAGE—A situation in which the same commodity (or security) has different values in different markets, thereby allowing a profit to be made by the simultaneous purchase and sale of the same or equivalent commodity (or security). In public debt-financing, arbitrage describes the common government practice of investing money in other debt markets immediately after it is borrowed so that the funds will increase in value before they are used for the purpose for which they were borrowed (e.g. constructing a building). Federal tax reform efforts since 1969 have placed major, complex restrictions on the ability of state and local governments to invest the proceeds of their tax-exempt obligations in higher interest treasury securities, or to "arbitrage" their borrowed funds in other ways.

BONA FIDE PURCHASER—A purchaser in good faith for valuable consideration, who takes without notice of any defect.

BOND—A written obligation which binds the signatory to pay a sum certain upon the happening of an event. In the context of state and local government finance, an oft-quoted, wordy definition is "evidence(s) of indebtedness, issued by states, cities, towns, or other corporate public bodies, negotiable in form, payable at a designated future time, and intended for sale ... with the object of raising money for municipal improvements, the expense of which is beyond the immediate resources of reasonable taxation, and payment of which is necessarily or logically should be distributed over a period of years."

A certificate or other evidence of indebtedness represents an express promise, made by the "issuer," to pay a specified person or the "holder" of the bond the purchase price of the bond (the principal), plus accrued interest. Payment of the principal normally is due at a specified time several years after issuance and sale, thereby making the bond a "long-term obligation." Interest payments are made periodically, usually at six-month intervals.

BONDHOLDER—The person who owns the bond. Although the bondholder purchases the bond, he or she may be considered a lender, because the amount of money spent by him or her to purchase the bond is actually a "loan," upon which the "issuer" will regularly pay interest and, on a specified date in the future, will repay the principal.

CAPITAL EXPENDITURES—This term has a variety of meanings, depending upon the context in which it is used. With respect to public debt-financing, it means spending for a product or facility to be used in the present and future, such as the construction costs of an auditorium or a highway. The term also refers to the money expended in acquiring, equipping and promoting that product or enterprise. Any or all of these costs may necessitate debt-financing as a means of funding the investment on a middle-term or long-term basis.

DEBT-FINANCING—The process of paying for capital expenditures, specific projects and/or enterprises, both public and private, through the issuance and sale of bonds, notes and other issuer obligations.

DEBT SERVICE—The funds used to retire a debt obligation through a series of periodic payments. When used with reference to regularly amortized loans, the term refers to periodic payments to the lender for both principal and interest on the outstanding balance. With respect to tax-exempt bonds, the term usually includes regular interest payments plus amounts paid into a sinking fund to retire the bonds when they become due. (With zero coupon bonds, accrued interest will only be paid at maturity.)

ISSUE—The term "issue" is used in two different manners in the field of state and local government finance. As a noun, the word refers to the entire body of bonds offered for sale at any one time or under a single authorization and having the same terms and conditions. As a verb, the word "issue" has several meanings, including the date the bond instrument was actually signed, but the most common refers to the actual delivery of the bonds to their original purchasers.

ISSUING UNIT OR ISSUER—The "borrower" or obligor which has issued the bonds or notes. The term includes government entities, such as states and municipalities; government agencies, such as housing development commissions; and private agencies, such as corporations.

NOTE—An instrument containing an express promise, made by the signer (issuer), to pay a specified person or the holder of the note a definite sum of money at a specified (usually relatively short) time. Notes generally possess characteristics similar to those of bonds, and are generally subject to similar requirements, except debt ceilings.

Notes generally mature within a shorter period of time than bonds, usually less than two years from the date of issuance and sale, making the note a "short-term obligation." Where the issuance of notes is specifically authorized by statute or constitution, notes usually are exempt from the issuing entity's debt ceiling or are limited in a manner different from the limitation upon bonds.

PAR VALUE—This term is often used to describe the value of an obligation as it appears on the face of the certificate. Technically, however, par value is the comparison of that face value to the obligation's actual selling value. When both values are equal, the obligation is said to be "at par." If it is sold for more than the face value, it is to be "above par," and if it sold for less, it is said to be "below par." Sometimes, bonds or other obligations sold above par are said to be sold at a "premium," while those sold below par are said to be sold at a "discount."

REVENUE—In the area of public debt-financing this term has two different meanings. It may be used to describe governmental funds derived from the assessment and collection of taxes, the imposition of service charges, or the receipt of intergovernmental aid. (See II, above). The term may also refer to the actual return, yield, or profit from an investment in a specific project or enterprise.

SHORT-TERM OBLIGATION—An important distinction is made between indebtedness of a more permanent nature (bonds) and temporary evidences of indebtedness, such as vouchers, notes and similar short-term devices for liquidating current obligations in anticipation of the collection of taxes or funds.

SINKING FUND—A separate fund composed of sums of money derived, on a regular basis, from particular taxes or sources of revenue and set aside for paying both the principal and interest on debt obligations of an issuer. Moneys in the fund are accumulated and invested until they are needed for particular interest or principal payments. Both the principal obligation and the fund "sink" as periodic payments are made from the fund to the bondholders.

PART C. LONG–TERM BONDS

As mentioned in IV A and IV B above, long-term bonds appear in many different forms. Basically, a long-term bond is one whose principal is not due for at least 10 years (but more frequently 20 to 40 years) following the date of issuance or sale. The various types of state and local government long-terms bonds are discussed and defined below.

Section 1. General Obligation Bonds

Subsection a.   General Characteristics.

General obligation bonds are bonds issued by a public body that has the power to tax. They are obligations of that body which are payable from its general revenues raised by taxation and other revenue sources (see II B(2), above). These bonds are often referred to as "full faith and credit" obligations, because the debt is secured by the promise that both principal and interest will be paid through the exercise of the body's taxing power unrestricted by the usual tax limits. (*See generally Flushing National Bank v. Municipal Assistance Corp.*, 40 N.Y.2d 731, 390 N.Y.S.2d 22, 358 N.E.2d 848 (1976), which is discussed in IV F(1), below). Tax limits are discussed in II B(2), above.

Usually, the amount of interest paid on a state or local government general obligation bond is low in comparison to the prevailing interest rates for comparable corporate bonds. The lower rates result primarily from the fact that interest on state and local government obligations is exempt from federal and state income taxation (in the state of issuance). The exemption from federal income taxation is provided by Section 103 of the Internal Revenue Code. The exemption from state and local taxation afforded these bonds is found in state constitutional or statutory provisions. The general pattern is for a state to exempt from its income taxes interest on any bonds issued by the state or its agencies or issued by local governments located within the state, but to tax interest derived from bonds issued by other states or their political subdivisions.

Subsection b. Public Purpose Requirements and Prohibitions on Lending of Credit.

There are many restrictions placed upon the issuance of general obligation bonds. One of the most important requires that a public body issue its bonds or other obligations only for "public," rather than private, purposes. This prohibition, and a related constitutional prohibition against leading public credit to private enterprises, constitute restrictions on both indebtedness and the spending of public money raised by such borrowing (or by taxation). (*See also* II A(2)(b) and III A(4), above.)

Nearly all states now have constitutional provisions prohibiting the state and its political subdivisions from "giving or lending its credit in the aid of any individual, association, or corporation," and many include a public purpose requirement. For example, article I, § 1 of the Connecticut Constitution states; "[N]o man or set of men are entitled to exclusive public emoluments or privileges from the community.... '' Even in states where these limitations are not expressed in specific constitutional or statutory provisions, the courts have sometimes found them by implication.

Because of inherent ambiguities in the two concepts and the vague manner in which these concepts are articulated in state constitutions, the courts are frequently called upon to construe their meaning and decide their appropriate application. Both the public purpose and lending of credit limitations are discussed in greater detail in IV F(2), below.

Subsection c.　Debt Ceilings.

Nearly early state has constitutional or statutory provisions limiting the amount of debt that may be incurred by their local governments. State general obligation debt is often subject to a debt ceiling as well. Debt ceilings are further discussed in IV I, below.

Subsection d.　Legislative and Electoral Approval for Issuance.

In most states, approval for the issuance of general obligation bonds involves at least two steps—legislative (or city council) approval, followed by voter approval. For state government debt-financing, there often is a requirement that the legislature specifically authorize and state the purpose of any bond issue.

In addition, some states must obtain prior approval for state bonds from a specially created board or agency, from state executive officials (the governor and/or state treasurer), or from both. For local borrowing, most states require that the governing body of the issuing local government enact an ordinance or resolution authorizing the issuance of general obligation bonds.

Voter approval is not always required for state debt, but most states require an election before local governments may incur indebtedness. In some of these states, an election is needed only if the particular bond issue will exceed the issuing government's debt ceiling. In other states, a bond election is required only if a petition for referendum is submitted by the requisite number of qualified voters. In other states, it is required prior to any issuance of local government debt.

In some states, the question of whether voter approval is required turns on a legal distinction previously made by the courts with respect to the language of an applicable statute. Thus, for example, in *Mann v. Granite Reeder Water and Sewer Dist.*, 141 P.3d 1117 (Idaho 2006), the Idaho Supreme Court concluded that a statute, requiring municipalities to submit any proposal to create indebtedness to voters, did not require a water and sewer district to hold an election before implementing a plan to issue water and sewer district bonds to fund a local improvement district. The bonds were to be retired by special assessments against benefited property within the improvement district. In upholding their validity, the court quoted a 1912 interpretation of constitutional debt as being a "debt of the city," which did not require voter ratification, as opposed to "a debt against the property benefited by [the] improvement [being financed]."

In another statutory construction case involving a multi-purpose project—a dam and reservoir designed to provide water for both a municipal water treatment facility and a recreational area—an Iowa court declined to enforce a statutory provision that required a special election for bond-financed projects that involved recreational facilities. The court upheld a city's decision to classify general obligation notes as being issued for an "essential corporate purpose" (constructing the water treatment plant), rather than serving the "general corporate purpose" of providing public recreational opportunities.

A somewhat less nuanced rejection of the applicability of voter initiatives to the issuance of municipal revenue bonds may be found in *City of Sequim v. Malkasian*, 138 P.3d 943 (Wash. 2006). There, the Washington State Supreme Court resoundingly approved the common practice of authorizing municipalities to issue revenue bonds without first submitting them to a vote of the people. Invalidating an initiative-called election, the court emphasized the specificity of state legislation that specifically authorized, and regulated, the issuance and sale of local revenue bonds.

The states are split on the question of whether a simple majority or a super majority of the voters is required to approve the issuance of general obligation bonds. The trend appears to be toward a simple majority, but a significant number of states still require a super majority. The most common super majority is two-thirds, but other levels, such as 60 per cent or four-sevenths, can be found, particularly for local government debt-financing. Some states require a simple majority for approval of general obligation bonds which are within the issuing entity's debt ceiling and a super majority if the entity seeks to exceed its debt ceiling. The U.S. Supreme Court has ruled that super-majority requirements for bond referenda do not violate the equal protection clause of the Fourteenth Amendment. (*See Gordon v. Lance*, 403 U.S. 1 (1971).)

Moreover, at least one court has upheld a state statute prescribing different supermajority requirements for school districts using town meetings to vote on bonds and school districts that utilize an official ballot system for bond approvals. *Walker v. Exeter Reg. Co-op. School Dist.*, 284 F.3d 42 (1st Cir. 2002).

Subsection e. Form of Bonds.

General obligation bonds may be issued in many forms. For example, they may have coupons attached, which represent successive (usually semi-annual) installment payments of interest from the time of issuance until maturity. They may also be issued without such coupons, so that at the time of maturity both principal and interest are paid to the bondholder in one lump sum. These are generally called "zero coupon bonds." General obligation bonds may be issued all at once or in a series of issues. Traditionally, they were payable to a specific person or to bearer. Amendments to Section 103 of the Internal Revenue Code, however, required that tax-exempt bonds be issued only in registered form. This change spawned an unusual (but ultimately unsuccessful) lawsuit, discussed in IV G(2), below, and a flurry of state legislative activity to bring state laws into compliance.

The form of the general obligation bond to be issued will depend upon the statutory requirements of the governing state. The two main provisions employed by most states are: (1) that the bonds be negotiable instruments, and (2) that they expressly state, on the face of the certificate, that they are obligations of the issuing unit.

Though the standard method of evidencing ownership of a bond is the issuance of a paper certificate, some states are now using "paperless issues," with ownership recorded by computer rather than by paper certificate. Usually, under this arrangement, the purchaser is given a choice and charged a premium to cover the extra costs of printing, signing, storing and delivery if he or she requests paper certificates.

Subsection f.   Issuance and Sale.

The entity issuing state general obligation bonds may be either a central administrative agency or the agency that will administer the program for which the bonds are issued. At the local level, the issuing entity usually is the local governing body.

Statutes governing the issuance of state and local government bonds often contain detailed restrictions. A common restriction is the requirement that the proceeds from the bond sale may only be used for specified purposes. For example, the Ohio Constitution provides that money obtained from the sale of bonds "shall be applied to the purpose for which it was obtained ... and to no other purpose whatsoever." In this way, the governing body ensures, for example, that proceeds from the sale of bonds issued to fund the construction of a highway will not be expended to construct a nuclear power plant. At the same time, however, issuing entities are generally afforded some discretion to modify the allocation of bond proceeds where several projects are contemplated (so long as the allocation is consistent with the overall purpose of the bond issue).

At the time of issuance and sale, the issuing state or local government is required to provide for payment of the bonds through the levy of ad valorem taxes sufficient to cover the periodic payments, and the payment of principal when the bonds mature. The funds arising from the levy of these taxes are placed in a sinking fund where they will earn interest. The extent to which interest may be earned on the sinking funds of tax-exempt state and local bonds, however, is severely restricted by the arbitrage provisions of Sections 103(b) and 148 of the Internal Revenue Code, as well as pertinent IRS regulations. (See IV E(2), below.)

Statutes generally require that the issuing resolution specify the details of the bond issue, including the amount, maturity dates, interest rates, and form of the bonds as well as the purposes for which the funds will be spent. Many of the statutes establish maximum interest rates and maturity dates for local bonds, because these factors are said to affect state borrowing policy. These statutes, however, generally allow the issuing local entities flexibility within those maxima to set the specific terms of their bond issue that do not affect general state policy, such as the form of the bond and the manner in which interest will be paid. Statutes in some states, however, set all the terms and give the issuer little discretion.

Subsection g. Public and Private Sales of Bonds.

General obligation bonds usually are required to be sold through a public process resembling a silent auction. Prospective investors are given the opportunity to submit their purchase proposals or bids, which must usually be sealed. The issuer opens all bids in public at the announced time and date. The best bid is selected, which generally is the bid offering the lowest net interest cost to the issuer. Bidders normally are underwriters or groups of underwriters (syndications) that intend to resell the bonds to individual investors.

A common (and increasingly popular) exception to the public sale requirement occurs in the event that bonds which have been offered for public sale are not purchased by the public. Such bonds may then be sold through private negotiations conducted by the issuing entity. These private, negotiated sales are more common for revenue bonds, especially those backed by a limited revenue stream, such as special assessments. See IV H, below, and IV C(2), below.

Sale through private negotiation often is restricted to certain types of purchasers. For example, many states provide that general obligation bonds may be sold only to the United States or to state agencies in the event that the bonds fail to be sold at public sale.

A few states do permit general obligation bonds to be sold either at a public or at a private sale, with the issuing government being given the discretion to determine which approach would best serve the public interest. This discretion usually is given only to general purpose local government units (*e.g.*, cities and counties).

State statutes establish specific requirements, which vary from state to state, to govern both public and private sales, including notice of the sale, publication of that notice, date and place of sale, and time allotted for submission of bids. The procedures for accepting bids also tend to vary from state to state. A majority of states, however, require that no bids of less than par value may be considered.

Subsection h.   Final Validation Procedures.

Many states have statutes establishing a final validation procedure for general obligation bond issues. This procedure provides a means of protecting the issue from attack after a specific period of time has lapsed.

Courts have interpreted final validation procedures to cover only procedural aspects of bond issuance, such as the form of the authorizing resolution and the format of the bonds. Thus, judicial review of substantive matters, such as authority of the issuer to incur debt and compliance with the public purpose and pledging of credit requirements, are not foreclosed by a final validation procedure. Substantive aspects of authorization are discussed in IV H(2), below.

There are three basic approaches to final validation of general obligation bonds issues. The first approach is based on publication of a notice that the bond issue has been authorized. Such notice will include a specific time period during which taxpayers have the right to contest the validity of the issue. If no suit or action is brought during that time, the issue is deemed legally valid and all actions and proceedings to contest the procedural validity of the issue are estopped.

In the second approach a state official, such as the Attorney General or the State Treasurer, reviews the procedures followed and the form of the bonds. If everything has been done according to the prescribed regulations, a certificate that the bonds are in proper form and have been issued in the proper manner will be given.

A third procedure, available in a few states, authorizes the issuer to apply to a court of proper jurisdiction for a declaration of the validity of the bond issue. Notice of the application is required, and if no objection is raised by citizens or taxpayers prior to the court's determination, the court may approve the validity of the bonds. After this judicial determination, all actions and proceedings brought by taxpayers to contest the procedural validity of the bond issue are estopped.

Finally, voter referenda and initiatives are used in some states as a means of challenging, or upholding, the validity of a bond issue. However, since referenda generally may be used only as to legislative as opposed to administrative decisions, their availability in this context is often limited. Moreover, courts have invalidated initiatives designed to repeal bond issue ordinances after contracts have been signed as an unconstitutional impairment of contract.

Subsection i.   Bondholders' Remedies.

A bondholder's interests in his or her investment are sometimes threatened by government action. For example, in *United States Trust Company v. New Jersey*, 431 U.S. 1 (1977), the Supreme Court examined a bondholder's challenge to a 1974 New Jersey statute that attempted to repeal the State's 1962 statutory covenant, which had been designed to restrict the power of the Port Authority of New York and New Jersey to finance mass transit rail operations from its revenues and reserves. The Court ruled that the 1974 statute violated Article I, § 10, clause 1 of the United States Constitution (the Contracts Clause), which forbids states to "pass any . . . law impairing the Obligation of Contracts." *U.S. Trust* and related issues are further discussed in IV F(3), below. There are often comparable bondholder protections in state constitutions (See IV C, above).

The final validation proceedings, described in IV C(1)(h), above, do not limit a bondholder's remedies when the issuing unit fails to honor its obligations or attempts to modify those obligations to the detriment of the bondholders. Many states list specific bondholders' remedies in separate statutes. In addition to these specific remedies, a bondholder may attempt to enforce his or her rights against the governmental entity that issued the bonds by mandamus or other legal or equitable proceedings. For example, the bondholder may seek judicial relief to compel the issuer to carry out the obligations imposed by the authorizing statute and resolution (see IV C(1)(d), above), as well as any specific bond covenants or agreements. The bondholder may also attempt to enjoin any unlawful acts of an issuing government unit that would reduce the security of his or her investment, for example attempts by the governing body of the issuer to lend public credit to private enterprises.

As in *U.S. Trust*, the bondholder may bring suit to restrain government actions that violate the federal Contract Clause. It should be noted, of course, that bondholder rights and remedies are limited by the terms of the "contract" formed between the issuer and the bondholder, which is created by statute, ordinance, and bond agreement (or certificate).

Section 2.   Revenue Bonds

Subsection a.   General Characteristics.

Revenue bonds have much in common with general obligation bonds. They are both tax-exempt, long-term obligations issued by public bodies. (Revenue bonds, however, are sometimes issued by quasi-governmental agencies, such as not-for-profit housing commissions, to finance projects that are later carried out by private corporations.)

The major difference, however, is that revenue bonds, unlike general obligation bonds, are not backed by the taxing power, or "full faith and credit," of the issuing governmental entity. (See IV C(1)(a), above). Instead, revenue bonds are payable from a particular revenue source, usually funds generated by the project financed by the revenue bonds. As a result, the courts, pursuant to the "special funds" doctrine, usually consider revenue bonds exempt from the constitutional or statutory general debt ceiling. (See IV C(2)(d), above.) That is, the general debt ceiling usually covers only general obligation bonds. (See IV C(1)(c), above.) Several states, however, impose separate limitations upon the amount of outstanding revenue bonds. (See IV C(2)(c), above).

Normally, revenue bonds are issued for the purpose of constructing, operating and maintaining a particular project, and they are usually payable solely from the revenues generated by the project. For example, revenue bonds may be issued to raise funds to construct a bridge, tunnel, airport, or sewage treatment plant, with the debt service on the bonds to be paid from bridge or tunnel tolls, airport fees and rental payments, or sewer service charges.

When sufficient uncertainty exists concerning the amount of funds that a project financed by revenue bonds is likely to generate, potential investors may be unwilling to purchase the revenue bonds at a reasonable price and/or a reasonable and interest rate, unless they are offered some additional security. In some instances, states provide that tax proceeds can be employed to help repay revenue bonds should the revenues earned from the project itself prove insufficient to pay both the principal and interest due upon maturity of the bond. These statutory provisions, however, generally make payment from tax proceeds discretionary rather than mandatory.

In some states, the legislature or other governmental body is authorized to decide the question of additional payments from tax revenues if and when it arises. Under these circumstances, the bonds are referred to as "moral obligation bonds." (See IV C(3), above.) Other states prohibit issuers from curing deficiencies in revenue bond retirement funds through the use of tax funds unless the bond issue—including the proviso that tax moneys can be used if needed—has first been approved at an election of qualified voters.

If tax proceeds are available to assure repayment of revenue bonds, the question arises whether indebtedness incurred through the sale of such bonds should be included within the general debt ceiling or should, like other revenue bond indebtedness, be excluded from the debt limitation calculations through the "special funds doctrine." A great deal of litigation has been generated by this question, and courts have reached differing results.

If the revenue bonds are issued in order to finance the cost of supplying a service, such as electrical power, additional security may be provided investors through long-term contracts, rather than through the pledge of tax revenues. Under these contracts, public and private investors agree to purchase the power or other service to be provided by the project.

In some cases, participating governmental units have agreed to make the required payments, whether or not the service is actually provided. Some courts have been willing to accept the characterization of this transaction as a service contract rather than a "debt" (for purposes of debt ceiling or referendum requirements), particularly where the municipality is specifically authorized to purchase services through long-term contracts (see IV I(6)(c), below). The risks associated with this common form of public utilities financing, called a "take or pay" or "dry hole" contract, are discussed in IV H(3), below.

As is the case with general obligation bonds (see IV C(1)(a), above), interest income derived from state and local government revenue bonds is exempt from taxation. Although investors in revenue bonds do not have the security of governmental taxing power behind the bonds and, therefore, usually demand a higher rate of return to compensate for the greater risk involved, revenue bond interest rates are still generally lower than interest rates for comparable taxable bonds.

Though a number of proposals have been made to tax the interest income from revenue bonds, all states continue to accord tax exempt status to revenue bonds issued by their own state agencies or political subdivisions. Section 103 of the Internal Revenue Code also allows the interest earned on revenue bonds to remain exempt from federal income taxation provided the bonds meet certain, specific requirements set forth in the Code itself.

Subsection b. Authorization.

The authority to issue revenue bonds often is delegated to specific agencies responsible for particular programs, such as the state highway commission, building commission, housing authority, or pollution control board. Statutory authorization and regulation of such specific revenue bonds often are located in those chapters of the statutes discussing the issuing agency, rather than in a general statute regulating the issuance of all bonds. For that reason, it is not unusual for the specific requirements for one type of revenue bond, such as a housing bond issue, to differ from those for other types of bonds, such as public building or pollution control revenue bond issues.

Many states do not require that elections be held to authorize the issuance and sale of revenue bonds. An authorizing resolution passed by the issuing governmental entity, similar to the resolutions required for general obligation bond issues, and review of that resolution by an appropriate agency, constitute sufficient authorization in most states for revenue bond issues. Moreover, where elections are required, a simple majority generally suffices for passage.

For state borrowing, the agency responsible for review and approval of revenue bonds varies from state to state. Some states require that approval be obtained from the state treasurer, or the governor, or both. Other states require approval from a special board or agency. Still others require a combination of both approaches before the proposed bond issue becomes authorized.

At the local level, the procedure is slightly different. Local legislative approval must be obtained for a bond issue through the enactment of an ordinance or resolution which specifies the purpose and terms of the issue. In a few states, the local governing body must also apply to a special state board or agency for approval of the proposed issue prior to enactment of the bond issue ordinance.

In some states, local government units are required to hold an election on all revenue bond issues as well as general obligation bond issues. In many states, however, local citizens must petition for an election subsequent to the governing body's adoption of the bond resolution or ordinance. Sometimes, elections are mandatory only if the particular bond issue exceeds a specified debt ceiling. At the state level, election requirements for revenue bond issues are fairly rare.

Subsection c. Public Purpose Requirements and Prohibitions on Lending of Credit.

Revenue bonds are also normally limited by the restriction that public funds be expended only for public purposes and that public credit not be loaned to private enterprises. (See IV C(1)(b), above). A great deal of litigation has been engendered by the question, "What constitutes a public purpose, or a private enterprise?" The question is more prevalent where revenue bonds, rather than general obligation bonds, are involved, because the very fact that the bonds will be supporting a revenue-generating activity can create the impression of private enterprise.

When the public purpose question arises, courts often focus on whether a distinct public interest will be served by the contested bond issue or project. For example, in *Idaho Water Resource Board v. Kramer*, 548 P.2d 35 (Idaho 1976), the Idaho Supreme Court reviewed a state statute authorizing local governments to issue revenue bonds to finance the cost of constructing a facility that would later be leased to a privately owned electric utility. In upholding the statute, the court found that the principal benefits of the proposed project inured to the public and that the benefit to the private utility was merely secondary.

Industrial Dev. Bd. of Gonzales, La. v. Citizens, 938 So.2d 11 (La. 2006), provides another illustration of the way some courts resolve the public purpose question. In that case, the Louisiana Supreme Court affirmed an appellate court's decision validating a bond issue that was intended to support a private retail sporting goods store and commercial development. The court ruled that the bonds in question, which were secured by a pledge of sales tax increments from the project, were not a "direct handout to private business" as objectors had contended. In support of that view, the court took note of the fact that the Louisiana statute, which permits revenues from both property taxes and sales taxes to be used to finance economic development projects, contains a broad definition of economic development.

The public purpose requirement and the related lending of credit limitations are further discussed in IV F(2), below.

Subsection d. Debt Ceilings and the "Special Funds" Doctrine.

As noted earlier, through the operation of the "special funds" doctrine, most state and local governments can issue revenue bonds without regard to the general debt ceiling. The "special funds" doctrine developed from judicial interpretations of constitutional and statutory debt ceilings, referenda requirements, and other provisions limiting state and local government debt. The term "debt" in these provisions has been construed to encompass only state or local government obligations which are payable from the general taxing power, especially the ad valorem property tax. Obligations payable solely from funds separate from general taxes ("special funds") usually are not considered "debt" under this interpretation and, therefore, are exempt from debt ceilings and related limitations on debt-financing. (*See also* IV I(6)(a), above.)

Those states that do place some restrictions upon the level of revenue bond financing, particularly for general purpose local governments, tend to permit more borrowing through revenue bonds than the same governmental entity can do via general obligation bonds. This may be due to the belief that there is less risk to the taxpayer from revenue bond default because taxes have not been pledged as security for the bonds. The expansion of revenue bond financing since the end of World War II, however, suggests that the risk of over-extension— which was the principal concern behind general obligation debt ceilings—may be as great, if not greater, in the case of revenue bonds.

Subsection e.   Form of Bonds.

The particular form a revenue bond takes depends upon the statutory requirements of the governing state. Basically, revenue bonds may be issued in any of the forms available for general obligation bonds. That is, revenue bonds may be issued with or without interest coupons and may be issued at one time or in a series (see IV C(1)(e), above). Like general obligation bonds, revenue bonds now must be issued in registered form in order to maintain the federal tax exemption on their interest (see IV G(2), below). Generally, revenue bond certificates must state that they will be paid solely from the revenues pledged and that they are not general obligations of the issuing governmental unit. Revenue bonds, like general obligation bonds, must be negotiable instruments.

Subsection f. Issuance and Sale.

The issuance and sale of revenue bonds are regulated by statutes similar to those regulating the issuance and sale of general obligation bonds. (See IV C(1)(f), above). The governing body of the issuing unit, however, often is given more discretion in setting the terms, amounts, maturity, interest rates, form, and other details of revenue bonds than it has when issuing general obligation bonds.

Use of proceeds from the sale of revenue bonds is limited in the same manner as the use of proceeds from the sale of general obligation bonds, *i.e.*, they may be expended only for the purposes for which the bonds were authorized. Use of the revenues gained from the project or enterprise being funded also is restricted. These revenues must normally be placed in a sinking fund where they will draw interest until the time for making debt-service payments on the bonds.

Subsection g. Public and Private Sale of Bonds.

A number of states permit revenue bonds to be sold either through private negotiations or through the public sale process, which is usually mandated for general obligation bonds. The governing body of the issuing governmental entity is granted discretion to determine which method of sale is in the "best interest" of the entity issuing the revenue bonds.

Arguments that private negotiations can result in better prices for the issuing entity in an increasingly volatile market, because of the issuer's ability to respond more quickly to market changes, have generally overcome fears that local governments could not be trusted to avoid favoritism if bonds and notes were not sold through a public bidding process. Since general tax revenues are not pledged for debt service on revenue bonds, the issuing entity must satisfy its obligations through the strengths of the project. As a result, there are fewer incentives for favoritism in the negotiations and more incentives for obtaining the lowest possible interest cost and best possible financing arrangement for the revenue bonds.

Subsection h. Contesting Validity.

Methods and procedures for contesting the validity of a revenue bond issue tend to be similar to those used to contest the validity of a general obligation bond issue. (See IV C(1)(h), (i), above.) Taxpayers may, however, have greater difficulty establishing their standing to sue in suits challenging revenue bonds. In the case of a general obligation bond issue, a taxpayer's tax dollars are involved, so she is in a stronger position to argue that she has a direct personal stake in the outcome of the litigation. Direct injury may be more difficult for a taxpayer to assert in the case of a typical revenue bond issue.

Notably, however, the fact that a taxpayer has challenged the issuance of general obligation bonds by no means guarantees that that person or entity will have standing to sue. For example, in *West Farms Mall, LLC v. Town of West Hartford*, 901 A.2d 649 (Conn. 2006), the owner of an existing shopping mall challenged a town's plans to finance, in part, a $158.8 million redevelopment of the municipal campus of the town. The Supreme Court of Connecticut concluded that the plaintiff lacked taxpayer standing because it had failed to establish injury-in-fact by showing that its taxes would increase if the project proceeded as planned.

In a number of states, statutes give resident taxpayers standing to challenge an illegal expenditure of public bond funds, such as one that has not been authorized properly or is for purely private purposes. The statutes involved generally are broad enough to cover challenges to revenue bond issues. The contesting citizen will often have to sue in the capacity of a "private attorney general" on behalf of the public.

Though revenue bondholders will usually not want to challenge the validity of bonds they have purchased, they may wish to challenge spending or financing practices of the issuer that undercut the security of their investment. They should have little difficulty obtaining standing to bring such claims. However, those claims may or may not succeed on the merits.

Subsection i.   Bondholders' Remedies.

Bondholders' remedies in the case of a revenue bond issue are substantially the same as those for holders of general obligation bonds. The primary difference is that liability on the part of the issuing unit is greatly limited where only revenues from the project or enterprise are pledged for repayment of principal and interest. Despite this, all express and implied promises that exist between the bondholder and the issuing unit may be enforced through recourse to any of the remedies generally available to bondholders. (See IV C(1)(i), above.)

Section 3.   "Moral Obligation" Bonds

Subsection a.   General Characteristics.

The "moral obligation" bond has sometimes been referred to as a "hybrid" of the general obligation bond and the revenue bond. That description, however, does not fully communicate the complexity of the moral obligation bond concept. A moral obligation is one that is not legally enforceable; it arises from a sense of fairness and equity when one party has received a benefit from another party without consideration. Yet, some promises involved in moral obligation bonds may be legally enforceable. The key to understanding this type of bond is understanding the legal promises that actually exist within the relevant agreements.

The moral obligation bond is a form of revenue bond, because payment is based primarily upon the pledge of revenues derived from the project or enterprise for which the bonds are sold. This pledge of revenues represents the express, *legal obligation* that exists between the issuing unit and holders of moral obligation bonds. As noted in IV C(2)(a), above, some revenue bonds periodically draw upon tax receipts when the revenues from the project or enterprise are insufficient to repay the bond's debt service. Such hybrid bonds are called moral obligation bonds when the issuer *does not specifically pledge* taxes for their repayment but does *promise that consideration will be given* to using tax revenues to cure deficiencies in the principal or interest accounts. The issuer's promise may be express or implied, but it is *not* legally binding because of the general principle that one legislative body may not commit a successor legislative body to enact a particular piece of legislation, such as the appropriation of tax revenues. It is this limited promise which sets the moral obligation bond apart from other revenue bonds. Because the promise is not legally enforceable, moral obligation bonds raise several issues not confronted by ordinary revenue bonds.

Subsection b.   History.

Moral obligation bonds originated in New York State as a response to the defeat of several bond issues at the polls in the late 1950s. In the 1960s and 1970s, moral obligation bonds were regularly issued by state housing finance agencies to finance multi-family housing for persons with low and moderate incomes. A series of housing bond issue crises in New York, Massachusetts and Pennsylvania in the mid–1970s exposed the weakness of the argument that the state would never be called upon to make payments on moral obligation bonds (because the bonds were issued as obligations of dependable "independent" agencies). In all three states, the agencies did call upon the moral obligation, and in all three cases the state legislatures eventually responded to their moral obligations by appropriating funds to meet financial shortfalls in bond anticipation note accounts of the housing agencies.

The moral obligation bond was sharply criticized as "dangerous" and "misleading" in the state of its origin by a commission set up to study the causes of a major default by the New York State Urban Development Corporation in 1975. The commission noted:

[T]he principal vice of the moral obligation concept lay in the official view that projects backed by the state's moral obligation were self sufficient, so that the moral obligation would never have to be called upon. This notion was fed by the political situation at the time the moral obligation concept was introduced and by the need to assure legality for the moral obligation bond by treating it as something other than a debt of the state.

Similarly, the Wyoming Supreme Court, in striking down an excise tax-backed revenue bond scheme to finance public facilities, characterized the moral obligation bond as a "sales gimmick" that raised substantial ethical questions.

   Subsection c.   Public Policy Issues.

One of the most important issues raised by the moral obligation bond concept is whether the moral promise to pay with tax proceeds in case of default changes a revenue bond into a general obligation. The statutory (or constitutional) language used to authorize moral obligation bonds generally implies that either the legislature or, in some cases, the qualified voters *may* provide for repayment with tax proceeds in case of default. Some states, however, have made such repayment mandatory with the use of the words "shall provide," or similar language. Courts that have been asked to construe these moral obligation provisions generally have concluded that the provisions do not create binding obligations on the part of the issuing units. Despite the apparently mandatory language, those courts have held that the legislature did not intend to create a binding obligation because it could not do so under the principle articulated in IV C(3)(a), above, which prohibits one legislature to bind future legislatures to act. These courts have further observed that the statutes authorizing moral obligation pledges also contain the standard revenue bond provisions, which limit repayment obligations to revenues generated by the project and specify that taxes are *not* pledged for repayment. (See IV C(2)(a), above.)

Another issue is whether the moral obligation provisions mislead bond purchasers into believing that the promise to pay is absolute and thus legal enforceable against the issuing unit. In fact, interest rates paid on moral obligation bond issues generally were lower than those offered on other revenue bonds, because the implied promise to repay appeared to lessen the bondholders' risk of loss on their investment. Indeed, as noted in IV C(2)(b), above, the New York, Pennsylvania, and Massachusetts Legislatures were called upon to make up deficits in moral obligation bonds and did in fact do so. Yet, the danger that moral obligation pledges might not be so honored in the future (or might result in delays in payment) has led to proposals to restrict or prohibit the use of moral obligation bonds.

Other issues raised by the moral obligation bond concept include the constitutionality of these bonds, whether they are restricted by the public purpose doctrine, and whether the amount of bonds sold should be further restricted by the referenda requirements or debt ceilings applicable to general indebtedness of the issuing unit (see IV I(3) and (4), below). The answers given to these and related issues necessarily vary from state to state.

Section 4. Industrial Development Bonds (IDBs) and Private Activity Bonds

Subsection a.   General Characteristics.

The industrial development bond (IDB) was developed in the 1930s to help Southern states attract industry and jobs (though some commentators trace its roots to the Nineteenth Century municipal subsidies to private railroads). Under the most common use of the IDB concept, a municipality issued and sold revenue bonds to fund the construction of a building or other facility suitable for a particular industry. Upon completion, the facility was leased to a private company in that industry. Typically, the rental payments were used as the *sole* revenue source for debt service (principal and interest) payments on the bonds. Alternatively, the transaction could be structured as an installment purchase, so the private company (user) would become owner of the facility when the IDBs were repaid. As a twist on that approach, the municipality might lend the IDB proceeds to the private company, which would use them to construct (or buy) the facility and would then make loan payments to the municipality at a level that would cover debt service on the IDBs.

Thus, these conduit bonds were often a form of corporate financing, with the advantage of tax-exempt interest payments. Though the bonds were nominally issued by the city involved, the corporate user of the facility was actually responsible for the debt-service payments (via its rental, installment purchase or loan payments). The interest payments on the IDB was lower than interest on a corporate bond or loan, because IDB interest was exempt from federal, and often state, income taxation. As a result, the user's rental (or installment purchase or loan) payments to the municipality were lower than would be possible in a purely private transaction.

Beginning in 1968, the Internal Revenue Code and Treasury regulations have provided that the interest on IDBs is exempt from federal income taxation only if the bond proceeds are used to finance specified activities. The allowable activities were restricted and refined by subsequent legislation, and in 1984 volume caps for each state were added (see IV E(1), below). The Tax Reform Act of 1968 placed additional restrictions on the proceeds of IDBs and placed them under the new umbrella, "private activity bonds." That term encompasses bonds issued for the benefit of charitable organizations that qualify under IRC § 501(c)(3), as well as bonds (formerly called IDBs) issued for the benefit of private businesses. (For further details, see IV E(1), below.)

Subsection b.   Public Policy Issues.

Industrial development bonds (IDBs) became increasingly popular, because of their potential for attracting jobs and improving the economic base of a community without interfering directly with state and local government general obligation debt. Many states authorized such bonds to be issued to finance a wide variety of commercial ventures. Before 1959, only 14 states were issuing IDBs; by 1967, that number had increased to 40.

IDBs, however, increasingly became the subject of severe criticism from several quarters. Critics pointed to a major risk for both bondholders and the local community—after a facility was constructed and leased, the lessee might go out of business, leaving the municipality with financial and accounting headaches (even though its own credit had not been pledged to repay the bonds), and with a facility that might be virtually useless. The job development potential of many projects financed by IDBs, such as fast food facilities, professional office buildings and bank branches, was questioned. Furthermore, critics were concerned that excessive use of IDBs might drive up the cost of revenue bond financing for sewer and water systems and other traditional public works projects.

Beginning about 1967, federal Department of the Treasury representatives became quite vocal and persistent in questioning the financing of privately owned projects through tax-exempt IDBs, because of the resulting loss of federal tax dollars. This strong opposition to IDBs, coupled with the other policy concerns, ultimately resulted in amendments to the Internal Revenue Code that severely restricted the projects eligible for IDB funding, imposed volume caps and other requirements, and made the significant name change to "private activity bonds." (*See* IV C(4)(a), above, and IV E(1), below.)

IDBs raise more difficult issues under the public purpose and prohibition against lending of credit requirements than do traditional revenue bonds (see IV C(2)(c), above), because of the much closer link between IDBs and private enterprise. As noted in IV C(4)(a), above, the public entity issuing the bonds may be little more than a conduit for the channeling of cheaper money (because of the tax exemption) to private interests, a concern that has caused courts to scrutinize IDB proposals more closely. However, the vast majority of modern courts that have considered these issues have resolved them in favor of industrial development bond projects under an expansive view of the public purpose requirement and a restrictive view of the lending of credit prohibition (see IV F(2), below). These courts have generally insisted upon a clear state legislative authorization for the particular project and have required the issuing entity to follow the specified statutory requirements.

PART D. SHORT–TERM NOTES

Section 1. Types of Notes—BANs, RANs, TANs

As explained in IV B, above, a short-term note or obligation is a debt instrument containing an express promise, made by the issuing unit, to repay the noteholder within a certain (fairly short) period of time. Notes have characteristics similar to those of bonds, except that notes are usually exempt from debt ceilings (or have their own limitations upon the total amount outstanding) and notes generally have a shorter maturity period.

The various types of short-term notes issued by state and local governments can be classified under three general headings: (1) Bond Anticipation Notes (BANs); (2) Revenue Anticipation Notes (RANs); and (3) Tax Anticipation Notes (TANs). The title of each communicates the nature of the note involved. For example, BANs are notes issued and sold in anticipation of the receipt of proceeds from the sale of bonds. RANs are issued and sold in anticipation of revenues to be derived from a particular project or enterprise. TANs are issued and sold in anticipation of proceeds to be received from the levy of taxes.

Notes usually are sold to obtain funds for the initial costs of constructing projects or enterprises or to bridge temporary cash flow shortages created by the time lag between the receipt of tax or other revenues—which are collected at periodic intervals—and governmental expenses—which are incurred daily. The notes then are retired with proceeds received from the bonds issued to fund the project or from taxes or other revenues collected by the issuing entity. Generally, notes may be issued for the same purposes for which bonds may be issued. As noted in IV C, above, these purposes tend to vary from state to state and to differ according to the type of bond (note) issued.

Section 2. Abuses of Notes

The availability of short-term credit on relatively easy terms can lead to overextension by any debtor, and state and local governments have been no exception. Problems can be expected to arise when governmental borrowing powers are employed in two inappropriate situations: (1) use of short-term credit to fund current operational expenses, and (2) borrowing more dollars on an interim (short-term) basis than can reasonably be converted into long-term debt (through the issuance of bonds).

The Cleveland and New York City financial crises involved both types of short-term credit abuses. In those cities, demands for public services increased dramatically while tax revenues fell because of substantial changes in the demographic characteristics of the resident population. Faced with the resulting cash flow dilemma, the cities did what many hard-pressed, private sector debtors do in similar situations, *viz.*, they borrowed money to respond to the cash crunch. The day of reckoning was postponed for years because of their successful use of a popular financing device—the "rollover" loan.

A loan is said to be "rolled over" when a new loan of a similar type, but usually for slightly different terms (such as a higher interest rate or larger principal amount), is issued, with the proceeds being used to pay off the old loan. Depending on the lenders' willingness to continue, the rollover technique can allow a debtor to postpone the date of final payment indefinitely. Of course, if the debtor becomes dependent upon this technique but the lenders lose confidence in the debtor's ultimate ability to repay the loan and refuse to roll it over, disaster can strike in the form of a loan default. Although the problems of Cleveland and New York City were much more complex than this short synopsis suggests, the dependence on rollover of short-term notes to fund operational expenses played a significant part in the fiscal agonies of those cities.

The New York State Urban Development Corporation (UDC) is an example of a public agency that got into financial difficulty by allowing too large an "overhang" for construction projects (continuation of interim financing after projects were completed) to accumulate, without funding the projects through the sale of long-term revenue bonds. That is, the UDC engaged in the second abuse described above.

A properly structured revenue bond project is funded during its construction phase by the issuance of enough BANs to pay the land acquisition and development costs. When construction is completed and the project is able to generate revenue, long-term revenue bonds can be (and should be) issued. The proceeds from the revenue bonds are then used to pay off the BANs. The revenue bonds are later repaid from the revenues generated by the project.

The municipal bond market had been very stable until the credit crunches of the late 1960s and early 1970s and the explosion of new types of revenue bonds (especially IDBs, see IV C(4), above) during the same period. As the market became less stable, bond-issuing entities particularly the newer "independent" entities such as the UDC and other state housing finance agencies, developed the practice of postponing the issuance of long-term bonds for completed projects and rolling over their BANs instead. Generally, they did this in order to avoid a long-term commitment to what they perceived as high long-term bond rates, but the approach ultimately resulted in an accumulation of excessive overhang.

The UDC fell into this trap and was forced to appeal to the New York State Legislature for a bail out under the moral obligation language of its bonds (see IV C(3), above) when holders of $135 million in UDC notes refused to roll them over in March of 1975. That event was one of the precursors to the New York City fiscal crisis of the mid–1970s.

PART E. MAINTAINING THE TAX–EXEMPT STATUS OF BONDS ISSUED BY PUBLIC ENTITIES

Section 1. From Industrial Development Bonds to Private Activity Bonds

Congress regularly has enacted significant changes in the Internal Revenue Code to curb perceived abuses in the use of tax-exempt bond financing. A major concern has been the growth in the use of tax-exempt bonds to finance what Congress now refers to as "private activities." Originally the term was used to describe industrial development bonds. It now embraces revenue bonds issued to finance a wide variety of activities such as college dormitories, hospital and housing construction, pollution control facilities and student loans. Bonds to finance these are similar activities are now called "private activity bonds." (See IV C(4), above.)

Private activity bonds increased substantially, both in volume and as a percentage of total state and local borrowings, in the 1970s and early 1980s. Critics of this growth, especially the Treasury Department, focused on three major concerns: (1) an increasing revenue loss to the federal government ($8.5 billion in 1983) at a time of severe federal deficits; (2) inflation in tax-exempt interest rates, which forced state and local governments seeking to issue government bonds for traditional public purposes (such as roads, schools, and public buildings) to meet higher borrowing costs either by raising taxes or by reducing the level of their services; and (3) a belief that the availability of tax-exempt financing caused some projects to be funded even though the economic value of the investment might be low, thereby diverting investment capital from more productive uses.

The first major restriction on tax-exempt financing (IRC § 103(c), later designated as § 103(b)) was enacted in 1968 and has been amended regularly ever since. It imposed limitations on the purposes for which industrial development bonds (IDBs) could be issued. However, there were many exceptions to these IDB limitations during the 1970s and early 1980s. So, the volume of these bonds did not begin to decline until the Tax Reform Act of 1984 imposed a ceiling on the amount of IDBs and student loan bonds that can be issued in a state in any one year. Subsequent statutory amendments and regulations changed how that ceiling or "cap" is calculated and the types of bonds it covers.

The Tax Reform Act of 1986 placed substantial restrictions on the proceeds of IDBs and used the term "private activity bond" to encompass both IDBs (issued for the benefit of profit-making businesses) and bonds issued for the benefit of charitable organizations (that qualify under Section 501(c)(3) of the Internal Revenue Code).

More precisely, private activity bonds are now defined as bonds whose proceeds are used for the benefit of a nongovernmental person that supplies the funds to pay the debt service on the bonds (see IRC (1986) § 141(a)), or whose proceeds are used by governmental entities to purchase output facilities (*e.g.*, investor-owned utilities, other than those that furnish water) from a nongovernmental person (see IRC (1986) § 141(d)). Section 103(b)(1) of the Internal Revenue Code provides that the interest on private activity bonds will not be exempt from federal income taxation unless they meet the Section 141(e) definition of "qualified bonds." The categories of "qualified bonds" are: exempt facility bonds, mortgage bonds and veterans' mortgage bonds, small issue bonds, student loan bonds, redevelopment bonds, § 501(c)(3) bonds, and Enterprise Zone Bonds.

"Exempt facility" bonds are used for specified types of transportation, residential rental, and waste disposal facilities. There is some overlap between the current list of "qualified exempt facility bonds" and the list of previously allowed purposes for industrial development bonds, but several purposes have been removed (*e.g.*, sports facilities, industrial parks) and some have been added (*e.g.*, hazardous waste disposal facilities). Each of the other types of private activity bonds listed above has its own detailed requirements in the Internal Revenue Code and accompanying regulations.

The current volume cap applies to all types of private activity bonds issued in the state during a calendar year, unless they are specifically excepted. (Seven key types of qualified private activity bonds are excepted from the cap.) Currently the volume cap is $150 million or the state's population multiplied by $50, whichever is more. (Congress authorized a phased-in increase from the year 2003 through 2007.)

Section 2. Arbitrage Bonds

As noted in IV B, above, issuers of tax-exempt bonds and notes can profit from the difference between the cost to them of borrowed money (the tax-exempt interest rates they pay to bond holders) and the interest income they can generate (by investing their bond proceeds until the proceeds are needed). For example, if the issuer must pay 5%

interest to the purchasers of its bonds but can invest the proceeds of those bonds in other securities offering a 7% return, the issuer will gain 2%. When multi-million dollar bond issues are involved, this investment profit for state and local governments (which themselves are exempt from federal income taxation) can be substantial. Since 1969, Congress has attempted to restrain the use of tax-exempt borrowing authority in this manner.

In general, the interest paid on "Arbitrage Bonds" is taxable to the bondholder (thus, these bonds lose the tax-exempt status usually available to bonds issued by state and local governments.) (See IRC (1986), § 103(b)(2).) As one commentator nicely summarizes the current rules, a bond issued by a state or local government "will be treated as an arbitrage bond if it is part of an issue any portion of the proceeds of which are reasonably expected (at the time of issuance of the bond) to be used directly or indirectly—'(1) to acquire higher yielding investments, or (2) to replace funds which were used directly or indirectly to acquire higher yielding investments.' " (Carol Olson, *Federal Tax Exemption History and Overview,* in 1 STATE AND LOCAL GOVERNMENT DEBT FINANCING, *quoting* IRC (1986), § 148.) Section 148, in turn, defines "higher yielding investment" as any investment made with state or local government bond proceeds that will produce a "materially" higher yield than the yield on the bond involved. Further, Section 148(f), subject to certain exceptions, requires that "arbitrage profit" from investment of bond proceeds must be "rebated" (paid) to the federal government. As this summary suggests, the statutory provisions and regulations governing the subject of arbitrage have become extraordinarily complex. Therefore, the applicable rules and their exceptions should be closely studied by persons involved in the issuance of state and local bonds and the investment of their proceeds.

PART F. STATE AND FEDERAL CONSTITUTIONAL ISSUES

Section 1. The Full Faith and Credit Obligation

The central feature of general obligation bonds is the issuer's pledge of its "full faith and credit" that the bonds will be paid off even if a tax increase is necessary to carry out that pledge. The sense of security that such a pledge can create is one of the major reasons for the popularity of general obligation bonds in investment circles. Likewise, the fact that the full faith and credit pledge carries with it the possibility that taxpayers may be called upon to submit to tax increases (to honor the pledge) is one of the major reasons why so many restrictions, often including a popular vote, are placed on the issuance of such bonds by constitutional and statutory provisions in most states. (See IV C(1)(a)–(d), above, and IV I(3)–(4), below.)

The meaning of the full faith and credit provision was discussed in *Flushing National Bank v. Municipal Assistance Corp.*, 40 N.Y.2d 731, 390 N.Y.S.2d

22, 358 N.E.2d 848 (1976), a case arising out of the New York City fiscal crisis. One of the main features of the New York State Legislature's response to the City's crisis was an emergency law imposing a three-year moratorium on actions to enforce the City's short-term obligations. The City had approximately $5 billion in outstanding tax anticipation notes (TANs), bond anticipation notes (BANs), revenue anticipation notes (RANs), budget notes and urban renewal notes (URNs). (See IV D, above.) All were scheduled to mature within 12 months and were backed by the City's full faith and credit, as required by article VIII, § 2 of the New York State Constitution. Under the moratorium law, the noteholders were given an opportunity to exchange their notes "voluntarily" for an equal principal amount of long-term revenue bonds issued by the Municipal Assistance Corporation for the City of New York (MAC), a new agency created by the State to bail out the City.

Because MAC was created as an independent agency, the MAC bonds did not carry the full faith and credit of either the State or the City. As a result, a holder of City notes who exchanged them for MAC bonds would not only move from a short-term to a long-term investment, but would also give up the security of the City's full faith and credit pledge in the process. A noteholder who refused to agreed to swap, however, was subjected to the three-year moratorium on efforts to collect on the principal of his or her City notes. During the moratorium period, the noteholders who declined to exchange their notes were to be paid interest at an annual rate of at least six percent. Most of the large New York banks and other institutional holders of notes accepted the exchange, but the Flushing National Bank challenged the scheme as a violation of the New York State constitutional requirement of a full faith and credit pledge by the City for general obligation debt.

The New York Court of Appeals, in an oft-quoted opinion, invalidated the moratorium, because the three-year deprivation of judicial remedies for default "makes meaningless the verbal pledge of faith and credit." The *Flushing Bank* Court's analysis of the full faith and credit provisions bears repeating:

A pledge of the city's faith and credit is both a commitment to pay and a commitment of the city's revenue generating powers to produce the funds to pay. Hence, an obligation containing a pledge of the city's "faith and credit" is secured by a promise both to pay and to use in good faith the city's general revenue powers to produce sufficient funds to pay the principal and interest of the obligation as it becomes due. That is why both words, "faith" and "credit", are used and they are not tautological. That is what the words say and that is what courts have held they mean when rare occasion has suggested comment. . . .

A "faith and credit" obligation is, therefore, entirely different from a "revenue" obligation, which is limited to a pledge of revenues from a designed source or fund. . . . It is also in contrast to a "moral" obligation, which is backed not by a legally enforceable promise to pay but only by a "moral" commitment.

Section 2. Public Purpose and Lending of Credit Limitations

As noted in IV C(1)(b), above, virtually all states, by constitutional or statutory provision, prohibit the lending of public credit to private enterprises. This prohibition is related to the requirement that public funds can be spent only for public purposes, but the two are distinct concepts. The lending of credit prohibition is also distinguishable from the standard debt ceiling (see IV I, below), even though the two provisions have a common Nineteenth Century heritage. Maine's constitutional provisions are illustrative.

Article IV, part 3, section 1 of the Maine Constitution gives the Legislature "full power to make and establish all reasonable laws and regulations for the defense and benefit of the people ... not repugnant to [the] Constitution...." The Maine courts have read the public purpose requirement into the words "benefit of the people."

Article IX, section 14 of the Maine Constitution states that the "credit of the State shall not be directly or indirectly loaned in any case," except for certain types of loans specifically authorized and other loans when the bonds are approved by two-thirds of both houses of the Legislature and a majority vote of the people. The same section provides that the "legislature shall not create any debt

... [which exceeds] $2,000,000 except to suppress insurrection, repel invasion or for purposes of war, and except for temporary loans...."

The public purpose doctrine has been a part of state and local government law since the inception of the Union. The limitation of credit doctrine, however, was added in reaction to some spectacular defaults of financial schemes involving railroad expansion in the Nineteenth Century. (See I A, above, and IV I(2), below.) Persons with memories of those times are long buried, and modern pressures have increased for more direct state and local government involvement in activities that traditionally were in the hands of the private sector, such as job development, economic expansion, housing, health services and student financial aid. As a result, the courts have had to deal with thorny separation of powers questions involving the proper role of the judiciary in reviewing legislative responses to these pressures.

Though state courts generally take a deferential view of legislative declarations regarding public purpose, they have been more willing to review the question than have the federal courts. A major principle that guides the state courts in this review is the requirement that the courts not debate the wisdom of a particular legislative policy. This does not mean, however, that a legislative declaration of public purpose will end the inquiry. Persons challenging the public purpose of a particular act of borrowing or spending may present evidence and arguments that, despite the legislative declaration of public purpose, no such purpose is actually present. The burden of proof on that question is a heavy one for the challengers because their evidence must overcome a presumption of legislative validity. If those challengers can only establish that reasonable persons might disagree regarding the wisdom or rationality of the particular spending or borrowing scheme, it probably will be upheld as having a valid public purpose.

Public purpose is not a static concept. Its meaning has changed as economic and social conditions have changed. In recent years, most courts that have considered the question have rejected arguments that public purpose involved only those activities that benefit the public directly, such as police protection and disease control, or that produce something the public has the right to use, such as public transportation.

Although it is generally conceded that no single set of objective criteria exists for making the required analysis, a number of factors have been identified by courts and scholars as useful indicators of public purpose. These factors include prior judicial characterizations, legislative declarations, voter approval, general economic benefit, availability of the facility to members of the public on an equal basis, degree of impact on the public welfare, number of beneficiaries and the extent to which society has an interest in benefiting those individuals, degree of necessity for public activity in the area (because of the nature of the problem or because of private inability to respond to it), and extent of competition with private enterprises. Largely private projects that produce indirect economic benefits to the public have been approved under a test that focuses on whether the benefit to the public, direct or indirect, outweighs any threatened detriment to the public. The courts generally conclude that the legislature is the proper body to weigh costs and benefits and that the judiciary should intervene only when the legislature's decision has no rational basis.

The Maine Supreme Court adopted this test, in upholding a complicated scheme, which involved State borrowing to assist the City of Portland in attracting a ship repair firm by expanding port and drydock facilities. In that case, the Maine Court concluded that the "ripple effect" of job development was a sufficient indirect public benefit to allow the scheme to pass constitutional muster. (*See Common Cause v. Maine*, 455 A.2d 1 (Me. 1983).)

The *Maine* Court also analyzed the port expansion project in terms of the lending of credit provision of the State's Constitution. Many courts have viewed the lending of credit limitation as simply an extension of the public purpose doctrine. Under that approach, if bonds were issued for a legitimate public purpose, the lending of credit limitation would also be satisfied. (*See Kizziah v. Department of Transportation*, 121 Cal.App.3d 11, 175 Cal.Rptr. 112 (1981).) In rejecting that approach, the *Maine* Court took an historical view of the concept and concluded that the lending of credit limitation had a life separate and distinct from the public purpose doctrine. Tracing the lending of credit provision to the Nineteenth Century railroad expansion era (see I A, above), the Court noted that the chief vice of the municipalities that led to the limitation was the practice of guaranteeing revenue bonds that were sold by privately owned railroad companies. As sureties, state and local governments were secondarily liable. When the railroads defaulted on the bonds, the governments were obligated to honor the railroad's obligations.

The *Maine* Court concluded that the proper analysis of the lending of credit limitation required recognition that the word "credit" was a term of art limited to the surety relationship between the primary obligor, a private individual or business, and the public body. In the *Maine* case, because the state was the primary obligor on bonds to be issued for the port development project, there was no suretyship relationship and, therefore, no violation of the lending of credit limitation.

The Court also noted that, over the years, Maine's constitutional provision had been amended to allow even certain types of suretyship arrangements, such as insuring mortgage loans for various industrial and agricultural activities, and for housing for veterans and Native Americans, as well as insuring payment of school building bonds. (These amendments were exceptions to the lending of credit limitation rather than to the debt limitation provision.)

Section 3.   The Takings Clause and Eminent Domain

The Fifth Amendment to the U.S. Constitution prohibits the taking of private property "for public use" without just compensation. In 2005 in an important (and highly controversial) decision, a sharply divided U.S. Supreme Court held that a city's use of its eminent domain power to condemn private land in furtherance of a plan for local economic revitalization constitutes a constitutionally permissible taking of that land for a public use. (*See Kelo v. City of New London*, 545 U.S. 469 (2005).) This decision, and state court cases following it, are relevant to bond financing since local governments sometimes rely upon their eminent domain authority to assemble land to be used for bond-funded projects and services.

In the aftermath of the *Kelo* case, state courts also confronted the question of whether economic development alone could satisfy state constitutional takings requirements. In *City of Norwood v. Horney*, 853 N.E.2d 1115 (Ohio 2006), the Ohio Supreme Court joined a number of other courts by parting with the U.S. Supreme Court's *Kelo* analysis. The *Horney* case involved a proposed mixed-use development in an inner ring suburb of Cincinnati, that was intended to convert residential properties to commercial uses in a "deteriorating area" located close to an interstate highway. The Ohio court held that while economic factors may be considered in determining whether private property may be acquired by eminent domain, "economic benefit alone [is not] a sufficient public use for a valid taking." The *Horney* decision viewed the dissenting opinions in *Kelo* as "better models for interpreting" the Ohio takings clause. The court expressed concern that an economic benefit along standard could subject private property owners "to the government's determination that another private party would put one's land to a better use."

Where bond-financed projects that involve eminent domain are especially controversial, project opponents may challenge governmental cost acquisition estimates which are required, in some jurisdictions, as a prelude to municipal use of eminent domain. In *Robert Siegel, Inc. v. District of Columbia*, 892 A.2d 387 (D.C. App. 2006), for example, the D.C. Circuit affirmed a dismissal of a challenge to a land acquisition cost estimate that had been made by the Chief Financial Officer (CFO) of Washington, D.C., prior to the acquisition of land within the proposed site of a new baseball stadium. The court concluded that any review of the CFO's reevaluation was the province of the city's Mayor and Council, who have the constitutional responsibility "to reconcile the demands . . . of needy citizens with the finite resources available to meet those demands." In the end, the court asserted, the matter was a budgetary issue within the province of the legislature, and not the judiciary.

Section 4. The Contract Clause of the United States Constitution

The basic relationship between state and local government borrowers and the purchasers of their debt securities is contractual in nature, so some discussion of the constitutional protection for bond and note covenants is in order. Purchasers of revenue bonds, in particular, are concerned about such covenants, because the purchasers' security depends upon the manner in which the public borrower handles the funds generated by the revenue bond project. Also state and local government issuers need to know the extent to which they can alter any of their general obligation or revenue bond covenants.

Questions of ordinary breach of contract are governed by general state contract law. However, if a state or local government repudiates its debt or repeals provisions which provide security for its debt, it might violate the contract clause of the United States Constitution. It provides: "No State shall ... pass any ... law impairing the Obligation of Contracts." Many state constitutions contain similar provisions.

Questions of contract impairment with respect to bond and note financing usually arise when the state uses its police power to rearrange relationships because of some financial exigency or other problem involving the general welfare. From the bondholders' perspective, the problem can be an acute one because of the long-term nature of their investment. No bondholder wants to be told in 2008 that a covenant restricting the use of project revenues standing behind bonds purchased in 2002, and not scheduled for redemption until 2017, has been repealed because the public welfare necessitates a reallocation of the project revenues, with a corresponding dilution of the bondholders' security.

In contract clause cases, courts ask whether there is a legitimate contract, what the terms of that contract are, whether the terms have been impaired by state or local government actions, and whether the impairment is both reasonable and necessary in light of the circumstances. The modern view is that the clause must take into account the state's police power and other "essential attributes of sovereign power." (*See United States Trust Co. v. New Jersey*, 431 U.S. 1, 21 (1977); *Home Building & Loan Ass'n v. Blaisdell*, 290 U.S. 398 (1934).)

There are two types of contract clause cases: (1) private contract cases, which allege that state action has constitutionally impaired a contract (or contracts) between private parties (*e.g.*, a statutory moratorium that alters existing private mortgage obligations), and (2) public contract cases, which allege that the state has impaired its own contractual obligations (*e.g.*, the repeal of a bond covenant). Though the test in both types of cases is essentially the same, the courts are somewhat less willing to defer to the state policy pronouncements in state contract cases.

In *United States Trust Co. v. New Jersey*, 431 U.S. 1 (1977), the Supreme Court invalidated a

1974 New Jersey statute that retroactively repealed a 1962 revenue bond covenant which had severely restricted the financing of commuter railroad facilities by the New York Port Authority. (The New York Port Authority is a bi-state authority created by an interstate compact; its key policy rules are set by identical New York and New Jersey statutes.) The 1962 statutory covenant had limited the use of Port Authority revenues to certain carefully defined railroad activities, but the 1974 statute permitted bridge tolls and other revenues to be used to subsidize the expansion of the Port Authority's mass transit system and the addition of direct rail services to John F. Kennedy Airport and Newark Airport.

In striking down the 1974 statute, the United States Supreme Court ruled that an impairment of a public contract can be constitutional only if it is both "reasonable" and "necessary" to serve an important public purpose. In applying this test, the Court refused to defer to legislative pronouncements of reasonableness and necessity because of the state's self-interest in making those declarations.

The Court agreed that the statutes served important public purposes—mass transportation, energy conservation and environmental protection. The Court refused, however, to engage in what it considered "a utilitarian comparison of public benefit and private loss," stating that even though the end was important, the means chosen (impairment of contract) could not be upheld unless it was both reasonable and necessary.

More specifically, the Supreme Court concluded that the contract impairment that was before it failed the "necessity" test, because the same results could have been achieved either by adopting a less drastic modification of the contract or by adopting alternative means of encouraging use of mass transportation, such as higher taxes on gasoline or higher tolls. The 1974 statute also failed the "reasonableness" test, because the problems it was designed to alleviate (environmental, transportation and energy conservation) were present and known when the original 1962 covenant was adopted. (Subsequent private contract clause cases include *Allied Structural Steel Co. v. Spannaus*, 438 U.S. 234 (1978), and *Energy Reserves Group, Inc. v. Kansas Power & Light Co.*, 459 U.S. 400 (1983); and *Condell v. Bress*, 983 F.2d 415 (2d Cir. 1993).)

One situation in which the Court was willing to sustain a unilateral modification of a public contract (a municipal bond covenant) involved the extreme situation of the bankruptcy of the municipality that issued the bonds. In a 1942 case, the Court sustained a state statute authorizing the state to place into receivership a bankrupt local government. Under the statute, a plan for the composition of creditors' claims, including municipal bondholders, could be imposed on dissenting creditors if two conditions were met: (1) the plan was approved by the receiver, the municipality, and 85 per cent of the creditors; and (2) a state court, after a public hearing, concluded that the municipality could not otherwise pay off the creditors, and that the plan was in the best interest of those creditors. The Court upheld the constitutionality of a plan adopted under the statute, in which the bondholders received new securities with lower interest rates and later maturity dates, because "unexpected financial conditions" made the plan necessary. The old bonds represented only theoretical rights because the city could not, as a practical matter, raise enough taxes to pay off its creditors under the old terms. Today municipal bankruptcy is largely governed by federal statutory law. (See IV G(3), below.)

Section 5. State Debt Ceilings and Referenda Requirements

State substantive ceilings on debt-financing and referenda requirements are discussed in IV I, below. They are treated separately from the state constitutional limitations discussed in this Part of the book, because of the importance of the subject and because those limitations are both statutory and constitutional.

PART G. FEDERAL STATUTORY REGULATION OF STATE AND LOCAL DEBT FINANCING

Section 1. Federal Securities Laws

Subsection a. Regulation of State and Municipal Securities Dealers.

As noted in IV C, above, state and local government debt obligations generally are negotiable instruments. Because purchasers of these obligations are investors in a common venture in which they have a reasonable expectation of profit derived from the entrepreneurial or managerial efforts of others, municipal bonds and notes are "securities" as that term is commonly understood.

A substantial industry has developed of brokers, dealers and banks which engage in the business of buying and selling negotiable municipal securities. Although this industry is subject to state regulation, prior to 1975 it was exempt from most of the registration and other regulatory requirements of the federal securities laws. Specific statutory provisions exempted any "security" issued by the United States, individual states, and their political subdivisions or instrumentalities from the regulatory provisions of those laws. However, a 1970 amendment to the securities laws, enacted to overturn a Securities and Exchange Commission (SEC) interpretation, expanded the definitional exemption for public securities to include industrial development bonds that are tax-exempt. (See IV C(4) and IV E(1), above.) Moreover, in 1975, Congress created a new regulatory structure for securities dealers under which they become subject to SEC anti-fraud requirements and to regulations regarding underwriting and trading in municipal securities.

The centerpiece of the federal regulatory scheme for securities is a detailed registration statement that must be filed with the SEC before covered securities may be sold in interstate commerce. The purpose of the registration statement is to implement what is essentially a self-regulatory system based on full disclosure of materials facts. Substantial civil and criminal penalties, as well as injunctive remedies, may be imposed for violations of the disclosure provisions.

Because municipal securities are partially exempt from the statutory definition of securities, state and local government issuers of securities have been spared the expense and effort required to prepare registration statements, not to mention the potential federal intrusion into their financial affairs. There was, however, heightened concern about investor confidence in the immediate aftermath of the New York City and Cleveland fiscal crises of the mid–1970's, and the default of the Washington Public Power Supply System in 1983 (see III E, above), as well as an increase in the number of individual bondholders. This concern led to a substantial increase in voluntary disclosure by state and municipal issuers since 1975.

Moreover, the statutory exemption is a definitional exemption from only certain specifically identified sections of the securities laws. It does not exempt *transactions* in municipal securities from the full reach of regulation under the federal securities laws. For example, purchasers of municipal securities may maintain an action under Section 10(b) of the Securities Exchange Act of 1934, which makes it unlawful to "use or employ . . . any manipulative or deceptive device" in connection with interstate commerce in securities. The expansive language of Section 10(b) has led courts to conclude that the section extends to transactions in municipal securities.

Initially, courts held that governmental entities were not "persons" within the meaning of the 1934 Act. As a result, claims under Section 10(b) and SEC Rule 10b–5 could be brought against underwriters (brokers, dealers and banks) who purchased municipal securities and resold them to the investing public but not against the state and local governments and governmental officials that issued the securities.

In 1975, however, Congress amended the 1934 Act by adding "government, or political subdivision, agency or instrumentality of a government" to the definition of "person." This amendment subjects governmental issuers of municipal securities to anti-fraud liability under Section 10(b) of the 1934 Act and SEC Rule 10b–5. In addition to the possibility of enforcement actions by the SEC itself, such issuers may also be subject to private anti-fraud lawsuits that were initiated by investors.

The Amendments of 1975 also established the Municipal Securities Rulemaking Board (MSRB), as part of the overall legislative scheme to subject municipal securities dealers to SEC registration requirements and other regulations while minimizing the direct regulation of municipal securities issuers. (Under the Act, no person may engage in a municipal securities business unless registered with the SEC or exempted by SEC action.)

The MSRB is a self-perpetuating 15 member board initially appointed by the SEC with five representatives of brokers and five representatives of the public. It is responsible for promulgating rules and regulations governing the qualifications and conduct of registered municipal securities professionals.

More generally, the MSRB is intended to prevent fraudulent, manipulative acts and practices by municipal securities dealers and to promote just and equitable principles of trade. The SEC may discipline by censure, suspension or revocation of registration any municipal securities professional who violates the securities statutes or rule of either the SEC or the MSRB.

The MSRB may require municipal securities brokers and dealers to furnish the Board or purchasers and prospective purchasers information (such as applications, annual reports and other documents) regarding a municipal issuer which are generally available from sources other than the issuer itself.

However, concern about the negative constitutional and public policy implications of federal interference with state and local government financial affairs led Congress to add a specific prohibition against SEC or MSRB attempts to require municipal issuers themselves to file any documentation with either agency or to furnish such documentation to purchasers or prospective purchasers prior to the issuance, sale or distribution of municipal securities. The legislative history of this provision, the so-called Tower amendment, includes an oft-quoted statement of former Senator John Tower of Texas that "states, cities, counties or villages [shall not be subjected] to any unnecessary disclosure requirements. . . ."

Subsection b.   Regulation of State and Municipal Securities Issuers.

Municipal issuers are not exempt from the disclosure requirements of Section 17 of the Securities Act of 1933. False statements or omissions of material facts, as well as fraudulent schemes, are proscribed for all issuers or sellers of "any securities."

This section provides a basis for SEC injunctive proceedings, as well as criminal prosecution if a violation is willful. Scienter (knowing or intentional misconduct) is required for a violation of the fraudulent schemes section, but negligence alone can form the basis of liability for false statements or omissions of material facts. On the other hand, however, most courts that have considered the issue have ruled that Section 17 does not create a private right of action.

Beyond this, in litigation stemming from the Washington Public Power Supply System default, courts established that governmental bond issuers owe a 'duty of disclosure' to investors, including secondary market bond purchasers. Courts also held that federal securities laws preempt state sovereign immunity doctrines, and that the Tenth and Eleventh Amendments to the U.S. Constitution provide no shield to governmental violators of securities law requirements. Moreover, in amendments to its regulations, the SEC has prohibited underwriters from participating in any public offering of municipal securities unless the issuer agrees, in writing, to provide certain annual financial information and operating data, as well as notices of material events that might affect the securities. Additionally, in an "interpretation" of its own rules, the SEC has taken the position that underwriters are obligated to "review in a professional manner" the accuracy of offering statements with which they are associated. To do so, they must "exercise reasonable care to evaluate the accuracy of statements in issuer disclosure documents."

Section 2.   Internal Revenue Code

In 1982, Congress took a new approach to the regulation of municipal securities by requiring that publicly issued obligations with maturities greater than one year must be issued in registered form, rather than bearer form, in order to qualify for tax-exempt status under the Internal Revenue Code. This requirement was upheld by the U.S. Supreme Court in *South Carolina v. Baker*, 485 U.S. 505 (1988). Furthermore, the Court stated, in *dicta*, that neither the Tenth Amendment nor the doctrine of inter-governmental tax immunity prevents Congress from taxing the income received by investors from state and local government securities.

As noted in IV C(1)(e) above, registered securities are issued in the name of the owner of the security. The owner's name is also entered on the books of the issuer. Principal and interest payments are paid directly to the record owner, without the necessity of presentation of the security. Ownership of the security is usually transferred by surrender of the old instrument to the issuer and re-issuance of the old certificate, or a new one, to the new owner. Transfer can also be effectuated by a book entry system maintained by the issuer. Through this process, the ownership of registered securities can be easily traced. The registration requirement was enacted by Congress in response to concern over compliance with estate and gift tax laws and concern about the increasing use of bearer bonds as substitutes for cash by persons engaged in illegal activities.

Prior to this 1982 amendment of the Internal Revenue Code, many state and local governments regularly issued securities in non-registered form. Indeed, some states required a non-registered form of issuance in order to enhance negotiability and thus marketability. (This was because bearer bonds are generally fully negotiable, but registered bonds are negotiable only if they qualify as a security under Article 8 of the UCC or other statute.)

The federal tax consequences of municipal securities were also profoundly affected by the Tax Reform Act of 1986, which amended the Internal Revenue Code in significant ways. For example, Section 265 of the amended Code prohibits the deduction of most expenses incurred in buying or owning municipal bonds (*other than* interest income). However, state income taxes imposed on municipal bond interest remain deductible under Section 164 of the Code.

The Tax Reform Act of 1986 substantially revised the Code provisions governing industrial development bonds. These bonds were made part of a larger category, called "private activity bonds" (whose proceeds are used for the benefit of nongovernmental persons who pay the debt service, or are used for certain purchases of output facilities from nongovernmental persons). The Act restricted the permitted uses for the proceeds of tax-exempt bonds, to ensure that those proceeds primarily benefit the public, rather than private businesses. It also contracted the types of public facilities that may be financed with tax-exempt bonds. (*See* IRC (1986), §§ 103, 141. *See generally* IV E(1), above.)

The 1986 Act also further curtailed the ability of state and local governments to raise money through the use of arbitrage. "Arbitrage Bonds" are defined as bonds issued with the purpose of reinvesting the proceeds in order to acquire higher yielding investments. (*See* IV E(2), above.) The 1986 Act classified interest paid on an Arbitrage Bond as taxable income to the bondholder. (*See* IRC (1986), §§ 103, 148.) It also added a limitation on the total number of times that a bond may be advance refunded, and it limited the period during which refunded bonds may remain outstanding. (*See* IRC (1986), § 148.)

Section 3.   Federal Bankruptcy Code and Insolvent Municipalities

The specter of municipal insolvency, dramatized by the fiscal crises of New York City and Cleveland in the 1970s (see III E, above), the collapse of the Washington Public Power Supply System in the early 1980s(see IV H(3), below), and the temporary insolvency of Orange County, California in 1994 (see IV H(4), below) has resulted in renewed attention to the subjects of municipal default and bankruptcy. Prior to these incidents, municipal insolvency had not been a matter of general concern since the handful of Depression-related fiscal problems of the late 1930s and early 1940s.

Chapter 9 of the Bankruptcy Reform Act of 1978 establishes a process by which municipalities that are overwhelmed by debt may gain breathing space from collection efforts while they develop a plan for reorganizing that debt. Under this Chapter, insolvent municipalities are afforded a court-supervised proceeding through which they may attempt to settle disputes with their creditors. While involved in a

Chapter 9 proceeding, the municipality is still required to provide necessary and basic municipal services (such as police, fire and electrical services). At the same time, however, Section 922(a) of the Bankruptcy Code provides for the automatic stay of all actions or proceedings against the debtor municipality, including lawsuits initiated by municipal bondholders and other creditors.

Subsection a.   Federalism Concerns.

The first federal municipal bankruptcy act was declared unconstitutional, as a violation of the Tenth Amendment, by the Supreme Court in 1936—only two years after its passage. A revised municipal bankruptcy act was passed in 1937, which included the general language of the current Section 903 of the Bankruptcy Code. One year later, the Supreme Court upheld the revised law. Section 903 recognizes what might be termed an uneasy truce between congressional power to make uniform laws concerning bankruptcies and the states' reserved powers under the Tenth Amendment.

As a reflection of federalism concerns, the Bankruptcy Code does not permit the federal bankruptcy court administering the process to interfere with the municipality's political or governmental power, its property or revenues, or its use of any income-producing property. Section 903 of the Bankruptcy Code states specifically that the Code does not limit or impair the power of the state to control the municipalities within its jurisdiction; and a city cannot be forced to take specific action without the state's consent. However, this Section preempts any state's attempt to prescribe debt composition plans that would bind non-consenting creditors.

In the 1978 Bankruptcy Reform Act, Congress deleted a provision prohibiting state composition procedures for municipalities. The House committee report accompanying the Act commented that it was advisable that states be given maximum flexibility in solving the debt problems of their municipalities. The report also noted that the general policy of the new Act was to encourage "work-outs" with consenting creditors short of bankruptcy court proceedings, and that deletion of the prohibition against state composition procedures recognized state power to assist municipal work-outs.

Subsection b.   Procedural Requirements.

Under Chapter 9 of the Bankruptcy Code, the insolvent municipality (defined as a political subdivision, public agency or instrumentality of a state), must be authorized by state law to file a Chapter 9 petition and must have negotiated in good faith with its creditors prior to filing the petition.

What constitutes a municipality, and what constitutes authorization to file a Chapter 9 petition, are determined by state law. Though a number of states have granted their political subdivisions general authority to file a Chapter 9 petition, some states regulate the process by requiring political subdivisions to obtain advance approval of a state agency. What little case law there is on the subject indicates that the courts will give a liberal interpretation to the authorization requirement. For example, independent special purpose municipal authorities, which are not specifically enumerated in a Pennsylvania statute that requires advance state agency approval for Chapter 9 filings, have been held to be generally authorized by state law to obtain the protection of Chapter 9 under state statutes that authorize them to sue and be sued, to acquire property, to borrow money and to "do all things necessary . . . to carry out (their) powers."

A number of courts have found that a general grant of powers consistent with Chapter 9 satisfies the Bankruptcy Code's authorization requirement. For example, in 1991 the State of Connecticut moved to dismiss a Chapter 9 petition filed by the City of Bridgeport on the basis that Bridgeport was not specifically authorized to be a debtor under state law. The bankruptcy court denied Connecticut's motion, reasoning that local governments are generally authorized to be debtors if they are delegated home rule authority over such matters as finances, property, borrowing and public service. Similarly, in a Colorado case, a bankruptcy court held that a special district's authorization for a Chapter 9 filing followed from its express legal ability to borrow money to refund any bond indebtedness, and to manage, control and supervise all of its own business and affairs.

Although the term "bankruptcy" often is used to describe the process available to the insolvent municipality, it is not totally accurate because the municipality does not have its debts discharged; nor does it "go out of business," as a bankrupt private corporation could. Instead, as noted above, a Chapter 9 proceeding gives the municipality time to reorganize its debt obligations, by refinancing or other means, so that eventually the debt can be satisfied.

Only voluntary proceedings initiated by the municipality are permitted. That is, an involuntary bankruptcy process, by which creditors can force private insolvent debtors into the bankruptcy courts, cannot be used against municipalities.

As mentioned above, bankruptcy is commenced when a qualified municipal debtor files a petition for an adjustment of its debt with the federal bankruptcy court. A petition filed in the prescribed manner operates as an automatic stay against all activities to enforce outstanding debts until the case is dismissed or a plan for the adjustment of debts is approved or rejected. This automatic stay applies to judicial, administrative or other proceedings; enforcement of judgments; creation, perfection, or enforcement of liens; obtaining possession of property; and efforts to force municipal officials to collect taxes. As is the case in private bankruptcies, the court has power to grant creditors appropriate relief from the automatic stay for cause, after notice and hearing.

Notice of filing of the petition must be published in the district where the case is pending. The municipal debtor must file a list of creditors and a proposed plan for the adjustment of the municipality's debts. The plan can be filed with the petition or at such later time as the court directs. Failure to file the list of creditors or the plan in a timely manner is grounds for dismissal of the bankruptcy petition.

Approval (confirmation) of a plan by the court is mandated if the court determines that: (1) the plan complies with all applicable provisions of the Bankruptcy Code (these generally relate to payment of administrative expenses, priorities of claims, treatment of secured and unsecured creditors, as well as procedures for handling modifications and objections to the plant); (2) the municipality has the power to carry out its plan; (3) the plan is feasible; (4) the plan is in the best interests of the creditors; and (5) each class of creditors has accepted the plan or is not impaired by the plan.

If the objecting creditors are impaired by the plan, the plan can still be approved if the court, upon request of the proponent municipality, finds that all other tests are met, that the plan does not discriminate unfairly, and that the plan is fair and equitable to the non-accepting creditors whose interests are impaired.

Municipal insolvency can affect the holders of municipal securities in a number of ways. The automatic stay provision may affect the timeliness of principal and interest payments. Security interests granted by the municipal debtor prior to the filing of a petition do not reach property acquired after the petition is filed, except in cases involving proceeds, product, offspring, rents or profits of that property. Thus, unless the creditor has a lien on the property producing the revenues, he or she may not be able to collect the revenues once the bankruptcy petition has been filed. Commentators have argued that this provision can be interpreted to shield a pledge of taxes for the payment of general obligation bonds and a pledge of assessments for the payment of special assessment bonds from the reach of the bondholder.

Because the Chapter 9 process does not result in the discharge of municipal debts or the dissolution of the municipal debtor, creditors of governmental entities which have the power to tax can be reasonably confident that the principal on their bonds (or loans) will eventually be repaid. What they may stand to lose is the total interest for which they originally contracted and repayment within the original time frame. As noted in IV F(3), above, delay in the time of payment will not necessarily violate the Contract Clause.

The Bankruptcy Code also provides that certain types of acceleration clauses are unenforceable, that certain transfers of property made while the municipality is insolvent and within 90 days prior to the filing of a petition are voidable, and that a non-recourse special obligation may, in certain circumstances, be treated as a general obligation.

PART H. COMPLIANCE WITH STATE ENABLING LEGISLATION

Section 1. Consequences of Issuing Unauthorized Debt

One of the most fundamental questions that must be answered by any issuer of state or municipal debt is whether the particular type of obligation contemplated is authorized by state law. The importance of careful analysis of applicable state constitutional and statutory provisions to determine whether proper authorization exists for a particular bond or note issue cannot be overemphasized. The consequences of the issuance and sale of unauthorized state or local government obligations are enormous.

The tax-exempt status of state and municipal obligations under Section 103 of the Internal Revenue Code, discussed in IV E, above, depends on proper state authorization of the obligations as well as compliance with the federal tax laws. In a 1984 case of first impression, the U.S. Court of Appeals for the Sixth Circuit upheld an Internal Revenue Service ruling disallowing the exclusion from a taxpayer's income of interest payments received on deferred payment contracts for the sale of heavy construction equipment to various city, county and state governmental entities in Tennessee. The contracts were not properly authorized by the governing bodies, as required by Tennessee law, and thus did not qualify as "obligations" within the meaning of Section 103 of the Internal Revenue Code. The court concluded that the fact that the contracts might be enforced by Tennessee courts, under an implied contract theory, despite their lack of proper authority, was irrelevant to the question of federal tax exemption.

Besides losing the advantage of tax-exempt treatment for the interest paid on unauthorized bonds, bondholders may even lose the security of repayment on such bonds. The latter subject is further discussed in IV H(3), below.

Liability of officials of the issuer for securities fraud under the anti-fraud and disclosure provisions of the federal securities laws, discussed in IV G(1), above, may flow from the unauthorized issuance of state or municipal obligations. One theory that has gained favor in such cases allows a plaintiff to argue that unauthorized municipal securities undermine investor confidence in the municipal markets generally and thus constitute a "fraud on the marketplace." Under this approach, the purchaser does not have to prove direct reliance on deceptive documents or actions of the issuer because the purchaser is entitled to assume that the availability of the bonds from the issuer indicates that they were lawfully issued. A case for fraud under Section 10(b) of the Securities Exchange Act of 1934 and SEC Rule 10b–5 can be established by proof that the obligations were unauthorized, and that the issuer and/or its advisors knowingly conspired to bring unlawfully issued obligations to market with the intent to defraud.

Notably, recent cases have established that potential liability for securities fraud and improper disclosure is not limited to officials of the municipality that issued the bonds. Instead, such liability can extend to underwriters, financial advisors, bond counsel, engineers, auditors and other professionals who were associated with a fraudulent or improper bond issue.

Section 2. Methods of Assuring There Has Been Proper Authorization

Because the consequences of unauthorized issuance are so severe, many states provide for a review by a state official, such as the attorney general or the state treasurer, of proposed debt obligations as a check against unauthorized issuance. The practice of seeking judicial imprimatur through a "test" case or "friendly" suit has also become prevalent.

In order to bring before the court such questions as compliance with the public purpose requirement, debt ceiling, and referenda requirements, the issuing agency will authorize a bond issue and begin the sale process. Some officials in the process will refuse to perform a necessary ministerial (non-discretionary) function, e.g., the secretary of administration may refuse to sign a warrant to requisition funds already appropriated by the legislature for the issuing agency, and suit will be brought seeking a court order requiring the official to perform that ministerial task. The defense will be lack of authorization, unconstitutionality, or similar invalidity of the bond issue, and the question will be tried, often with a stipulation of facts. The result will be appealed so that an opinion can be rendered in which the validity of the proposed debt obligation is decided. (See also IV C(1)(h), C(2)(h), above.)

Section 3. The Washington Public Power Supply System Cases

Several cases involving the shutdown of two nuclear power plants by the Washington Public Power Supply System (WPPSS) offer a fascinating look at the authorization question.

WPPSS was a municipal corporation established in 1957 as a "joint operating agency," originally consisting of four Washington cities (Ellensburg, Richland, Seattle and Tacoma) and 10 public utility districts. By state statute, it had authority to acquire, build, operate and own electrical power generating plants and transmission systems. It had no taxing power nor general obligation borrowing power, but it did have statutory authority to issue revenue bonds payable from funds derived from the operation of its utility facilities.

In response to questions concerning the uncertainties of nuclear power plants, WPPSS put together an extremely complicated financing package whose centerpiece was a Participants' Agreement, under which some 88 public participants (including cities, utility districts and rural electric cooperatives in six states) agreed to pay their pro rata share of the costs of producing electric power whether or not they ever received any power. Similar agreements, generally called "dry hole," "take or pay" or "hell or high water" agreements, have been used in other states, with or without specific statutory authority, for various types of utility projects.

During the 1970s, WPPSS constructed three nuclear generating plants and began construction on two more. The first three projects were completed, and they provide electricity to a number of public utilities in several Northwestern states. They were financed through complicated agreements that, ultimately, allocated the risk of non-completion of the plants to a federal agency, the Bonneville Power Administration (BPA). The remaining two plants, which did not have such a BPA guarantee, were only partially built when they were canceled in 1982. At that time, approximately $2.25 billion in revenue bonds had been issued by WPPSS. Repayment with scheduled interest would have come to more than $7 billion.

When WPPSS announced the cancellation of the two unfinished nuclear power plants, considerable questions were raised about the viability of the outstanding bonds. The trustee for the bondholder, Chemical Bank of New York, brought a declaratory judgment action in Washington state court seeking a determination that the participants were obligated to pay to WPPSS sufficient funds to finance the bonds, with interest.

The decision in *Chemical Bank v. Washington Public Power Supply System*, 666 P.2d 329 (Wash. 1983), *cert. denied sub nom. Chemical Bank v. PUD No. 1*, 471 U.S. 1075 (1985) (No. 84–1258), sent tremors through the bond market. The Washington Supreme Court reversed the trial court and concluded that the Participants' Agreement was void because it was beyond the powers of the local governments involved. The court construed the agreement as a contract to purchase project capability that amounted to an "unconditional guarantee of payments on the revenue bonds, secured by a pledge of the participants' utility revenues, in exchange for a share of any power generated by these projects." In the court's view, the contract exceeded the participants' authority in several respects:

1. Purchase of project capability ("take or pay") did not qualify as a purchase of electricity under state statutes authorizing such purchase.

2. The Participants' Agreement, with the unconditional guarantee given to WPPSS, did not constitute the construction or purchase of electric generating facilities under statutes authorizing cities and towns to do so because the participating local governments had no effective ownership interest in or control over the WPPS project.

3. The implied power to pay for service contained in the statutory authority to acquire or construct generating plants and provide electricity did not include the power to make unconditional pledges to pay for services whether or not they were received.

4. Statutes authorizing joint operating and joint development agreements contemplated a sharing of control and payment conditioned upon services

rendered, neither of which was present in the WPPSS case.

The Supreme Court of Idaho, in *Asson v. City of Burley*, 670 P.2d 839 (Idaho 1983) *cert. denied sub nom., Chemical Bank v. Asson*, 469 U.S. 870 (1984), reached a conclusion similar to that of the majority on the Washington Supreme Court. It found no authority under Idaho law for the purchase of "project capability" from WPPSS. The Idaho Court concluded that the agreements amounted to long-term indebtedness which could not be issued without a two-thirds vote of the electorate. An exception to the referendum requirement for ordinary and necessary expenses was held inapplicable because the project capacity provision was not within the purview of statutes (similar to those in Washington), which authorized construction and operation of power plants and purchase of energy.

Nine months after the WPPSS decision in Washington, the Oregon Supreme Court reached the opposite conclusion in *DeFazio v. WPPSS*, 679 P.2d 1316 (Or. 1984), in which it held that the Oregon cities that joined the ill-fated venture had authority under the Oregon Constitution and implementing statutes to make the agreements. The Oregon case was initiated by a group of ratepayers in a participating city who objected to the prospect of having to pay for electricity they were not going to receive because of the cancellation of the plants.

The Oregon Supreme Court, in an articulate opinion by Justice Linde reviewing the authorities, concluded that charter cities operating under Oregon's broad home rule provisions had authority to enter into the challenged contracts. The court rejected the argument that the contracts were a form of "forbidden" credit for WPPSS. Noting that any long-term contracts may be needed by a supplier in order to obtain financing to produce and supply the goods or services, the court reasoned there was no legal difference between the authority to contract to purchase something, however small the amount and large the cost, and the authority to contract to pay for the costs "if small and costly deliveries should turn out to be none at all."

Though the agreements proved unwise in retrospect, and were perhaps unwise when made, the Oregon Court did not regard that as a basis for finding them to be unauthorized. Authority to provide electric power or other public services "cannot well be construed to permit wise but to exclude unwise contracts."

The Oregon Court concluded with a brief essay on the relationship of the vertical and horizontal levels of government in America:

The design of the agreements at issue in this case went to the bounds of Oregon law. The argument that the bounds were crossed has been ably and strongly presented, but ultimately it asks us to hold that the design was illegal as a whole though it remained within each separate rule. Retrospective judicial evaluation of individual transactions by such a standard would not be rule of law ...

The WPPSS default also gave rise to litigation concerning other significant legal issues, especially questions of securities law and constitutional law. (See IV G(1)(b), above.) Among other things, this litigation established that professionals who provide advice or guidance with regard to improperly issued municipal bonds run a very real risk of incurring liability. In *In re Washington Public Power Supply System Securities Litigation*, [1989 Transfer Binder] Fed.Sec.L.Rep. ¶ 94,325 (W.D.Wash.1988), a federal court denied motions for summary judgment by the bond issuer's financial advisor, based in part upon that advisor's substantial involvement in the offerings themselves, the advisor's development of official statements, and the advisor's awareness of undisclosed information. Similarly, the same court denied summary judgment motions by consulting engineers to the bond issuer, based upon their preparation of engineering projections included in the official statements for offerings of the Supply System's bonds.

Section 4.　The Orange County Financial Crisis

Another relatively recent event with important implications for the integrity of the municipal bond market, as well as municipal investment practices, was the December, 1994 bankruptcy of Orange County, California. In that situation (in an effort to avoid the stringent limitations imposed by California's "Proposition 13" on their ability to increase real estate taxes and to use their revenues to pay

for debt service) 187 cities, school districts and
county units pooled $7.8 billion of revenues in an
investment fund run by the Orange County Treasurer. That fund borrowed billions of dollars more,
posting collateral in the form of fixed income securities.

Interest rates on the borrowed funds then increased, however. This rate change forced Orange
County to pay more for debt service on its borrowings than it was earning on its investments. Eventually, the County missed a sizeable payment to a
creditor which had extended it a collateralized loan.
In response, the creditor liquidated the collateral
standing behind its loan. Following this, Orange
County filed for federal bankruptcy court protection. That step was taken to reduce litigation by
bondholders and other creditors, and to prevent
other creditors from also liquidating their collateral.
(For a discussion of the federal Bankruptcy Code
and insolvent municipalities, see IV G(3), above.)

After the bankruptcy filing, Orange County's access to capital funding was damaged. The County
has had to pay relatively high interest rates since
that time, and it may well need credit enhance-
ments for any debt floated in the future. In addition, in June 1995, Orange County's voters rejected
a proposed .5% county sales tax increase, a tax
change that would have eased some of the County's
fiscal problems.

Despite this, in 1996, Orange County was able to
float a new bond issue for $800 million. That bond

sale imposed substantial debt service obligations on the County. Nonetheless, it did provide sufficient funds to enable Orange County to terminate its bankruptcy proceedings, and to make long overdue payments to various noteholders and vendors.

Orange County's massive losses, through its substantial and ill-advised investments, have given rise to widespread concerns about the need for increased disclosure, and for additional restrictions on municipal investment practices. They have also raised questions about the wisdom of Proposition 13—and its implications for investment and financing by municipalities in California.

PART I.   DEBT CEILINGS AND OTHER RESTRICTIONS ON THE AMOUNT OF STATE AND LOCAL DEBT

Section 1.   Overview

The amount of debt a state or local government has outstanding at any particular time is usually restricted by state constitutional or statutory debt ceilings. As noted in IV C(1)(c) and IV C(2)(d), above, debt ceilings usually apply only to general obligation debt, rather than to debt financed from a "special fund," such as revenue bonds or special assessment bonds.

Most states employ referenda requirements in addition to, or as a substitute for, substantive debt ceilings. A few states also require local government debt to be approved by a state administrative agency.

Over the years, several mechanisms have evolved for avoiding or evading these substantive debt ceilings and procedural requirements.

Section 2. Nineteenth Century Origins of Debt Ceilings and Related Restrictions

Ceilings upon state debt first appeared in state constitutions in the mid-Nineteenth Century, in response to state defaults and suspensions of payments on state debt in the 1840s. In the last decade of the Nineteenth Century, local debt ceilings were added to state constitutions to restrict the debt-financing activities of municipalities, just as the earlier limits had restricted debt-financing by states. Restrictions upon the lending of public credit (see IV C(2) and IV F(2), above) were also adopted to restrain states, and later local governments, from using their tax revenues to finance unsuccessful private entrepreneurial activities. The investments, crises, and defaults that preceded these constitutional restrictions upon state and local debt are described in Part I A, above.

Nineteenth Century debt ceilings restricted the amount of outstanding debt for the state or local government involved to a specified percentage of the assessed (or full) value of the real property located within its boundaries. Though property values may have been a reasonable basis for measuring the capacity of Nineteenth Century state and local governments to service their debt, several modern commentators have argued that this approach is outdated given the wide range of revenue sources now available to state and local governments (*see* II, above).

Section 3. Current State Constitutional and Statutory Debt Ceilings

The vast majority of modern constitutional and statutory limitations upon the level of state and local government debt continue to follow the pattern established by the Nineteenth Century debt ceilings. For example, Iowa's constitutional debt ceiling provides, much as its 1857 predecessor did:

> No county, or other political or municipal corporation shall be allowed to become indebted in any manner, or for any purpose, to an amount, in the aggregate, exceeding five per centum on the value of the taxable property within such county or corporation—to be ascertained by the last State and county tax lists, previous to the incurring of such indebtedness.

Statutory debt ceilings are structured in a similar manner. Some states base the computation of the debt ceiling upon the average assessed (or full) value of property for several years (rather than just a single year as in the above example), in order to reduce fluctuations caused by property reassessments.

Pennsylvania deviates from the pattern of relying solely upon real property values in calculating the local government debt ceiling. Its constitution provides that the State Legislature, in setting a local government's debt ceiling, shall use a "debt limit base" which is "a percentage of the total revenue . . . of the unit of local government computed over a specific period immediately preceding the year of borrowing. . . ." It should be noted, however, that the implementing legislation, while including most sources of local revenue in the debt limit base, excludes state and federal "subsidies or reimbursements" from that base. Furthermore, the Pennsylvania Constitution subjects Philadelphia to a more traditional form of debt ceiling—13½% of the annual "assessed valuations of the taxable realty therein"—despite the availability to Philadelphia of municipal income tax revenues (*see* II D, above).

Section 4.   Referenda Requirements

Several states require that state and/or local government bonds be approved by voter referenda prior to issuance. Referenda requirements often apply to revenue and other kinds of bonds, as well as to general obligation bonds. This procedural approach, which is also traceable to the Nineteenth Century, is used by some states as a complete substitute for substantive debt ceilings. Other states, such as Ohio and Pennsylvania, set local government debt ceilings but allow local voters to approve the issuance of debt above the ceiling. Still other states use referenda as an adjunct to administrative control over the level of local government debt.

One question that has arisen respecting referenda requirements is whether a pledge by local officials to request an annual appropriation of funds to pay part of the principal and interest on a bond issue must be invalidated following a county charter amendment requiring voter approval of county financial assistance to certain bond projects. The issue arose in *Moschenross v. St. Louis County*, 188 S.W.3d 13 (Mo. App. 2006), where a home rule county adjacent to St. Louis, Missouri, entered into a contract with a state agency, the Missouri Development Finance Board, to finance part of a new major league baseball stadium through a $46 million revenue bond issue. Under the agreement, the county promised to include requests to pay for the bonds in its annual budget proposals to the county council. After the bond financing was in place, however, St. Louis County voters approved an initiative petition that required a vote of the people before the County could provide financial assistance for the development of a professional sports facility. Despite this, the financing agreement was upheld by a trial court, whose judgment was later affirmed by the Missouri Court of Appeals. The appellate court concluded that the agreement was a valid contract that was not affected by the county charter amendment which (by its own words) operated prospectively.

Section 5. Administrative Approval Requirements

Though state debt often must be approved by an administrative agency, only a few states require administrative approval prior to the issuance of local government debt. Louisiana and North Carolina require local governments to obtain prior approval both from their local voters and from a state administrative agency. In Nevada, approval must be obtained from the county General Obligation Bond Commission.

Section 6.   Devices for Avoiding or Evading Limitations on the Amount of Outstanding Debt

Several mechanisms have been developed by state and local officials to enable them to circumvent substantive debt ceilings and/or procedural requirements (*e.g.*, the voter or administrative approvals described above). Insofar as these mechanisms are legal, they can be regarded as "avoidance" devices. Insofar as they are illegal, the mechanisms should be considered to be "evasion" devices.

Subsection a.   Exceptions to Debt Ceilings and Referenda Requirements.

Many states exclude debt incurred for certain purposes, (*e.g.*, financing of water and sewer improvements) from the substantive debt ceiling applicable to their state and/or local governments. As a result, debt can be incurred to finance these activities and projects even after the governmental entity involved has reached its debt ceiling.

Also, bonds whose debt service is paid from a "special fund" (a source separate from the general taxing power which backs "full faith and credit" general obligation bonds) are usually exempt from the debt ceiling. (*See* IV C(1)(c) and IV C(2)(d), above.) This includes most revenue bonds, private purpose bonds (which include former IDBs), and many moral obligation bonds. These bonds may, however, be subject to voter referenda or administrative approval requirements. (See IV I(4)-(5), above.)

Subsection b.   Special Authorities and Special Districts.

A common mechanism for avoiding constitutional or statutory debt ceilings is the creation of a special authority or special district, such as a school district or a transportation authority, with the power to incur debt. These separate governmental entities, which are now used to build and operate a wide range of capital facilities and programs, either are subject to no debt ceiling at all or have a ceiling which is separate from (and in addition to) the debt ceiling of contiguous or coterminous municipalities. Courts in nearly every state have upheld this arrangement, even where the special district and the municipality have overlapping boundaries. As a result, a municipality that needs certain capital improvements but has already reached its debt ceiling often can (if authorized by state law) create a special district or can persuade the state legislature to create a special authority, with power to issue bonds to construct the capital improvements.

Special authorities and special districts typically finance their capital projects with the proceeds of revenue bonds and pay for debt service on these bonds with service charges generated by the capital facility involved. For example, a transportation authority might build a bridge, finance its construction with revenue bonds, and pay debt service on these bonds with tolls collected from persons using the bridge. In some states, however, special authorities also have the power to levy their own real property or other taxes.

Many commentators have criticized the proliferation of special authorities and special districts. Though these separately incorporated governmental entities might have certain advantages, in terms of expertise and management efficiency, they often are created solely to undercut the debt ceiling. Also, the existence of several quasi-independent governmental entities, within a single metropolitan area, may reduce public accountability and increase the cost of debt financing.

Subsection c.　Lease–Financing.

Another mechanism for circumventing debt ceilings is leasing, instead of purchasing, capital facilities. Courts generally have ruled that annual payments on a "true lease" can be paid from current revenues, and the capital value of the asset involved will not constitute "debt" within the meaning of debt ceiling and referenda requirements. Similarly, a "service contract," by which a municipality agrees to purchase services (usually the provision of utilities) over a period of years and to pay for those services as they are delivered, generally is not treated as "debt." On the other hand, an "installment purchase contract," by which a municipality agrees to pay specified sums for a period of time (installment payments) at the end of which it acquires ownership of the asset involved, does constitute debt, so the capital value of the asset usually will be counted against the municipality's debt ceiling.

Payments on true leases and service contracts generally are excluded from the debt ceiling and referenda requirements because of the "contingent obligation" doctrine. The theory behind this doctrine is that payments are not due until a particular condition has occurred (the delivery of the service or availability of the rental property) and the contract may be terminated before this condition is satisfied. As a result, the municipality is not bound for an extended period as it is with traditional debt. It is often difficult to determine whether a particular payment made by a municipality pursuant to a contract is a service (or rental) payment rather than an installment payment. The difficulties are compounded for leases with an option (by the municipality) to purchase the capital facility involved. Courts have often been generous in concluding that a particular arrangement is a lease or service contract, and therefore exempt from the debt ceilings and referenda requirements. Some commentators, however, have criticized this use of lease-financing as a borrowing device unregulated by the debt limits.

Subsection d.   Evasion of Debt Ceilings.

Governmental entities on the brink of fiscal crisis have abused short-term debt and have employed various so-called "creative" accounting devices to mask the extent of their financial problems or to delay the day of reckoning. New York City employed several of these evasive devices just before its fiscal crisis, and several other local governments and some states have also used them, but on much smaller scale.

Subsubsection i. Abuse of Short–Term Debt. Short-term notes are legitimate devices for borrowing to meet temporary cash-flow difficulties created by the time lag between the receipt of taxes and other revenues and the payment of expenses. Notes are exempt from debt ceilings and are generally exempt from referenda requirements. These exemptions reflect the short-term nature of TANs, RANs, and BANs. (See IV D(1), above.) As explained in IV D(2), above, these legitimate short-term credit devices can be abused by being used regularly to fund current expense items (that should be paid from current revenues) and by being continually "rolled over" (so that they become gradual accretions to a municipality's outstanding debt, unregulated by the debt ceiling).

Subsubsection ii. "Creative" Accounting Devices. "Creative," but generally illegal and inappropriate, accounting devices have been employed by financially pressed states and cities. One such device involves overestimating revenues while underestimating expenses. For example, a city might overestimate the revenues standing behind its tax anticipation notes by including revenues from tax delinquent or tax-exempt properties. Similarly, it might overstate the amount of state or federal intergovernmental aid available to back revenue anticipation notes. In response to such abuses, several states have provided that their local governments can issue notes for only a specified percentage (*e.g.*, 50% or 75%) of estimated taxes or revenues, and these states have imposed more stringent accounting and auditing requirements, including Generally Accepted Accounting Principles. (*See* III A(2), above.)

Another "creative" device involves mixing or changing accounting bases during the middle of a fiscal year. The "cash basis" requires both revenues and expenditures to be recorded only when they are received, in cash. By contrast, under the "accrual basis," revenues are recorded as soon as they are earned and expenditures are recorded as soon as they are incurred, regardless of when payments are actually made (or received). If a state or local government mixes its accounting bases by recording its revenues, such as real property taxes, as soon as the tax bills are issued (accrual basis) but recording its expenses, such as salaries and purchases, only when they are paid (cash basis), that state or local government will falsely convey the appearance of a balanced budget. It then might have to rely upon short-term debt to bridge the resulting fiscal crisis when its obligations become due.

Another "creative" accounting device, discussed in II B(3), above, involves capitalizing expense items, *i.e.*, borrowing to pay for current expenses.

This is really a mechanism for evading tax limits, but it also has the effect of swelling the capital budget. The danger is that when officials are faced with such a swollen capital budget, they might, in turn, employ other "creative" accounting devices or abuse short-term debt.

*

TABLE OF AUTHORITIES

Cases, statutes, articles and books used in the preparation of this Nutshell are listed by chapter, section and subsection. Although many sources were consulted, special mention should be made of several key ones. The authors drew upon MANDELKER, NETSCH, SALSICH, WEGNER, STEVENSON AND GRIFFITH, STATE AND LOCAL GOVERNMENT IN A FEDERAL SYSTEM (6th ed. 2006); and STATE AND LOCAL GOVERNMENT DEBT FINANCING (M. David Gelfand ed., 1991 & annual supplements). We found a useful discussion of sales and use taxes in PAUL J. HARTMENT, FEDERAL LIMITATIONS ON STATE AND LOCAL TAXATION, Ch. 10 (1981).

Other casebooks and treatises in the field that were consulted include: M. DAVID GELFAND, CONSTITUTIONAL LITIGATION UNDER SECTION 1983: A TREATISE FOR CITY ATTORNEYS, PUBLIC INTEREST LITIGATORS, AND STUDENTS (2d ed. 1996 and Supp.); JEROME R. HELLERSTEIN AND WALTER HELLERSTEIN, STATE AND LOCAL TAXATION: CASES AND MATERIALS (7th ed. 2001); JOHN MARTINEZ, C. DOUGLAS SANDS AND MICHAEL E. LIBONATI, LOCAL GOVERNMENT LAW (1982 & Supps.); EUGENE MCQUILLIN, THE LAW OF MUNICIPAL CORPORATIONS (3rd ed. rev. 2005); OLIVER OLDMAN and FERDINAND P.

SCHOETTLE, STATE AND LOCAL TAXES AND FINANCES TEXT: PROBLEMS, AND CASES (1974).

I A & B   HENRY C. ADAMS, PUBLIC DEBTS: AN ESSAY IN THE SCIENCE OF FINANCE 317–31 (1887); ROBERT S. AMDURSKY & CLAYTON P. GILLETTE, MUNICIPAL DEBT FINANCE LAW: THEORY AND PRACTICE 12–25 (1992); RICHARD T. ELY, TAXATION IN AMERICAN STATES AND CITIES 131 (1888); JEROME R. HELLERSTEIN & WALTER HELLERSTEIN, STATE AND LOCAL TAXATION: CASES AND MATERIALS 1–19 (6th ed. 1997); EDWIN R.A. SELIGMAN, ESSAYS IN TAXATION 16–17 (9th ed. 1931); M. David Gelfand, *Debt Ceilings and Other Restrictions on Debt Financing: Compliance, Avoidance, and Evasion*, in 2 STATE & LOCAL GOVERNMENT DEBT FINANCING (M. D. Gelfand ed., 1991 & Supps.); M. David Gelfand, *Seeking Local Government Financial Integrity Through Debt Ceilings, Tax Limitations and Expenditure Limits: The New York City Fiscal Crisis, The Taxpayers' Revolt, and Beyond*, 63 MINN. L. REV. 545 (1979).

II A(1)   M. David Gelfand, *Comparative Urban Finance: Are the London and Brooklyn Bridges Falling Down?*, 55 TUL. L. REV. 651, 667–68 (1981); M. David Gelfand, *Taxes and Other Revenue Sources Standing Behind Bonds and Notes*, in 2 STATE AND LOCAL GOVERNMENT DEBT FINANCING (M. D. Gelfand ed., 1991 & Supps.).

Corp., 417 U.S. 369 (1974); Norfolk & Western R. Co. v. State Tax Comm'n, 390 U.S. 317, 325 n.5 (1968); A. Magnano Co. v. Hamilton, 292 U.S. 40, 44 (1934); Heiner v. Donnan, 285 U.S. 312 (1932); Brushaber v. Union Pac. R. Co., 240 U.S. 1, 24 (1916); Quill Corp. v. North Dakota, 504 U.S. 298 (1992).

II A(2)(f)(i)   Alden v. Maine, 119 S. Ct. 2249 (1999); College Savings Bank v. Florida Prepaid Postsecondary Educ. Expense Bd., 119 S. Ct. 2219 (1999); Montana v. Crow Tribe of Indians, 523 U.S. 696 (1998); Printz v. United States, 117 S. Ct. 2365 (1997); City of Boerne v. Flores, 117 S. Ct. 2157 (1997); Seminole Tribe v. Florida, 116 S. Ct. 1114 (1996); United States v. Lopez, 514 U.S. 549 (1995); United States v. Morrison, 529 U.S. 598 (2000); Gonzalez v. Raich, 545 U.S. 1 (2005); Cipollone v. Liggett Group, 505 U.S. 504 (1992); New York v. United States, 505 U.S. 144 (1992); South Carolina v. Baker, 485 U.S. 505 (1988); Aloha Airlines, Inc. v. Director of Taxation of Hawaii, 464 U.S. 7 (1983); Federal Maritime Comm'n v. South Carolina State Ports Authority, 535 U.S. 743 (2002); Board of Trustees of the Univ. of Alabama v. Garrett, 531 U.S. 356 (2001); Kimel v. Florida Board of Regents, 528 U.S. 62 (2000); Garcia v. San Antonio Metropolitan Transit Auth., 469 U.S. 528 (1985); EEOC v.

LAW. 447, 449, 454–61 (1977); M. David Gelfand, *Comparative Urban Finance: Are the London and Brooklyn Bridges Falling Down?*, 55 TUL. L. REV. 651, 668–71 (1981); Roseburg School Dist. v. City of Roseburg, 851 P.2d 595 (Or. 1993); Knapp v. City of Jacksonville, 2007 WL 121861 (Or.); Oregon Const. Art. XI § 11b(2)(b).

II B(2)　　MANDELKER, NETSCH, SALSICH, WEGNER, STEVENSON AND GRIFFITH, STATE AND LOCAL GOVERNMENT IN A FEDERAL SYSTEM: CASES AND MATERIALS 354–363 (6th ed. 2006); United States Advisory Commission on Intergovernmental Relations, State Limitations on Local Taxes and Expenditures (1977); United States Advisory Commission on Intergovernmental Relations, State Constitutional and Statutory Restrictions on Local Taxing Powers (1962); M. David Gelfand, *Seeking Local Government Financial Integrity Through Debt Ceilings, Tax Limitations, and Expenditure Limits: The New York City Fiscal Crisis, The Taxpayers' Revolt, and Beyond*, 63 MINN. L. REV. 545, 551–54 (1979); M. David Gelfand, *Taxes and Other Revenue Sources Standing Behind Bonds and Notes*, in 2 STATE AND LOCAL GOVERNMENT DEBT FINANCING, ch. 10 (M. David Gelfand ed., 1991); Nordlinger v. Hahn, 505 U.S. 1 (1992); City & County of San Francisco v. Farrell, 648 P.2d 935 (Cal. 1982); Los Angeles County Trans.

Jurgens Co. v. Wilkins, 848 N.E.2d 499 (Oh. 2006).

II D(1)
D. BERMAN, STATE-LOCAL RELATIONS: PARTNERSHIPS, CONFLICT, AND AUTONOMY 53 (ICMA Municipal Yearbook, 2005); MUNICIPAL INCOME TAXES (R. Connery ed. 1968); 1 State Tax Guide, paras. 15–100, 15–691, 15–780 (CCH 2d ed.); 1 State and Local Taxes Serv. (All States Unit) (P–H) paras. 1001, 1007; United States Advisory Commission on Intergovernmental Relations, Significant Features of Fiscal Federalism, M–190 (June 1994), at 78–79; U. S. Bureau of the Census, City Government Finances in 1981–82, Series GF 82, No. 4, Table 5 (1983); M. David Gelfand, *Comparative Urban Finance: Are the London and Brooklyn Bridges Falling Down?*, 55 TUL. L. REV. 651, 671–76 (1981); Abb C–E Nuclear Power, Inc. v. Director of Revenue, 215 S.W.3d 85, 2007 WL 274838 (Mo.); Northwest Medical Imaging, Inc. v. Dept. of Revenue, 151 P.3d 434, 2006 WL 3824919 (Alaska); RSMo § 32.200 art. IV(1).

II D(2)
City & County of Denver v. Sweet, P.2d 441 (Colo. 1958); Dooley v. City of Detroit, N.W.2d 724 (Mich. 1963); Grant v. Kansas City, 431 S.W.2d 89 (Mo. 1968); Carter Carburetor Corp. v. City of St. Louis, 203 S.W.2d 438 (Mo. 1947); Mario Foundry Co. v. Landes 147 N.E. 302 (Ohio 1925);

Mich. Comp. Laws § 141.501 *et seq.*
(1999); Ohio Rev. Code Ann.
§ 718.01 (West 1999); Pa. Stat. Ann.
Tit. 53, § 6902 (West 1999).

II D(3)   W. Hellerstein, *Some Reflections on
the State Taxation of a Nonresident's
Personal Income*, 72 MICH. L. REV.
1309 (1974); Lunding v. New York
Tax Appeals Tribunal, 522 U.S. 287
(1998); Austin v. New Hampshire,
420 U.S. 656 (1975); Wisconsin v.
J.C. Penney Co., 311 U.S. 435 (1940);
Travis v. Yale & Towne Mfg. Co., 252
U.S. 60 (1920); American Commuters
Ass'n v. Levitt, 405 F.2d 1148 (2d
Cir. 1969); Thompson v. City of Cin-
cinnati, 208 N.E.2d 747 (Ohio 1965).

II (E)1   THE COUNCIL OF STATE GOVERNMENTS,
25 THE BOOK OF THE STATES 300, 331,
341 (1984); DUE & MIKESELL, SALES
TAXATION: STATE AND LOCAL STRUCTURE
AND ADMINISTRATION 277 (2d ed. 1994);
HARTMAN, FEDERAL LIMITATIONS ON
STATE AND LOCAL TAXATION, ch. 10
(1981); J. HELLERSTEIN & W. HELLER-
STEIN, STATE AND LOCAL TAXATION, ch.
9 (6th ed. 1997); United States Advi-
sory Commission on Intergovern-
mental Relations, State & Local
Roles in the Federal System 133
(1980); M. David Gelfand, *Taxes and
Other Revenue Services Standing Be-
hind Bonds and Notes*, in 2 STATE
AND LOCAL GOVERNMENT DEBT FINANC-
ING, ch. 10 (M. D. Gelfand ed., 1991

and Supps.); Pierce, *The Place of Consumers' Excises in the Tax System*, 8 LAW & CONTEMP. PROB. 430 (1941); Studenski, *Characteristics, Developments and Present Status of Consumption Taxes*, 8 LAW & CONTEMP. PROB. 417 (1941); Louisville v. Sebree, 308 Ky. 420, 214 S.W.2d 248 (1948).

II E(2)(a)   Virden v. Schaffner, 496 S.W.2d 846 (Mo. 1973); Automatic Retailers of America, Inc. v. Morris, 386 S.W.2d 901 (Mo. 1965); RSMo. § 144.010.1(7), RSMo. § 144.010.1(8), RSMo. § 144.011 (1996), RSMo. § 144.020.1.

II E(2)(b)   DUE & MIKESELL, SALES TAXATION (1994); Farm & Home Sav. Ass'n v. Spradling, 538 S.W.2d 313 (Mo. 1976); Op. Atty. Gen. Mo. No. 38 (Schechter, 11–14–68); Virden v. Schaffner, 496 S.W.2d 846 (Mo. 1973); Automatic Retailers of America, Inc. v. Morris, 386 S.W.2d 901 (Mo. 1965); Piedmont Canteen Service, Inc. v. Johnson, 256 N.C. 155, 123 S.E.2d 582 (N. C. 1962); White v. State, 306 P.2d 330 (Wash. 1957); Code of Ala. 1975, § 11–51–200; Ga. Code Ann. § 48–8–82 (1995); Ill. Rev. Stat. 1990, Ch. 24, Par. 8–11–1; RSMo. 94.500 (1996); RSMo. § 144.285 (prior to 1982 amendment); RSMo. § 144.285 (1996).

Dakota By & Through Heitkamp, 504 U.S. 298 (1992); Borders Online, LLC v. State Bd. of Equalization, 29 Cal. Rptr. 3d 176 (Cal. App. 2005); Pub. L. No. 108–435, 118 Stat. 2615 (2004).

II E(2)(d)   Bruskin and Parker, *State Sales Taxes on Services: Massachusetts As A Case Study*, 45 TAX LAW 49 (1991); M. David Gelfand, *Taxes and Other Revenue Sources Standing Behind Bonds and Notes*, in 2 STATE AND LOCAL GOVERNMENT DEBT FINANCING, ch. 10 (M. David Gelfand ed., 1991); Weber, *Florida's Fleeting Sales Tax on Services*, 15 Fla. St. U. L. Res. 613 (1987); Southern Bell Telephone and Telegraph Co. v. Department of Revenue, 366 So.2d 30 (1st DCA Fl. 1978); Federated Department Stores, Inc. v. Kosydar, 340 N.E.2d 840 (Ohio, 1976).

II E(2)(e)   Washington Times–Herald v. District of Columbia, 213 F.2d 23 (D.C. Cir. 1954); RSMo. §§ 94–510, 540, 550 (1996); RSMo. §§ 66.615 to 66.620 (1996); NMSA §§ 7–19–4, 7–20–1, 7–21–51 (1993); New York Tax Law §§ 1210 *et. seq.* (McKinney 1999); Nev. R.S. § 374.010 (1993) (mandatory county sales tax).

II E(3)(a)   P. HARTMAN, FEDERAL LIMITATIONS ON STATE AND LOCAL TAXATION, §§ 10:1, 10:5 (1981); RSMo. §§ 144.600, .610, .615, .635 (1996).

McCulloch v. Maryland, 17 U.S. (4 Wheat.) 316 (1819); City of Mesa v. Home Builders Ass'n of Cent. Ariz., Inc., 523 P.2d 57 (Ariz. 1974); City of Alameda v. Premier Communications Network, Inc., 202 Cal. Rptr. 684 (Cal. Ct. App. 1984); 49 U.S.C. § 1513, Pub. L. No. 93–44, § 7(a), 87 Stat. 88, 90 (1973); RSMo. § 73.110 (1996); Tenn. Code Ann. § 67–751 (repealed in 1983).

II H(1)(a)   MANDELKER, NETSCH, SALSICH, WEGNER, STEVENSON AND GRIFFITH, STATE AND LOCAL GOVERNMENT IN A FEDERAL SYSTEM: CASES AND MATERIALS 319–348 (6th ed. 2006); 14 McQUILLIN, MUNICIPAL CORPORATIONS §§ 38.01, 38.05 (4th ed. rev. 2005); J. MARTINEZ, C. SANDS & M. LIBONATI, LOCAL GOVERNMENT LAW §§ 24.28–24.42 (1982); Conrad v. Lexington–Fayette Urban County Gov't, 659 S.W.2d 190 (Ky. 1983); McNally v. Township of Teaneck, 379 A.2d 446, 450–451 (N.J. 1977); Haynes v. City of Abilene, 659 S.W.2d 638, 640–642 (Tex. 1983).

II (H)(1)(b)   H.L. Munn Lumber Co. v. Ames, 176 N.W.2d 813 (Iowa 1970); Chicago & N.W. Ry. v. Seward, 88 N.W.2d 175 (Neb. 1958); LeRoy v. Rapid City, 193 N.W.2d 598 (S.D. 1972).

II H(1)(c)   MANDELKER, NETSCH, SALSICH, WEGNER, STEVENSON AND GRIFFITH, STATE AND LOCAL GOVERNMENT IN A FEDERAL SYSTEM: CASES AND MATERIALS, 315–320

(6th ed. 2006); St. Louis Post Dispatch, at 1D, col. 6 (Jan. 4, 1982); City of Winter Springs v. State, 776 So.2d 255 (Fla. 2001); City of Fort Lauderdale v. SSM Properties, Inc., 825 So.2d 343 (Fla. 2002); Harrison v. Board of Supervisors, 118 Cal. Rptr. 828 (Cal. App. 1975); Mobil Oil Corp. v. Town of Westport, 438 A.2d 768 (Conn. 1980); Davies v. City of Lawrence, 545 P.2d 1115 (Kan. 1976); Conrad v. Lexington–Fayette Urban County Gov't, 659 S.W. 2d 190, 197 (Ky. 1983) (*citing* Mathews v. Eldridge, 424 U.S. 319 (1976)); Thibodeaux v. Comeaux, 145 So.2d 1 (La. 1962), *cert. den.*, 372 U.S. 914 (1963); Johnson v. City of Inkster, 258 N.W.2d 24 (Mich. 1977); Blades v. Genessee Drain District No. 2, 135 N.W.2d 420 (Mich. 1965); Parking Systems, Inc. v. Kansas City Downtown Redev. Corp., 518 S.W.2d 11, 15 (Mo. 1974); Sears v. City of Columbia, 660 S.W.2d 238 (Mo. App. 1983); Western Amusement Co. v. City of Springfield, 545 P.2d 592, 594 (Or. 1976); Haynes v. City of Abilene, 659 S.W.2d 638 (Tex. 1983); City of Houston v. Blackbird, 384 S.W.2d 929 (Tex. Civ. App. 1964); Heavens v. King County Rural Library District, 404 P.2d 453 (Wash. 1965).

II H(1)(d)   MANDELKER, NETSCH, SALSICH, WEGNER, STEVENSON AND GRIFFITH, STATE AND LOCAL GOVERNMENT IN A FEDERAL SYSTEM: CASES AND MATERIALS 319–320

(6th ed. 2006); McNally v. Township of Teaneck, 379 A.2d 446 (N.J. 1977).

II H(2)(a) INTERNATIONAL CITY MANAGEMENT ASS'N, MANAGEMENT POLICIES IN LOCAL GOVERNMENT FINANCE 315–346 (2004); MANDELKER, NETSCH, SALSICH AND WEGNER, STATE AND LOCAL GOVERN- MENT IN A FEDERAL SYSTEM: CASES AND MATERIALS, 337 (6th ed. 2006); C. SANDS & M. LIBONATI, LOCAL GOVERN- MENT LAW § 24.06 (1982); M. David Gelfand, *Taxes and Other Revenue Sources Standing Behind Bonds and Notes*, in 2 STATE AND LOCAL GOVERN- MENT DEBT FINANCING, ch. 10 (M. D. Gelfand ed., 1991 and Supp.); Kafo- glis, *Local Service Charges: Theory and Practice*, in STATE AND LOCAL TAX PROBLEMS 164–166 (H. J. Johnson ed., 1969), *reprinted in* OLDMAN & SCHOETTLE, STATE AND LOCAL TAXES AND FINANCE 856 (1974).

II H(2)(b) MANDELKER, NETSCH, SALSICH, WEGNER, STEVENSON AND GRIFFITH, STATE AND LOCAL GOVERNMENT IN A FEDERAL SYS- TEM: CASES AND MATERIALS 302–312 (6th ed. 2006); Englewood v. City and County of Denver, 229 P.2d 667 (Colo. 1951); Collins v. Town of Goshen, 635 F.2d 954 (2d Cir. 1980) (*citing* Washington v. Davis, 426 U.S. 229, 244–45 & n. 12 (1976), *and* Hawkins v. Town of Shaw, 437 F.2d 1286 (5th Cir. 1971)); Town of Ver- non v. Public Utilities Comm'n, 318 A.2d 121, 125–26 (Conn. 1971); Con-

tractors and Builders Ass'n v. City of
Dunedin, 329 So.2d 314, 319 n. 5
(Fla. 1976); Apartment and Office
Bldg. Ass'n v. District of Columbia,
415 A.2d 797, 799 (D.C. App. 1980);
Lewis v. Mayor and City Council of
Cumberland, 54 A.2d 319, 324 (Md.
1947); Rutherford v. City of Omaha,
160 N.W. 2d 223, 228 (Neb. 1968);
Apodaca v. Wilson, 525 P.2d 876, 883
(N.M. 1974) (*quoting with approval*
City of Niles v. Union Ice Corpora-
tion, 133 Ohio St. 169, 12 N.E. 2d
483, 488–489 (1938)); City of Texar-
kana v. Wiggins, 151 Tex. 100, 246
S.W. 2d 622, 624–629 (1952).

II H(3)

MANDELKER, CUNNINGHAM, & PAYNE,
PLANNING AND CONTROL OF LAND DEVEL-
OPMENT 614–628 (4th ed. 1995); J.
MARTINEZ, C. SANDS & M. LIBONATI,
LOCAL GOVERNMENT LAW § 15.03
(2006);City of Monterey v. Del Monte
Dunes, 526 U.S. 687 (1999); Dolan v.
City of Tigard, 512 U.S. 374 (1994);
Nollan v. California Coastal Cmn.,
483 U.S. 825 (1987); Associated
Homebuilders of Greater East Bay,
Inc. v. City of Walnut Creek, 4 Cal.
3d 633, 484 P.2d 606 (1971), *app.
dis.*, 404 U.S. 878 (1971); Westfield–
Palos Verdes Co. v. City of Rancho
Palos Verdes, 141 Cal. Rptr. 36 (Cal.
App. 1977); Contractors and Builders
Ass'n of Pinellas County v. City of
Dunedin, 329 So.2d 314 (Fla. 1976);
Pioneer Trust & Sav. Bank v. Village
of Mount Prospect, 176 N.E.2d 799

(Ill. 1961); Divan Builders, Inc. v. Planning Bd., 334 A.2d 30 (N.J. 1975).

II H(4)   Roberts v. McNary, 636 S.W.2d 332 (Mo. 1982); Solvang Municipal Improvement District v. Board of Supervisors, 169 Cal. Rptr. 391 (Cal. App. 1980); Mills v. County of Trinity, 166 Cal. Rptr. 674 (Cal. App. 1980); County of Fresno v. Malmstrom, 156 Cal. Rptr. 777 (Cal. App. 1979).

II H(5)(a)   *See, e.g.*, Wilson v. C.I.R., 340 F.2d 609 (5th Cir. 1965), *app. dis., cert. den.*, 382 U.S. 108, *reh. den.*, 382 U.S. 1021 (1966); Wisconsin Gas and Electric Co. v. United States, 138 F.2d 597 (7th Cir. 1943), *aff'd*, 322 U.S. 526 (1944); Noble v. C.I.R., 70 T.C. 916 (1978); 11 U.S.C. §§ 902(2), 943(a) (1984); 26 U.S.C.A. § 164(C)(1) (1978).

II H(5)(b)   *See generally* 4 COLLIER ON BANKRUPTCY, paras. 902.02–.03 (15th ed. rev. 1999); 11 U.S.C.A. §§ 902(2) and (3), 943(a) (1979).

II I   CLOTFELTER & COOK, SELLING HOPE: STATE LOTTERIES IN AMERICA (1989); KARCHER, LOTTERIES (1989); M. David Gelfand, *Taxes and Other Revenue Sources Standing Behind Bonds and Notes*, in 2 STATE AND LOCAL GOVERNMENT DEBT FINANCING, ch. 10 (M. D. Gelfand ed.,1991 and Supps.); Presi-

II K(2)

U.S. Census Bureau, *2002 Census of Governments, Volume 4, Number 5: Compendium of Government Finances: 2002*, GC02(4)–5 (2002) (*available at* www.census.gov/prod/2005pubs/gc024x5.pdf); United States Advisory Commission on Intergovernmental Relations, Significant Features of Fiscal Federalism, No. 1, M–190, Table 60 (Dec. 1994); U.S. Bureau of the Census, City Government Finances in 1982–83, Series GF 83, No. 8 (Nov. 1984); U.S. Bureau of the Census, County Governmental Finances in 1982–83, Series GF 83, No. 8 (Nov. 1984); M. David Gelfand, *Comparative Urban Finance: Are the London and Brooklyn Bridges Falling Down?*, 55 TUL. L. REV. 651, 688 (1981); 30 ILL. COMP. STAT. 115/1 to 115/11.

II L(1)

J. HELLERSTEIN & W. HELLERSTEIN, STATE AND LOCAL TAXATION: CASES AND MATERIALS 980–1020 (6th ed. 1997); Mullane v. Central Hanover Bank & Trust Co., 399 U.S. 306 (1950); Turner v. Wade, 254 U.S. 64 (1920); Londoner v. City & County of Denver, 210 U.S. 373 (1908); Hodges v. Muscatine County, 196 U.S. 276 (1905).

II L(2)

J. HELLERSTEIN & W. HELLERSTEIN, STATE AND LOCAL TAXATION: CASES AND MATERIALS 980–1020 (6th ed. 1997); Lujan v. Defenders of Wildlife, 504 U.S. 555 (1992); Hunt v. Washington State Apple Advertising Comm'n, 432 U.S. 333 (1977).

1972); Mallory v. Barrera, 544 S.W.2d 556 (Mo. 1976); Shapp v. Sloan, 391 A.2d 595 (Pa. 1978), *app. dis. sub nom.* Thornburgh v. Casey, 440 U.S. 942 (1979); Colo. Gen. Assemb. v. Lamm., 700 P.2d 508 (Colo. 1985); Laws of Pa., Gen. Appropriations Act of 1975, 1975 Act No. 8A, § 8(b); Pa. Stat. Ann. tit. 72, §§ 4613, 4615 (2006).

III A(4)   Menorah Medical Center v. Health & Ed. Fac. Auth., 584 S.W. 2d 73, 78–79 (Mo. 1979); State ex rel. City of Jefferson v. Smith, 154 S.W. 2d 101 (Mo. 1941).

III B   M. DAVID GELFAND, CONSTITUTIONAL LITIGATION UNDER SECTION 1983: A TREATISE FOR CITY ATTORNEYS, PUBLIC INTEREST LITIGATORS, AND STUDENTS § 2–4(A) (1996 and Supp. 2004); MANDELKER, NETSCH, SALSICH, WEGNER, STEVENSON AND GRIFFITH, STATE AND LOCAL GOVERNMENT IN A FEDERAL SYSTEM: CASES AND MATERIALS, 519–533 (6th ed. 2006); Anderson, MacDonald, & O'Reilly, *Impasse Resolution in Public Sector Collective Bargaining—An Examination of Compulsory Interest Arbitration in New York*, 51 ST. JOHN'S L. REV. 453 (1977); Clemow and Mooney, *Impasse in Public Sector Bargaining*, 9 CONN. L. REV. 579 (1977); Tener, *The Public Employment Relations Commission: The First Decade*, 9 RUTGERS-CAMDEN L.J. 609

(1978); South Bend Community School v. National Education Association, 444 N.E.2d 348 (Ind. App. 1983); City of Des Moines v. Public Employment Relations Board, 275 N.W.2d 753 (Iowa 1979); Garden City Educators' Ass'n v. Vance, 585 P.2d 1057 (Kan. 1978); New Jersey v. Town of Irvington, 403 A.2d 473 (N.J. 1979); City of Atlantic City v. Laezza, 403 A.2d 465 (N.J. 1979); Philadelphia Federation of Teachers v. Thomas, 436 A.2d 1228 (Pa. 1981); 29 U.S.C. § 152–(2) (1976).

III C   M. David Gelfand, *Seeking Local Government Financial Integrity Through Debt Ceilings, Tax Limitations, and Expenditure Limits: The New York City Fiscal Crisis, the Taxpayers' Revolt, and Beyond*, 63 MINN. L. REV. 545, 554–55, 575–78 (1979); Ariz. Const. art. 9, §§ 17–20 (2006); N.J. Stat. Ann. § 40A:4–45.2 (2006); Cal. Const. art. XIII B, § 1 (2007).

III D(1)   M. DAVID GELFAND, CONSTITUTIONAL LITIGATION UNDER SECTION 1983: A TREATISE FOR CITY ATTORNEYS, PUBLIC INTEREST LITIGATORS, AND STUDENTS §§ 3–2(A), 3–2(B) (1996 & Supp.); MANDELKER, NETSCH, SALSICH, WEGNER, STEVENSON AND GRIFFITH, STATE AND LOCAL GOVERNMENT IN A FEDERAL SYSTEM: CASES AND MATERIALS 798–805 (6th ed. 2006); R. REISCHAUER & R. HARTMAN, REFORMING SCHOOL FINANCE 6 (1973); Arlington Central Sch. Dist.

692 A.2d 384 (Vt. 1997); Randolf County Bd. of Educ. v. Adams, 467 S.E. 2d 150 (W. Va. 1995); Pauley v. Kelly, 255 S.E.2d 859 (W. Va. 1979); Vincent v. Voight, 614 N.W.2d 388 (Wis. 2000); Campbell County School Dist. v. State, 907 P.2d 1238 (Wyo. 1995); Washakie County School Dist. v. Herschler, 606 P.2d 310 (Wyo. 1980).

III E   M. David Gelfand, *Comparative Urban Finance: Are the London and Brooklyn Bridges Falling Down?*, 55 TUL. L. REV. 651, 690–99 (1981); Wolman & Peterson, *State and Local Government Strategies for Responding to Fiscal Pressure*, 55 TUL. L. REV. 773 (1981).

IV A   MANDELKER, NETSCH, SALSICH, WEGNER, STEVENSON AND GRIFFITH, STATE AND LOCAL GOVERNMENT IN A FEDERAL SYSTEM: CASES AND MATERIALS 391–421 (6th ed. 2006); E. MCQUILLIN, MUNICIPAL CORPORATIONS, §§ 43.01–43.161 (3d ed. rev. 2005); C. SANDS & M. LIBONATI, STATE AND LOCAL GOVERNMENT §§ 25.01–25.28 (1982); VALENTE & MCCARTHY, LOCAL GOVERNMENT LAW, 4th 766–808, (4th ed. 1992); M. David Gelfand, *Debt Ceilings and Other Restrictions on Debt Financing: Compliance, Avoidance and Evasion*, in 2 STATE AND LOCAL GOVERNMENT DEBT FINANCING, ch. 9 (M. D. Gelfand ed., 1991 and Supps.).

(Wyo. 1978); Lonegan v. State, 801 A.2d 91 (N.J. 2002).

IV C(4)   See sources cited for IV E(1), below.

IV D(1)   M. David Gelfand, *Seeking Local Government Financial Integrity Through Debt Ceilings, Tax Limitations, and Expenditure Limits: The New York City Fiscal Crisis, the Taxpayers' Revolt, and Beyond*, 63 MINN. L. REV. 545 (1979).

IV D(2)   MANDELKER, NETSCH, SALSICH, WEGNER, STEVENSON AND GRIFFITH, STATE AND LOCAL GOVERNMENT IN A FEDERAL SYSTEM: CASES AND MATERIALS (6th ed. 2006); Peter Salsich, *Housing Finance Agencies: Instruments of State Housing Policy or Confused Hybrids?*, 21 ST. LOUIS U. L. J. 595, 608, n. 83 (1978).

IV E(1)   House Report No. 98–432, Part II, Pub. L. No. 98–369, at 1683, in 6B U.S. Code Cong. & Ad. News 611–12 (1984); MANDELKER, NETSCH, SALSICH, WEGNER, STEVENSON AND GRIFFITH, STATE AND LOCAL GOVERNMENT IN A FEDERAL SYSTEM: CASES AND MATERIALS 387–391 (6th ed. 2006); Arkuss, *New Federal Legislation Affecting Tax Exempt Obligations*, 16 URB. LAW. 805, 812 (1984); Mark–David Adams, *Private Activity Bonds*, in 1 STATE AND LOCAL GOVERNMENT DEBT FINANCING, ch. 6 (M. D. Gelfand ed., 1991 & Supps.); Carol Olson, *Federal Tax Exemption: History and Overview*, in *id.* at §§ 5.22–5.33; IRC (1986),

thority, 105 S.Ct. 1005, 83 L.Ed.2d 1016 (1985), *overruling* National League of Cities, 426 U.S. 833 (1976); National League of Cities v. Usery, 426 U.S. 833, 852 (1976); City of Philadelphia v. S.E.C., 434 F. Supp. 281 (E.D. Pa. 1977), *app. dis.*, 434 U.S. 1003 (1978).

IV G(2)   Carol Olson, *Federal Tax Exemption History and Overview*, in 2 STATE AND LOCAL GOVERNMENT DEBT FINANCING, ch. 5 (M. D. Gelfand ed., 1991 and Supps.); Dean Weiner, *Arbitrage and Refunding*, in *id.* at ch. 7; South Carolina v. Regan, 104 S.Ct. 1107 *appointment of special master*, 104 S.Ct. 2148 (1984); Pollock v. Farmers' Loan and Trust Co., 157 U.S. 429 (1895); Tax Reform Act of 1986, Pub. L. No. 99–514, 100 Stat. 2085, 26 U.S.C. § 103, *amending* § 310(b)(1) of the Tax Equity and Fiscal Responsibility Act of 1982 (TEFRA), Pub. L. No. 97–248, 96 Stat. 596.

IV G(3)   COLLIER ON BANKRUPTCY, 15th ed. rev., Vol. 2, para. 109.03 and Vol. 4, para. 900.03; Robert Amdursky, *Federal Securities Law*, in MUNICIPAL FINANCE LAW 579–586 (Practicing Law Inst. 3d ed. 1984); James E. Spiotto, *Municipal Insolvency: Bankruptcy Receivership, Workouts, and Alternative Remedies*, in 3 STATE AND LOCAL GOVERNMENT DEBT FINANCING, ch. 13 (M.

D. Gelfand ed., 1991 and Supps.); *In re* Fort Cobb, Okl., Irrigation Fuel Authority, 468 F. Supp. 338, 342 (W. D. Okla., 1979), *app. dis.*, June 24, 1980 (10th Cir.); *In re City of Bridgeport*, 21 B.C.D. 1504, 128 BR 688 (B.C. Conn. 1991); Villages at Castle Rock Metropolitan District No. 4, 145 B.R. 76, 7 C.B.D. 2d 137 (BCD Colo. 1990); *In re* City of Wellston, 43 B.R. 348 (Bkrtcy. E.D.Mo. 1984); *In re* Pleasant View Utility Dist. of Cheatham Cty., 24 B.R. 632 (Bkrtcy. M.D. Tenn. 1982), *leave to appeal denied*, 27 B.R. 552 (M.D. Tenn. 1982) (construing Tenn. Code Ann. § 7–82–306 (1980)); *In re* North and South Shenango Joint Municipal Authority, 14 B.R. 414 (Bkrtcy. W.D. Pa. 1981), *petition for mandamus or prohibition denied sub nom.*, Pennbank v. Washabaugh, 8 B.C.D. 509, 673 F.2d 1301 (3d Cir. 1981); State *ex rel.* Williamson v. Garrison, 348 P.2d 859 (Okla. 1959); 11 U.S.C. § 927 (1999); 11 U.S.C. §§ 901, 922, 934(a); 11 U.S.C. §§ 101(29), 109(c) (1984); Fla. Stat. Ann. § 218.01 (2006); N.Y. Loc. Fin. Law § 85.80 (McKinney 1999–2000); Pa. Stat. Ann. Tit. 53 § 5571 (2006); Tenn. Code Ann. § 7–82–304 (2005).

IV H(1)   Ann J. Gellis, *Application of Securities Laws and Disclosure Standards*, in 2 STATE AND LOCAL GOVERNMENT DEBT FINANCING, ch. 8 (M. D. Gelfand ed., 1991 and Supps.); Power Equipment Co. v. U.S., 748 F.2d 1130 (6th Cir. 1984); T. J. Raney & Sons v. Fort Cobb, Okl., Irr. Fuel Auth., 717 F.2d 1330 (10th Cir. 1983), *cert. den.*, 104 S.Ct. 1285 (1984); Shores v. Sklar, 647 F.2d 462 (5th Cir. 1981); *In re* Washington Public Power Supply System Sec. Litig. [1989 Transfer Binder] Fed. Sec. L. Rep. (CCH) ¶ 94,235 (W.D. Wash. 1988).

IV H(2)   Clayton Gillette, *Constitutional and Statutory Aspects of Municipal Debt Finance—Recent Developments*, Municipal Finance Law 37 (Practising Law Inst. 3d ed. 1984); State *ex rel.* Warren v. Nusbaum, 59 Wis.2d 391, 208 N.W.2d 780, 794 (Wis. 1973); Wash. Rev. Code Ann. § 43.52.250 *et seq.* (2006).

IV H(3)   *In re* Washington Public Power Supply System Sec. Litig. [1989 Transfer Binder] Fed. Sec. L. Rep. (CCH) ¶ 94,325 (W.D. Wash. 1988); Asson v. City of Burley, 670 P.2d 839, 850–854 (Ida.1983), *cert. denied sub nom.* Chemical Bank v. Asson, 105 S.Ct. 219 (1984); De Fazio v. WPPSS, 679 P.2d 1316, 1338, 1343–1345 (Or. 1984); Chemical Bank v. Washington Public Power Supply System, 666 P.2d 329, 334–342, 348 (Wash. 1983), *cert. denied sub nom.*, Chemical Bank v. PUC Dist. No. 1, 105 S.Ct. 2154 (1985).

*

INDEX

323

APPROPRIATIONS

In general, 146–152
    Process, 146–152
        Specific, 148–149, 150–151

ARBITRAGE BONDS

See Bonds

ARBITRATION

See Collective Bargaining and Alternative Dispute Resolution

ASSESSED VALUATION

See Real Property Taxes

ASSESSMENT

Bonds,
    See Bonds, Types; Special Assessment
Challenges to assessments, 137–138, 143
Districts, 106
"Jeopardy assessment," 136
Levels,
        See also, Real Property Taxes
    Full value, 51–52
Methods,
    Area, 113
    Appraisal, 114
    Front-footage, 114
Process of assessment, 46–47
Property reassessment as debt limit avoidance device, 49–50
Self-assessment vs. government assessment, 135
Special,
    In general, 5, 48, 104–126
        Federal tax treatment, 124–125
        Impact taxes as a form of, 119
        Treatment under federal bankruptcy code, 125–126
Special benefit, 5, 120

AUDITING PRACTICES

    See also, Accounting Practices
Tax audit, 135

AUTHORIZATION

Lending of credit, 225–230
State debt, 252, 254–255
State purchases, 148–149
Taxes, generally, 9

BANK DEPOSITS
See Personal Property Taxes

BANKRUPTCY AND DEFAULT
Federal Bankruptcy Code,
    In general, 245–251
        Chapter 9, 247–251
Municipal insolvency, 250–251
Procedural considerations, 247–251
Treatment of special assessments in bankruptcy, 125–126
Workouts, 247

BLOCK GRANTS
See Intergovernmental Aid, Federal

BONA FIDE PURCHASER
Definition, 176

BONDHOLDER
Definition, 177
Lender, As, 173–174
Remedies, 192–194, 205
Standing to sue, 204

BONDS
Anticipation note accounts, 175, 214
Arbitrage, 176, 220–222, 244–245
Authorization,
    General obligation, 182–183
    Moral obligation, 208–209
    Revenue, 199–200
    Review by state officials, 191, 254–255
Bearer, 186–187
Definition, 176–177
General obligation,
    See Bonds, Types
Interest rate limitations, 181–182
Issuance and sale,
    In general, 181
        Referendum requirement, 183–186, 198–199, 268
Judicial review of authority to issue, 191–194, 203–205
Legislature,
    Approval by, 183, 195
    Authorization by, 198
Long-term, 174, 181
Maturity dates, 186, 188–189
Maximum interest rates, 189

DEBT CEILINGS
See also, Debt–Financing
In general, 183, 194, 200–201, 236, 254–255, 264–267
    Avoidance and evasion of,
        See also, Accounting Practices, "Creative" Accounting Devices
        Capitalizing expense items, 240–241, 244
        Lease-financing, 242–244
        Special authorities and special districts, 241–242
    Exceptions, 240–241

DEBT FINANCING
See also, Bonds; Debt Ceilings; Notes
In general, 1–5, 152–154
    Definition, 157

DEBT OF THE CITY
Distinguished from Debt Against Property Benefited, 184–185

DEBT SERVICE
See also, Bonds, Interest Rate Limitation
In general,
    Definition, 157

DEBT, SHORT–TERM
See also, Notes
Abuse of, 215–217, 271

DIFFERENTIAL RATES
See Real Estate Taxes, Rates; Constitutional Issues, State, Uniformity Requirements

DISCLOSURE
Liability under federal securities laws, 238, 253

DISCRIMINATION
Against interstate commerce, 36–39
School financing,
    Federal challenges, 166–169
    State challenges, 169–170
Severance taxes, 97

DUE PROCESS CLAUSE
See Constitutional Issues, Federal

EDUCATION
See Schools, Financing of

SUSPECT CLASSIFICATION
See Constitutional Issues, Federal, equal protection clause

TANGIBLES, TAXATION OF
See Personal Property Taxes

TAX LIMITATIONS
See Real Property Taxes, Rates, Limitations Upon

TAX REFORM ACT OF 1986
Arbitrage bonds and, 244–245
Industrial development bonds and, 244

TAXES
Economic characteristics, 7
    Cyclical and countercyclical, 7–8, 45–46, 58
    Income elastic and inelastic, 7, 58, 64
    Regressive and progressive, 7, 57, 64, 71
Types of,
    See Entry Under the Specific Tax in this index

TAXES, CONSUMPTION
See Sales and Consumption Taxes

TAXES, CORPORATE INCOME
See Income Taxes

TAXES, PRIVILEGE
See License Fees and Taxes

TAXES ON SERVICES
    See also, Sales and Consumption Taxes, Transactions Subject
        to
In general, 75–77
    Exemptions for commercial art and advertising, 75–76
        True object test, 76
    Exemptions for professional services, 75

TAXING AND SPENDING CLAUSE
See Constitutional Issues, Federal

TELEPHONE CHARGES
See Sales and Consumption Taxes, Transfers Subject to

TENTH AMENDMENT
See Constitutional Issues, Federal

TOBACCO, TAXATION OF
In general, 85–86

TOURISM, TAXATION OF
In general, 91–92

TRANSACTION THEORY
See Sales and Consumption Taxes, Theory of

TRANSFER OF PROPERTY
See Sales and Consumption Taxes, Transactions Subject to

TRANSPORTATION DISTRICTS
See Special Districts

TRUE OBJECT TEST
See Taxes, Services

TWENTY-FIRST AMENDMENT
See Constitutional Issues, Federal

UNIFORMITY OF TAXATION
See Constitutional Issues, State

UNIONS
See Collective Bargaining and Alternative Dispute Resolution

UNITARY BUSINESS TEST
See Constitutional Issues, Federal, Commerce Clause

USE TAXES
In general, 80–84
    Authorization and administration, 81–84
    Constitutional issues, 82–83
        Commerce clause,
            Substantial nexus test, 83

USER CHARGES
See Service Charges and User Fees

USER FEES
See Service Charges and User Fees

VETO BY THE EXECUTIVE
Appropriations process, 148

WASHINGTON PUBLIC POWER SUPPLY SYSTEM
In general, 255–260
    Authority of municipalities to enter,
        Idaho, 258
        Oregon, 258–259
        Washington, 256–258

WASHINGTON PUBLIC POWER SUPPLY SYSTEM—Cont'd
In general—Cont'd
  Financing package, 255–256
  Take-or-pay agreements, 255–256

WHOLESALE TRANSACTIONS
See Sales and Consumption Taxes, Gross Receipts Taxes

WORK-OUTS
See Bankruptcy and Default

†